D0475944

THE UNKNOWN FLEET

The Army's Civilian Seamen in War and Peace

WDV *Marquess of Hartington* rescuing the crew of the sinking ketch *United Friends* 26 miles off Cork during a gale on 9 July 1896. The ketch, bound for Cork from Newport (Mon.) with a cargo of coal, was of a type commonly used for coastal trading at the time

(Major B.V. Wynn-Werninck)

THE UNKNOWN FLEET

The Army's Civilian Seamen in War and Peace

REG COOLEY

ALAN SUTTON

First published in the United Kingdom in 1993 by
Alan Sutton Publishing Limited
Phoenix Mill · Far Thrupp · Stroud · Gloucestershire
in association with The Royal Naval Museum, Portsmouth

First published in the United States of America in 1993 by
Alan Sutton Publishing Inc · 83 Washington Street · Dover · NH 03820

A catalogue record for this book is available from the British Library

ISBN 0–7509–0384–8

Library of Congress Cataloging in Publication Data applied for

Typeset in 11/13pt Bembo.
Typesetting and origination by
Alan Sutton Publishing Limited.
Printed in Great Britain by
The Bath Press, Avon.

The idea and inspiration for a history of the War Department's Civilian Fleet sprang from the desire of the late Mr Charles Codner, a proud member of the Fleet from boyhood in the thirties to his retirement in 1951, to see historical justice done to a service which history seemed to have passed by.

His personal recollections of the Fleet's ships and activities and his enthusiastic and determined research, formed the basis and inspiration for this work, and greatly helped to infuse into it a sense of the spirit of the Fleet which he himself embodied.

To Charles, then, who sadly died early in 1991, this book is dedicated. Not solely, however. Some years ago he had prepared his own dedication for the history he hoped would one day be written:

To the memory of old shipmates, Officers, both Deck and Engineers, who manned and operated the Fleet long ago and who gave loyalty and devotion to the Fleet and to the Crown.

Song of the WD Fleet

Not for spoil of sea or river,
Not for trade or merchants' gain,
Sail we o'er Britannia's waters,
Plough we through our Island's main.

Plying hither, thither, always,
Whither duty may command,
Guns for fort and stores for fortress,
Thus we serve our native land.

Nought we know of deeds of glory,
Struggles in a well fought fight,
Servants we to Britain's Army,
Resting neither day or night.

Oft the storm-cloud gathers o'er us,
Dangers of the deep are nigh,
Swift to hear and aid to render,
When distressed our brethren cry.

Humbly toiling for the War-God,
Never may our labours cease,
Till the warriors' work is ended,
And the whole world rests in peace.

C.B. Taylor, Staff-Sgt
(Published in the ASC journal, May 1907)

CONTENTS

ACKNOWLEDGEMENTS

Charles Codner's part in this book is acknowledged in the dedication, and I couple with his name that of his friend of many years, John Smale of Shoreham-by-Sea who also died early in 1991. John was of great help and encouragement and second only to Charles in his knowledge of WD shipping, and many of the photographs come from his unique collection, very kindly made available by Mrs Joyce Smale, through whose generosity they have now found a home in the Royal Corps of Transport archives.

I acknowledge the tremendous debt I owe to so many who have helped me with advice, information and encouragement. Among the foremost of these I number Alan Blight, the former Superintending Engineer and Constructor of Shipping, who gave me my starting point and generous access to his own papers, and Maj. Bill Wynn-Werninck, for his technical help, experience, wise advice and, not least, for his artwork. I acknowledge the great contributions made by the late Frank Bourne, the last Master Superintendent, and the late Capt. Jack Cains, MBE, upon whose lively memories of his long Fleet experience I was privileged to draw. Lt.-Col. Mike Young, the Regimental Secretary, who supplied many a titbit from the archives, and constant encouragement, Lt.-Col. John Hambleton, Secretary of the Institution of the Royal Corps of Transport, John Roe, for his lively reminiscences of Cairnryan, Brig. K.A. Timbers of the RA Institution, and Maj. P.J. Lee, late RA, for valuable information on coastal defences and training and Mrs Magnuson of the Institution of Royal Engineers Corps Library for similar help on submarine mining and Inland Water Transport, and the Secretary of the Institution for permission to publish the material.

I am also especially grateful to the staff of the Public Records Office, not only for their courtesy and assistance, but also for permission to use material in their archives. I also acknowledge the use of British Crown Copyright/M.o.D. material by permission of the Controller of HMSO, the Naval and Army Historical Branches of the M.o.D. for assistance and for the use of the Dunkirk log of the WDV. *Haig*, the British Newspaper Library for permission to use material from nineteenth-century newspapers, and so many other agencies whose sources and references, listed elsewhere, I have also used. I do apologize if I have inadvertently committed any errors of omission in this respect.

I would like to thank the following newspapers for the use of copyright material: *Galloway Advertiser & Wigstown Free Press*, (26 January 1956), *Illustrated London News*, (30 September 1876), *Scottish Sunday Express*, (20 March 1955) and *The Times Newspaper*, (11, 12, 28 March 1892).

My thanks are also due to the following for their advice and unstinting assistance:

Mr and Mrs David Woods of the Society for Spritsail Barge Research, Miss Patricia O'Driscoll, Maj. J. Goodrick and Maj. R. Masters, TD, late RA, Lt.-Col. G.C.E. Crew, Lt.-Col. C.J. Piper, late RCT, Maj. P. Watson, TD, and Capt. R.V. Webber, late RASC, Maj. H.F.R. Mason, Maj. J.A. Robins of the Army Transport Museum, Maj. D. Nicholas, Maj. W. Moorhouse, Maj. G. Williamson, all late RCT, Capt. R. Hynes, S. and T. Corps, Irish Army, Mr Peter Robinson, late RASC, PC D. Lines, Thames River Police, Mr R.E. Davey, MBE, Messrs W. Aitchison, E.A. Cowdry, A.B. Wales, E. Kimber, W. Hawkins, M. Houghton, all late of the WD Fleet, Mr Martin Langley of Plymouth, Mrs E. Downing, Bermuda Maritime Museum, Sgt. Marilyn Smith, Maritime Command Museum, Halifax, NS, Mrs Blacklaw of the Ministry of Defence Library, the staff of British Newspaper Library and the York and Leeds Reference Libraries, The Royal Humane Society, and so many others, from whom I beg forgiveness for any unwitting omissions. Lastly, I acknowledge the great support I have always received from my long-suffering wife, Peggy, who has been a word-processor widow for so long.

INTRODUCTION

At Cairnryan, on a drizzling day in September 1957, an old RASC coaster, the 61-year-old *Sir Evelyn Wood*, embraced her sister, the 1886 *Marquess of Hartington* in an alongside tow. With a mournful farewell whistle, the two vessels edged slowly, reluctantly, away from the jetty, into the grey waters of Loch Ryan and out of the fleet they had served so well for a combined total of 132 years. An honourable discharge for two fine and well-loved ships, whose record of service to War Department and RASC fleets had been a credit not only to their civilian masters and crews, but to their builders and, not least, to those ashore who had maintained them in peace and war.

It is not generally appreciated that, until the Second World War, the story of War Department sea-going transport had been a uniquely civilian one. The departure of these two old coasters, epitomizing the spirit and traditions of the Fleet and its predecessors, marked the beginning of the end of a long era of military maritime history. Coincidentally, the *Marquess* had entered the Fleet in the same year that it became the responsibility of the Commissariat and Transport Staff, the predecessor of the Army Service Corps.

The decline of the civilian fleet and its 'blue water' role dated from the end of the 1939–45 war as the RASC Fleet inevitably and inexorably shed many of its wartime duties. It continued for the following decade, and beyond, to play a very important part in the transition period to peacetime conditions, but in 1956 the decision was taken to place the sea-going fleet on a military operational basis.

The history of the civilian WD Fleet has received scant attention from military historians. It is almost as though the Fleet sprang into existence in the nineteenth-century, fully rigged and manned, from the water, rather like the classical Cadmean warriors who sprang fully armed from the soil. Not so, of course; although the Fleet traces its modern beginnings back only to the latter part of the nineteenth-century, it nevertheless has a pedigree reaching back to the Middle Ages.

It is not difficult to appreciate why history seems to have overlooked the civilian fleet. Theirs was truly 'the trivial round, the common task' with few headlines, few laurels, even few disasters; just dull, steady, reliable and loyal service to the Army and, in earlier days, to the Royal Navy. If the latter did not already bear the 'Silent Service' appellation, then it could surely have been equally justly claimed by this small navy and its predecessors.

And what a variety of ships ploughed the Channel, the Northern Seas, the Mediterranean, the China Seas, the Caribbean, the North Atlantic, or busied themselves in the harbours of Britain and the Empire. From hoys, barges, wherries and schooners, to paddle and screw steamers, motor passenger vessels, steam and motor launches, high speed target towers and patrol craft, LCTs and tongkangs! This multiplicity of shipping types reflected the multiplicity of tasks the Fleet carried out. Heavy gun barrels from Woolwich Arsenal to Shoeburyness for proofing, powder to Purfleet Ordnance factory, arms and armament to warships, ordnance stores and explosives from Woolwich to all parts of Britain and Ireland, the Continent and Mediterranean, men and stores to coastal defences and the Irish forts, water supply to the Royal Navy, ammunition dumping, target-towing and range patrolling for coastal defence batteries . . . the list is endless.

The latter tasks, assumed towards the end of the last century, grew to be one of the Fleet's most important commitments between the wars and led to its expansion just before the outbreak of the Second World War. Conversely, the disbandment of coast artillery after the war was a major factor in its demise.

There were, of course, other factors − the considerable reduction in stores maintenance by sea, the bread and butter role of the Fleet, in favour of much swifter and more flexible use of rail and road transport, and the growth and development of an operational role for water transport, to which we have already referred.

In these days of built-in obsolescence, the longevity of many of the old coasting steamers remains a source of wonder. They clanked from port to port, from year to year, in peace and war, plying their steady and unspectacular trade in all weathers. Apart from the *Marquess*, the queen of them all, and *Sir Evelyn*, her consort, one might say, there was the 125 ton *Gordon*, built in 1907, sold in 1947; *Haslar*, a former Royal Engineers' submarine mining vessel of 175 tons, 1903 to 1951;

the *Haldane*, which registered forty-one years of service; and the *Moore*, which went to the scrap-yard in 1950 after forty-three years of service.

It was often possible for crews, being wholly civilian, to stay with their vessels indefinitely and indeed there were some who spent practically all their working lives on the same vessel. Those who transferred on advancement often returned as masters and mates to the vessels in which they had learned their seaman's trade as boys. Small wonder, then, at the tremendous feeling of pride in, and loyalty to, these iron work-horses. There can be no doubt that the tradition of service which motivated these sailors, and continues to motivate the present day Army seaman, drew its inspiration from those who manned the schooners, hoys, powder vessels, barques, barges and wherries of a bygone era.

It is a tradition which springs not only from an innate sense of duty, but also from loyalty – to the Crown, certainly, but also, in a great measure, to the vessel itself.

This loyalty is not surprising to any true seaman. As Capt. Jack Cains, MBE, one of the great personalities of the Fleet, said, 'One got a great deal of affection for a ship . . . . There's more to a ship than wood or iron; there's a certain amount of soul in a ship'.

It would be surprising if the spirit, loyalty and pride which actuated bygone seamen had not expressed itself in family traditions of service comparable with those that go to strengthen and renew the spirit of service in the Armed Forces.

Jack Cains was one of five brothers in the Fleet; 'Tom' Thomas, to whom the Fleet was 'his very life', was the third generation to serve, not only in the Fleet, but in the *Marquess of Hartington*, and another Master Superintendent, Mr James Day, equalled his father's record of fifty years of service with the Fleet.

Writing in 'Ships Monthly', a one-time boy seaman in the Fleet, Mr William Hawkins, said, 'I never cease to be amazed by the fact that the WD Fleet is so unknown to the vast majority of seafarers. In its time it must surely have been the oldest and largest (in number of vessels) non-naval fleet in history'. He added that the Fleet was very much a family concern, and those who joined from the RN or Merchant Navy found a totally different lifestyle with small boat seamanship and personal loyalty far more evident. Complaining, the traditional prerogative of the British seaman, was rare.

It is right and just that the history of this hitherto unsung branch of the service, no longer a part of the Army, should now be recorded. History is sometimes a condemnation of the past; more often, perhaps, a salute. This history is intended as a long overdue salute.

It is also a requiem – for a fleet, but not for its traditions. Traditions need no requiems.

1
MEDIEVAL BEGINNINGS

At the outbreak of the Second World War, the Army was served by a mixed fleet of coastal and sea-going freighters, harbour vessels, high-speed target towing craft, dumb barges and a miscellany of other small craft. The blue ensign with crossed swords was a familiar sight in the ports and harbours of the United Kingdom and its overseas colonies. And everywhere it was entirely manned and operated as a civilian organization under a civilian Inspector of Shipping, although administered and controlled for the War Department as a branch of the Royal Army Service Corps.

The War Department Fleet, as it was then known, was soon to lose its wholly civilian nature as operational requirements dictated the necessity for a military water transport service. Although the civilian fleet continued, virtually as a separate entity within the RASC Fleet, as it became known at the war's end, a unique transport era had ended. The history and origins of this civilian fleet went back for several hundred years and were, strangely, perhaps, intimately connected with both Army and Navy.

In the early Middle Ages, warlike supplies were provided at the king's expense through his household organization which, though bearing the title of the 'King's Wardrobe', had, by 1300, extended its responsibilities to many of the functions which, in the words of Brig. O.F. Hogg:

> in the course of time have devolved upon the Defence Services and Paymaster General, acting as a naval and military office, a recruiting organization, a Ministry of Infantry, RCT, RAOC, and a Ministry of Supply. Hence it controlled the purchase, manufacture and repair of equipment and coordinated such engineering, mechanical and technical services as were then existing.

The fourteenth and fifteenth centuries saw the seemingly endless succession of military adventures in France known as the Hundred Years

War. During this period, which must have been an increasingly busy one for the king's bowyers, crossbowyers and armourers, not to mention the keepers of tents, artillery began to assume more and more importance and so it became clear that the nation's warlike needs had outgrown the now archaic wardrobe. Accordingly, in 1414, the year before Agincourt, Henry V issued Letters of Patent appointing one Nicholas Merbury to be his Master of Ordnance. This, incidentally, was the first time the word 'ordnance' was to appear in an official document. This new department of state, the Office of Ordnance, was established in the Tower of London, which had long been the nation's arsenal.

There being no standing army, the Office of Ordnance became mainly occupied in supplying ships of the developing Navy with stores, equipment, cannon, munitions, and even gun crews, and continued to do so throughout the sixteenth century. This period saw the beginning of the age of discovery and the development of the concept of sea power. Ships grew in size, guns increased in power and range; Britain's Navy was beginning to take shape. Royal dockyards, with supporting Ordnance storehouses, were built at Portsmouth, Sheerness, Chatham and Devonport, each with its gunwharf. And, most important for the future War Department Fleet, a Royal dockyard was established at Woolwich in 1518, with an Ordnance storehouse and gunwharf.

In 1670, Tower Place, a gentleman's residence, became the Ordnance depot and, from its location on Woolwich Warren, became known as The Warren. By 1682 The Warren, re-named the Royal Arsenal in 1805 by George III, was the main gun repository in the country. From this sixteenth-century establishment grew the great Royal Arsenal from which the Army and Navy throughout the British Empire would be supplied with stores, equipment and munitions.

After 180 years of service, the Office of Ordnance came under a cloud and, following a Royal Commission in 1597, which found fraud, profiteering and other malpractices, was reconstituted as the Board of Ordnance. This new board, under its Great Master, the 2nd Earl of Essex (executed, alas, for treason four years later) was given similar responsibilities for every aspect of Ordnance business by land and by sea. It lasted in this form as an office of the Crown until the Civil War, when it was taken over by Parliament and virtually lapsed until its revival at the Restoration in 1660. In 1683 it was reconstituted as a Civil Department of State and charged with the duty of providing armament for all ships and forts.

To head the Board, Charles II recreated the post of Master-General of the Ordnance, which had lapsed in 1611. Henceforward this appointment would go to a distinguished soldier and, until 1828, would carry with it a seat in the Cabinet. The MGO and his lieutenant had dual military and civil roles. Militarily they were Commander-in-Chief and Second-in-Command of the Royal Artillery and Royal Engineers (though not necessarily with any experience in either arm of the service) and, on the civil side, they controlled works, barracks, hospitals, contracts and Ordnance factories. These responsibilities devolved upon four principal officers, the Clerk of the Ordnance, the Surveyor-General, the Principal Storekeeper and the Clerk of the Deliveries.

Under these worthy civil servants were officials known as Inferior Officers and Under-Ministers. One of the latter was the Purveyor and he was charged, under the Board, 'To provide such ships, vessels, lighters and boats as the affairs of the Board might require at favourable contract rates.' As we shall see, his duties were to assume considerable importance in the development of water transport for the land service; transport by water was a vital link in the stores distribution system, at home no less than abroad. While laden storeships chartered by the Board lumbered east and west to the far harbours of the new Empire, humbler hired craft, hoys, galleys, ketches, schooners, brigs, delivered the sinews of war to warships, to gunwharves and to military stations and forts around the coasts of the British Isles.

It is not over-stating the case to describe water transport as a vital and indispensable link in the distribution system in the United Kingdom. The state of roads in Britain before the nineteenth century was appalling. Highways of soft earth and gravel were frequently impassable and became bogs in winter. Many were boulder-strewn, pot-holed, and scarcely wide enough to take a wagon. Footpads and highwaymen were additional inconveniences to be borne by the traveller. Even in the London area travel could be hazardous; Board of Ordnance officials travelling between the Tower and Woolwich prudently went by boat. Small wonder, then, that wheeled vehicles were little used before the seventeenth century and that water transport by sea and navigable river, though slow and subject to the vagaries of wind and weather, was usually the safest and most practical method of moving artillery and other military and naval armament and stores. Nonetheless there is evidence (*vide The Ordnance Office and the Navy*, Andrew Thrush), in Ordnance Office papers of the

hire of carts and wains to move stores from the Tower by road – even as
far as Bristol.

So the 'affairs of the Board' came to require a considerable volume of
hired shipping but, as will be seen, the time came when it was found
practical and economic for the Board to own and operate its own sea-
going vessels in addition to its inland water transport. The Board's control
of shipping continued until 1855 when, as a direct result of the
calamitous collapse of military organization and administration which
occasioned so much suffering among troops in the Crimea, its Letters of
Patent were cancelled. So, after centuries of Ordnance administration, it
disappeared into clouded history.

The Board's functions and responsibilities were transferred to, and
gratefully received by, the War Department, which inherited twenty
vessels. Thus it was that the War Department Fleet came into being and
thus, too, the reason for its civilian status, no move being made to
militarize it. Indeed, to have done so would have meant training a whole
new military organization, an undertaking to be deferred for nearly
ninety years.

The clouds of opprobrium under which the Board of Ordnance
disappeared would, of course, have extended over all its multifarious
activities. However, the almost complete absence in existing records of
references to the day-to-day functions or malfunctions of the Board of
Ordnance Fleet would seem to indicate that the masters and crews of this
small collection of vessels went about their mundane tasks with that self-
effacing efficiency and reliability which was to characterize the service
throughout its subsequent history.

The date usually ascribed to the 'launching' of the Fleet is 1818,
probably because in that year Capt. Thomas Dickinson, RN (Retired),
described as Superintendent of Ordnance Shipping, was ordered to
report on the use and justification for Ordnance vessels worldwide. These
terms of reference imply that the Fleet was already in existence, as indeed
it was. However, at home it consisted only of river and harbour craft for
the arming and disarming of HM Ships and maintenance of the sea forts,
powder vessels for the conveyance of gunpowder to and from powder
works and warships, floating magazines for the safe storage afloat of
explosives.

The operation of ferries also fell under Board of Ordnance auspices.
These operated across the Thames, notably between Gravesend and

Gravesend Ferry, *c.* 1780, operated by the Board of Ordnance. The craft appear to be forerunners of Second World War landing craft

Tilbury Fort and between Woolwich and the north bank of the Thames. A contemporary print shows the Gravesend ferry boats to bear a striking likeness to modern ramped landing craft and well able to carry vehicles and guns. There was also a ferry service between Portsmouth and the Isle of Wight, for which a master at £54 per annum and a mate at £48 were established. This ferry service was controlled by a Superintendent of Embarkations and appears to have been assisted in some way by two staff serjeants. They were paid 2s. 4d. a day from Board of Ordnance funds plus 1d. beer money and 1d. for lodgings.

There is earlier evidence from which one might date the beginnings of the Fleet. The Board employed its own lightermen in the seventeenth century and, in 1729, a hoyman, one Anthony Swift, was added to the establishment of The Warren. So it is clear that the Board, and, no doubt, its predecessor, the Office of Ordnance, had been operating a river fleet for some centuries. In addition, there was of course considerable reliance on contractors and agents for the river and coastwise movement of Ordnance material. The acquisition of its own vessels by the Board for coastwise movement appears to have started in the latter part of the eighteenth century, prompted by the steady increase in the demands of the armed forces during that troubled age.

The best evidence for this is the appointment in 1777 of the first Superintendent of Shipping, a Capt. John Dickinson (it was not known if he and his successor were related). He was charged with the duties of operator, purveyor and repairer of shipping. He was responsible directly to the Board of Ordnance, with most of his work centred on Woolwich Arsenal. His purveying duties would have echoed those of his predecessor, the Purveyor, insofar as the hire of vessels 'at favourable contract rates' was concerned. An important sideline of his responsibilities in those days of unremitting sea warfare was to survey all hired vessels to ensure that they were well-found as, under the charter party agreement, the Board would be obliged to compensate the owner with the full value of any ship captured or sunk by the enemy.

The post of Superintendent of Shipping was superseded by that of Inspector of Shipping in about 1865. One 'perk' of his post, according to the *History of the Royal Arsenal*, was a reserved pew in the (unofficial) Gentlemen-cadets Chapel in the Royal Academy at the Arsenal. He sat between (or perhaps was straddled by, bearing in mind one of the future roles of the Fleet) the Inspector of Artillery on the one side, and the Assistant Inspector of Artillery on the other. One may imagine that those in peril on the sea received full attention during his devotions, as, perhaps, was the intention.

Overseas, in over a dozen exotic (and unhealthy) stations, from Quebec to Van Diemen's Land, from Demerara to Malta, craft variously described in official papers as government boats, army vessels, governor's barges, colonial vessels and garrison boats, plied the harbours and rivers of the Empire. Not all would have been Board of Ordnance vessels, however, as the Commissariat Department was also operating water transport. There is also evidence that, in the pirate-infested waters of the West Indies, it must have been thought prudent to arm Board of Ordnance vessels for in 1828, an unfortunate Edward Williams was awarded a pension of £16. Williams, who had served seventeen years in the West Indies (a remarkable achievement in what was considered, with full justification, to be a white man's graveyard), lost an arm while firing a salute.

2
THE BOARD OF ORDNANCE FLEET, 1818–55

Capt. Thomas Dickinson's remit in 1818 to report on the use of and justification for Ordnance vessels worldwide was followed a few years later by a parliamentary committee. This committee was convened to consider how best and most economically the Board of Ordnance's shipping requirements could in future be met. At this time, shortly after the end of the Napoleonic Wars, the Board was at the height of its powers and commitments. It was responsible for the entire business of Ordnance in its widest sense, for both naval and land service. Not a warship sailed that was not equipped with its stores, equipment and armament, from guns to marline spikes, from oakum to sails, whether alongside at a gunwharf, or over shipside off one of the Royal dockyards, and around the coasts of the British Isles, not a fortification or a battery but was maintained by the Board and serviced by its shipping both public and hired.

There is no contemporary report now available but from later evidence it is known that the main question for decision was whether or not government ownership of vessels would be preferable and more economic than the continuation of hiring. It is not too difficult to appreciate why the question arose at this particular time.

The Napoleonic era was now at an end and with it the threat of invasion had long gone. However, the legacy of a chain of fortifications, particularly along the south coast, remained. These forts and stations were still to be maintained and had necessitated the setting-up of many local Ordnance storehouses which, given the state of the road system at that time, ill-adapted for heavy loads and lawless, could only be regularly and safely served by sea. Many of the forts, like those which loom out of the Portsmouth approaches, could in any case only be served by water transport. This considerable increase in the Board's shipping activities is reflected in the expansion of the Royal Arsenal's wharfage and the addition of twelve new cranes in 1803, and three more in 1812. More wharfage and cranage was added in 1823–4. It must, of course, be remembered that Woolwich was the centre and, through the Principal Storekeeper, the controller of the Board's Fleet.

The other major task in which the Board was involved was the disarming of ships of the line; the expansion of the Royal Navy during the anxious Napoleonic years had now been thrown into helter-skelter reverse and in consequence the harbours of the south coast were crowded with de-commissioned men of war. Some idea of the magnitude of the task may be deduced from the fact that, of ninety-eight ships of the line in commission in 1813, only thirteen remained a scant four years later.

So it may be supposed the time had come when the cost of this considerable growth in waterborne activity had to be questioned. We do not know whether Capt. Dickinson's investigation led to, or was prompted by, the parliamentary committee. Official affairs were conducted in a much more leisurely fashion in those days and so there may have been a close connection, the committee having apparently sat sometime in the mid-1820s.

The only certain evidence we have of the results of the parliamentary committee are contained in the *Report on the Account of Army Expenditure for 1887–88*. It was clear from this brief report that the same question of cost effectiveness of public versus hired vessels had again been considered. The report admits 'that vessels used as floating magazines, or as gun hoys must be the property of the department; and the same view was not controverted when the subject was discussed more than 60 years ago'. The authors added that it had then been proved 'that by the employment of public craft a considerable saving was effected as compared with the cost of hiring'.

The 1888 report came to the same conclusion. It was stated that

There were no precise means of ascertaining the sums we should have paid shipowners for the whole of our coasting work, but taking the best data available, the conclusion was that Government vessels work cheaper so long as their number is kept down to, or perhaps below, the requirements of the work, and that our vessels paid a good percentage on the money sunk in them.

The report gives a clear indication of the growth of the Fleet during the nineteenth century when comparing the expenditure for 1889–90 of

£20,464 for a shipping tonnage of 4,016, with 1825, when four coasting vessels, a total of 226 tons, cost £1,550. This exemplified the 'enormous increase caused by the larger force and military preparations at home, and by the advance in armaments'. This latter factor was on the point of ending the Fleet's long-standing naval commitments.

The Board of Ordnance Fleet, although serving the Army and the Navy, was still very much a part of a Civil Department of State. Naval and military history passed it by; even Lloyd's Register knew it not. Its activities were routine, its disasters rarely recorded, its triumphs never. Transfer to military control as the War Department Fleet did not greatly affect this virtual anonymity until publication of the Army Service Corps journal began in 1891. The story of the development of the Fleet and its commitments has perforce to be gleaned mainly from lists of shipping and their tasks as recorded in the dry pages of the annual Ordnance Estimates.

There are no lists of Ordnance vessels available for the early part of the century; the first authentic roll extant from official sources appears to be that published with the 1839/40 Ordnance Estimates which lists twelve ships. Although eight are shown to have been built between 1804 and 1828, we cannot be certain as to when they actually entered the service. We do know, however, that around this time there were the four coasting vessels referred to above, three powder vessels, the *Lady Chatham* (63 tons), the *Lord Howe*, and *Lord Townshend*, and a floating magazine, the 900 ton *Manship*. These vessels were apparently employed by the Royal Laboratory at Woolwich. None of the vessels figures in the 1839 list, but it is known that *Manship* was replaced by a much smaller 200 ton brig, *Convert*, in 1823, a clear consequence of the reduction in armament production.

Ordnance Estimates for the years from 1827 to 1843 show that the cost of 'Ordnance vessels, gun hoys and floating magazines, including every expense of masters, mates, seamen and repairs' ranged through various amounts between £4,000 and £5,000, the highest figure being for 1827, at £4,825. The acquisition of two vessels in 1841, *Nettley* (82 tons) and *Lord Vivian* (89 tons), caused a £360 increase in the estimate to £4,546. There were now thirteen vessels in the Fleet and two more were added in 1853 and 1854.

From the 1844/5 Estimates (see Appendix V) one gets a clear picture of the deployment of the Ordnance vessels and their duties. All, of course, were sailing vessels. Five, including the latest and largest, the 89 ton *Lord Vivian*, were stationed at Woolwich and engaged in 'conveying stores to and from the various Stations in Great Britain and Ireland'. The veteran 36-year-old *Richard* was based at Purfleet as a powder vessel, conveying powder to and from Purfleet, Faversham Powder Works, and Bow Creek. Chatham was served by two even older vessels, *Marlborough* (1804) and *Ebenezer* (1805) whose duties consisted in arming and disarming HM Ships at Chatham and Sheerness; they also doubled as powder and as stores vessels.

At Portsmouth two further vessels were also engaged in arming and disarming HM Ships and other duties based, of course, on the gunwharf which was to become the main focus of the Fleet's activities in the next century. Down in the West Country, at Devonport, *Beresford* and *Gosport* were also engaged with HM Ships and finally, the 1809 50 ton *Earl of Chatham* carried out the perilous duties of a powder vessel at Priddy's Hard, supplying ships at Spithead.

The largest vessels were the stores vessels at Woolwich, and all except one had crews of seven: master, mate, four seamen and a boy. There were nine boys in the total fleet complement of sixty-five, the total cost of whose wages was £4,170. A seaman's wage was between £32 and £54 a year at this time.

The year 1855 was a landmark in the history of the civilian fleet. The mismanagement of the war in the Crimea led to a debate in the House of Lords in January 1855 when, in the words of Brig. Skentelbery (*The Ordnance Board – An Historical Note*),

> Lord Panmure, the Secretary-at-War, seized the opportunity to attack the Board of Ordnance (the MGO being absent in the Crimea). Despite the strongest protests from many influential people, the attack succeeded and the London Gazette of 25 May 1855 promulgated the Queen's decree revoking the Letters Patent of the Master-General, the Lieutenant-General and the Principal Storekeeper of the Ordnance, and vesting the administration of the Ordnance in Lord Panmure.

This decree brought to an end a remarkably complicated disposition of responsibility for the direction of military affairs. As Secretary-at-War at Horse Guards, Lord Panmure superintended the financial operation of the Army as regards personnel, but had no control over artillery and engineers or over Army material, those aspects belonging to the Board of Ordnance.

There was also a Secretary of State for War and the Colonies, at the Colonial Office. He had a general but rather vague control practically limited to time of war, but no responsibility for details of army management. The Commander-in-Chief of the Army had absolute control under the sovereign, but could do nothing involving financial results without the concurrence of the Secretary-at-War, neither was there any defined responsibility between the two posts.

The reorganization separated responsibilities for war and the colonies. A Secretary of State for War was appointed with control over all other administrative officers. The Ordnance Board's civil functions were handed over to the Secretary of State, and its military functions to the Commander-in-Chief. Thus the War Department Fleet came into being, its controlling authority at War Office being the Store Branch, headed by a naval officer with the resounding title of Director of Stores and Naval Director-General of Artillery.

There is no reason to suppose that these momentous changes would have disturbed the even tenor of life in the Fleet very much. Masters of WD vessels would, however, have perused with interest *RULES and REGULATIONS to be strictly observed by Masters, Mates and Seamen of the several Vessels belonging to or employed by the War Department* published under the name of Captain (later Rear Admiral) J. Crawford Caffin as War Office Circular No. 471 on 24 August 1859. These contained thirty-one clauses and covered every aspect of the master's duties, and are the earliest extant instructions. They are reproduced in full in Appendix I.

It is probable that Fleet members would have found more exciting the prospects of promotion attendant upon the increase of five ships for which £6,000 had been allowed in a supplementary estimate to the 1854/55 Estimates. This provision was obviously to meet a long-term requirement and may therefore be taken to be a further indication of the steady growth in Ordnance business and, of course, of confidence in the unfailing ability of the Fleet to satisfy all demands made upon it.

Now at its greatest strength of twenty vessels, the Fleet had deployed the additional five vessels, one to Portsmouth, two to Chatham, one to Priddy's Hard, and increased the fleet at Woolwich from five to six. The pattern of work, unvaried over very many years, was now gradually changing. The Crimean War had sounded the death knell of the sailing navy and the first steam-driven ironclads were beginning to appear. History does not record the reaction of the Fleet (or sailors) to the introduction of steam winches and derricks for loading and unloading heavy armament from Her Majesty's Ships of the Line, a hitherto labour-intensive task accomplished mainly by sweat and sheer-legs.

J.M.W. Turner's painting, *A First-Rate taking in Stores*, (Cecil Higgins Art Gallery, Bedford) graphically illustrates this aspect of the Fleet's work. Some appreciation of the task of arming and disarming wooden-walled warships will also be gleaned from the amount and dead-weight of the armament they carried. Lt.-Col. Maurice-Jones, in his *History of Coast Artillery*, points out that a First Rate warship mounted a hundred or more guns, consisting of twenty-eight to thirty 42, 28, and 12 pounders, plus a dozen or so 6 pounders. The total weight of this armament was about 2,200 tons.

There were four Rates of Ships of the Line, each carrying proportionately less armament, down to about fifty to seventy guns, and Fifth and Sixth Rate vessels of up to fifty guns. To the tonnage swung in and outboard must, of course, be added the weight of ammunition required to serve them, ranging from 6 to 42 lb shot. It will be recalled that, at the end of the Napoleonic Wars, eighty-five ships of the line were de-commissioned and most of their armament returned to Woolwich or stored at gunwharves.

The basic craft used to carry heavy artillery was the hoy. The hoy was a work-boat of Flemish origin, usually rigged as a sloop, that is to say, with a foresail and mainsail. These boats, sometimes with one deck, sometimes with none depending on their purpose, were extensively used on the river for both passenger and goods traffic. The well-known nineteenth-century author, R.S. Surtees, in his *Jorrocks Jaunts*, depicts Mr Jorrocks as an unhappy passenger in a hoy trading between Margate and Blackwall with bulky goods and, therefore, *sans* deck. He had a most uncomfortable journey. It is interesting to note that the nautical term 'Ahoy!' derives from this humble sailing vessel.

In addition to its gun- and stores-carrying tasks for the Navy, the Fleet continued to supply and maintain the coastal defences of Great Britain, the Channel Islands and Ireland; during this period, up to 1856, much of the ordnance of ships and batteries was common to both services. This task reached its peak during the Napoleonic Wars when there were over

Landing a heavy gun barrel at Shoeburyness. The barge is either *Gog* or *Magog*

200 forts, fortresses and batteries to be supported. Inevitably, after 1815 there was a rundown, but, as with the Navy, there was still plenty of work for the Fleet on this account. And, of course, there was always the bread-and-butter stores traffic between the Arsenal and the Ordnance storehouses or depots around the coast.

The Crimea not only had a far-reaching effect on military administration; the coastal batteries of Sebastopol had shown a hitherto complacent Admiralty that the long and illustrious career of the wooden-wall was over. The day of the ironclad was at hand and in the succeeding decades, the development of armour prompted increasingly sophisticated and complex counter-developments in armaments to an extent that made it essential that the Navy should assume full responsibility for its own Ordnance. This came about in 1891, but in the meantime the Fleet continued to expand. The Royal Arsenal, its wharfage and cranage facilities significantly extended in 1856, continued to be the main focus and base of the Fleet which, by 1862, had grown to thirty-three vessels.

Technical control of the Fleet was the responsibility of the Inspector of Shipping, but operational control was now vested in a Principal Military

Loading an 81 ton gun at Woolwich into the WD barge *Magog*

Storekeeper. War Office Circular No. 266 of 12 June 1858, under a heading of 'Passes for Stores', affirmed:

> All stores may be shipped by the Heads of Departments, but no craft or boat is to leave the wharves or causeways of the Arsenal without a permit to be granted by the Principal Military Storekeeper or to a clerk or clerks nominated by him.

Although 1856 was a watershed in the history of the development of naval and military ordnance; the range of artillery had already been increasing to the extent that existing facilities on Woolwich Common and Plumstead Marshes for the proof testing and further development of guns had become inadequate. The Board of Ordnance had already bought land at Shoeburyness for this purpose and in 1859 the forerunner of the present-day Proof and Experimental Establishment was

Loading a gun at the turn of the century was obviously a labour intensive business. *Georgina* was originally purchased as a sailing barge for duty as a powder vessel

established. Thus arose a new commitment for the Fleet; henceforth, and until after the Second World War, heavy gunbarrels, many weighing over 100 tons, were towed to and fro between Woolwich and Shoeburyness.

The *City Press* of 23 September 1876 reports that during the week an 81 ton gun constructed at Woolwich Arsenal had safely arrived at Shoeburyness in a barge (*Magog*), which had to be specially built for it at a cost of £2,300. This event must have fired the public interest, as an artist's impression of the loading at Woolwich was featured on the front page of the *Illustrated London News* of 30 September 1876.

An article in *R.E. Professional Papers, 1877*, describing the landing of the gun, states that 'it was therefore decided that a barge of special construction should be built to take the gun, on its proof carriage, on rails . . .'. The reasons given were that the largest sheers at Shoeburyness could only lift 50 tons, and there was no railway within 5 miles. In 1886, therefore, *Magog* was joined by the 400 ton *Gog*. Guns were now loaded by crane onto bogies at Woolwich and unloaded at Shoeburyness by hauling engine, via a rail slipway.

Magog was replaced by a 250 ton barge, bearing the same name, in 1900 and did yeoman service on this task until 1948, towed first by the steam tug *Katharine* (1882 to 1930) and then her successor, *Katharine II*, about which, more later. Normally an uneventful task, there was to be one notable and fully-chronicled exception in 1928 when severe weather conditions in the River Thames tested the seamanship of *Gog's* skipper to the limit, as related in Chapter 10.

3
THE WAR DEPARTMENT FLEET IS BORN

Nineteenth-century history appears to have little to say about the Fleet's operation overseas in the Empire. It is known from the 1818 investigation entrusted to Capt. Thomas Dickinson that the Board of Ordnance operated vessels outside the United Kingdom. However, some awards of pensions to seamen in the West Indies, referred to in Ordnance Estimates for 1828, provide the only evidence of overseas activity so far discovered. On the other hand, an abstract of Commissaries' Accounts for 1825–6 shows expenditure on army vessels, garrison boats, colonial vessels, government schooners, and even clothing for the crew of the Governor-General of Canada's boat. These accounts covered eighteen colonial locations from Quebec to New South Wales and Van Diemen's Land, reflecting the Commissariat Department's little-known responsibilities for marine transport abroad, which may have paralleled, but would not have duplicated, the water transport activities of the Board of Ordnance.

A picture of the Fleet's overseas deployment does not come to light until 1895 (see Chapter 6 and Appendix V), though the list of shipping compiled from Fleet Repair Branch records has references to vessels built in Hong Kong, Singapore, Bermuda and Jamaica. One, the steam launch *Lily*, built in 1878, is shown as stationed at Halifax, Nova Scotia, up to 1905, leading a small fleet of eighteen boats and an unnamed lighter. Halifax's history as a garrison town dates back to the arrival of Lord Cornwallis in the 1750s; throughout that period, until the arrival of steam, contact between the fortress, the Citadel, and the outlying forts had been maintained by 26 ft eight-oared whalers of the civilian fleet.

Writing in a Canadian Services publication in 1959, Lt. S.L. Roman, RCASC, says:

When steam replaced oars, the SS *Lily* took over water transport duties in Halifax harbour, moving personnel, rations, ammunition and other stores and equipment to George's and McNab's Islands and to the batteries on the coast. With the arrival of *Lily* target towing became an additional responsibility. Crews were formed of devoted and long-suffering civilians.

He adds a note that one man was known to have served for forty-two years, and the master of the first CASC vessel, *Alfreda*, retired in 1919 after thirty-five years' service, with a gratuity of $900. In 1920, Canadian Water Transport was militarized but remained a separate service under the aegis of the RCASC. It was, sadly, disbanded in 1948.

Up to the time of the birth of the War Department Fleet, the only steam vessel thought to have been in military service had been a paddle-steamer, *Lord Blaney*, whose painting hangs in Byam House, Marchwood. The artist describes her as a War Office (not Board of Ordnance) vessel and her ensign carries the Royal Cipher; however, she appears in Lloyd's Register as a Liverpool steam packet in private ownership.

There is therefore no reason to question a 1907 Army Service Corps journal report naming *Balaclava* as the first steamship in the Fleet. She was, however, 'unfortunately lost on the Wexford coast in November, 1865'. Regrettably, the circumstances are unknown. The *Balaclava* was built around 1857, to be followed in 1859 by *Lord Panmure*, rewardingly named for the Secretary of State at War who had precipitated the demise of the Board of Ordnance. *Lord Panmure* was based at Woolwich and for many years was engaged on a regular schedule carrying stores to and from Portsmouth Gunwharf. She served the Fleet until the turn of the century but, as related in Chapter 5, narrowly escaped an early grave in 1869.

Another steamer, *Stanley*, which entered the Fleet in 1880, was dispatched to the Mediterranean with a cargo of 100 ton guns in 1882. Her skipper was a Mr T.N. Moors, who had qualified by obtaining a BOT certificate for foreign trading. We have no way of knowing whether this was the first such voyage by a WD Fleet vessel, but it was certainly not the last. The *Marquess* and *Sir Evelyn*, for instance, made not a few during their long service.

But although steam had now made its appearance on the scene, sail was still predominant, and the changeover was very gradual indeed. After the entry of the *Lord Panmure* into the Fleet, there is no record of the addition of further steam vessels until 1874 when two launches, *Falcon* and *Grand Duchess*, built respectively at South Shields and Portsmouth,

The *Marquess of Hartington* at HM Gunwharf, Portsmouth, in 1936. She served the Fleet for seventy-one years

Sir Evelyn Wood served the Fleet for sixty-one years. She is seen here at Hobbs Point, Pembroke Dock

were recorded. *Falcon* was a paddle-steamer, then the only one in the Fleet, but was later converted to screw. One wonders if one of the reasons for the conversion might have been the accident in the paddle-box which cost AB G. Barnes a leg in 1894. The unfortunate Barnes was discharged a year later with one year's pay (£63, which now would be of the order of £2,100). The RA officers at Portsmouth subscribed a crutch and wooden leg, but Barnes later got £15 from the Treasury for an artificial limb, and a job at the Royal Arsenal applying dubbin to harness at 3s. 3d. (16.25p) a day. In addition, his son was appointed to *Seagull* at 11s. (55p) a week. Another seaman involved in the accident was able to return to work.

The following year, the ship's boy, jumping aboard from the pier, slipped and fell between vessel and quay, narrowly escaping the paddles. He was hauled out with a boat-hook. At about the same time, *Falcon*, seeing a schooner standing into danger on Ryde Sands, during a gale, notwithstanding warning guns from the Warner lightship, hoisted warning signals herself and, steaming towards the schooner, succeeded in alerting her to the danger. Later the same day she picked up a launch full of distressed marines, with broken oars, and towed her to HMS *Victory*. The master was Mr George Day, later Inspector of Shipping, who served for fifty years in the Fleet, an achievement equalled by his son.

From 1877 a large number of steam vessels, most of them launches, joined the Fleet and the new Royal Engineers Submarine Mining Service. This service, a brief account of which is given in Appendix II, had been set up in 1871 and had quickly grown into a worldwide fleet of specialist craft.

This period of steam building saw the arrival, in 1886, of the best-loved and most durable vessel ever to grace the Fleet, the *Marquess of Hartington*, named for a former Secretary of State for War. Built by Hawthorn, Leslie and Co. at Hebburn at a cost of £10,000, displacing 670 tons and with a carrying capacity of 200 tons, she was the largest vessel so far to join the service. She was joined by the even larger *Sir Evelyn Wood*, named for a former Quartermaster General, in 1896. *Sir Evelyn*, displacing 850 tons, was built at Paisley by Fleming and Ferguson at a cost of £10,850. The service of these two ships was henceforward to form a continuous thread in the many-stranded fabric of the Fleet's history.

At 144 tons displacement, the 1891 *General Skinner* was among the largest of the Royal Engineers'
submarine mining vessels

Although the War Department had now clearly accepted that steam
had arrived, they still saw a limited role for sail; indeed, both the new
freight steamers were sail-rigged. The sailing barge *Sir George Murray*
joined the Fleet in 1900, and the following year the last hoy, *Seagull II*,
entered the service at Pembroke Dock. Even in 1915, nearly sixty years
later, the *Naval Service Pocket Book* records no less than six sailing vessels
and two hoys, the oldest being *Clyde* (1858) and *Havelock* (1859), both
cutters stationed in Bermuda. Built at a cost of £300 each, (about
£11,000 at today's prices) they must certainly have proved cost-
effective.

The *Naval Service Pocket Book* of 1914 does not, however, mention
another small group of sailing vessels in WD service which, remarkably,
continued operating well into the Second World War. These, though not
part of the WD Fleet, were in some cases crewed by Fleet seamen. The
operations of these powder vessels, for such they were, are dealt with in
Chapter 5.

Towards the end of the nineteenth century there were several
developments which were to have an important effect on the future of
the WD Fleet. The first of these was the transfer of responsibility for the

day-to-day running of the Fleet from the Royal Arsenal to the Commissariat and Transport Staff in 1886 and hence, in 1888, to the new Army Service Corps. As it has not been possible to trace an official record, the reasons for the change in a centuries-old arrangement are open to conjecture. It would not be difficult to comprehend that the considerable expansion of the Fleet since the 1850s would have made necessary a re-appraisal of the Principal Military Storekeeper's responsibilities. The supply, transport and ordnance services of the Army were now on a military footing and this factor, added to the considerable experience of the Commissariat in the operation of water transport for the conveyance of supplies, gained in a number of small wars, would have presented an irrefutable case for combining the Army's land and water transport operations under one head.

By 1892, the WD Fleet numbered 119 vessels at home and 127 abroad, and continued to be centred on Woolwich. A new department was set up at the Royal Arsenal under an ASC Colonel with the appointment of Deputy Assistant Adjutant-General Transport (DAAG), Royal Arsenal. This department was directly under the QMG and was not, as hitherto, a part of the Ordnance factory. The DAAG controlled all sea and land transport throughout the United Kingdom but for all Royal Arsenal transport operations he was responsible to the Commissary-General of Ordnance. He enjoyed the right of direct access to the Commander-in-Chief and to General Officers Commanding. The post was later re-designated, more in keeping with its powers and responsibilities, as Assistant Director of Military Transport (ADMT), Woolwich.

The first officer to hold the post was Col. C.E. Walton, CB, and he was followed by Lt.-Col. F.E. Stevens, whose substantial compilation, *Notes and Information regarding the Conveyance of War Office Stores, Explosives, and Supplies by Rail, War Department Vessels, and Hired Water Transport* is considered in Chapter 6. The military (ASC) staff of the Transport Office numbered over twenty, including a captain and QM as executive officer, and a staff sergeant-major as chief clerk. There were also a number of 'civilian subordinates' – civilian clerks – on the establishment. The offices were in a two-storey building facing a wharf so the vessels were easily accessible to the office staff who would thus often benefit from a gift of cigars from a master on returning from a Channel Islands run. There was a mess for the unmarried clerks in the dockyard and transport to and from the office for meals was provided by a WD launch.

It is obvious that a very happy relationship existed between the Fleet members and the ADMT staff. This is evidenced by a report in the ASC journal in February 1902 that the clerical staff of the Transport Office were

> most enjoyably entertained at the Royal Mortar Hotel, Woolwich. . . . Among those present were Mr Oliver and Mr T.N. Moors (Inspector and Assistant Inspector of Shipping), the masters of the WD vessels *Sir R. Buller, Sir E. Wood, Marquess of Hartington* and *Katharine*.

The veteran Mr Oliver was given the honour of replying to the toast 'The Officers'.

At around the time control of the Fleet was transferred to the Commissariat and Transport Staff, the expenditure arising from the maintenance by the War Department of a coasting fleet had been specially reviewed – no doubt as part of the deliberations on its future control. A brief summary of this review, taken from the *Report on the Account of Army Expenditure, 1887–88*, is contained in Chapter 2. The report also draws attention to the fact that the proportional output of stores from Woolwich for the Navy had increased to 43 per cent. In terms of tonnage, 12,389 were Army and 9,190 were Navy stores. The report added, prophetically, that the strength and allotment of the WD vessels would probably be much affected in a short time by the decision as to the Admiralty undertaking the storekeeping duties of naval ordnance, adding that a large portion of the vessels would naturally be transferred to the Navy.

From the very earliest days funds for the provision of armament for land and naval service had been provided from the same compartment of the public purse. By the 1880s, however, this arrangement had become more and more unsatisfactory from the Navy's point of view. Up to the mid-eighteenth century, when Army and Navy were, for the most part, similarly equipped, this system of supply had been quite rational. Thereafter, however, the vast changes in naval design, in strength of armour, in size and power of armament, meant that land and naval service requirements, and the costs of production, had diverged to an extent that the Admiralty were no longer content to be at the financial mercy of the War Office. By the same token the War Office was not easy with a situation which saw the Admiralty's share of expenditure out-stripping its own.

The inevitable split between votes and responsibility was commenced in 1886 and completed in 1891 with the setting up of the Naval Ordnance Department. This department was, however, established at the Royal Arsenal and initially staffed by the transfer of officers from the Ordnance Stores Department, whose duties therefore remained virtually unchanged. So far as can be ascertained about sixteen vessels were transferred.

As regards officers and seamen, a contemporary list (not necessarily complete) names thirty-one who transferred on 1 October 1891. These included eleven masters and seven mates in charge, but, only one ordinary seaman. He was only eighteen, and in his three years service had already served in six vessels. No less than twenty-five of those transferred had joined the Fleet as boys. There is no doubt that the Navy gained a wealth of experienced seamen from the transaction.

Another important change, undoubtedly connected with the above split, was the transfer of procurement of WD shipping from the Admiralty to the War Office, responsibility being vested in a new office, that of the Superintending Engineer and Constructor of Shipping. The first-fruits of the new regime, the 100 ton steam launch WDV *Drake*, designed by the first holder of the post, Mr J.A.C. Hay, was launched on 9 April 1891, christened by Mrs Taylor, the wife of the Senior Ordnance Stores Officer, Western District, at Devonport.

These changes now set the pattern for the future. Although they had resulted in the loss of part of the Fleet's commitments, another task was to follow which would last well beyond the Second World War. It would not only see a considerable increase in the Fleet over the years, but would bring about an even closer relationship with coastal defences throughout the Empire.

4
NEW TASKS

The history of coastal artillery from Tudor times to the mid-nineteenth century had been one of neglected defences, out-of-date guns, unfit and even senile garrisons. The doctrine that the Royal Navy was able to defend coasts far more efficiently than fixed defences, known as the Blue Water School, carried great weight and provided governments with excuses to cut expenditure on the Army and spend it on the Navy or elsewhere. Only during brief periods of great potential danger, as between 1797 and 1805, were great efforts made to undo the many years of neglect.

Coastal artillery, with its forts, defence works, guns, stores and so on both at home and abroad, was the responsibility of the Board of Ordnance. Under the Master-General of the Ordnance, a Lieutenant-General was responsible for artillery but as he was never a gunner, the Board's knowledge of this subject was virtually nil. A civilian organization, it was ruled by civilians more interested in economy than efficiency. Intolerably stingy and parsimonious, its officials would spend time trying to save twopence while gun carriages rotted.

Between the sixteenth and nineteenth centuries neither the armament of ships nor of coastal defences had changed very much. For the gunner, the potential target had always been a great slow-moving wooden wall, relying on wind and presenting a large broadside target at virtually point-blank range. The heaviest gun then mounted in both ships and in batteries was the 42 pounder, which had an extreme range of about 3,000 yd. The only new threat that had appeared up to the early nineteenth century had been the bomb vessel, whose vertical attack by mortar had to be countered by overhead protection.

It was not until the latter half of the nineteenth century when, in common with all other branches of Imperial defence, coastal artillery really began to come into its own. Steam-powered armoured warships mounting rifled guns firing tubular and pointed shell would now present a vastly different adversary. Like had to be met with like and so development followed development with bewildering rapidity. Warships continued to increase in size and power; some could steam at up to 18 knots, and had 12 in armour. In 1877 the first torpedo-boat, whose defence was its speed of 21 knots, came on the scene. To keep pace with this rapid evolution new methods, new instruments, more powerful guns, stronger fortifications, were required and produced, with the result that coastal artillery became the leaders in accurate and effective shooting and pioneers in scientific gunnery.

Until the 1880s, however, the exciting developments of the previous thirty years had made little difference to practice firing, which from time immemorial had been aimed at beach targets or floating anchored barrels and 9 ft square screens as simulating the almost static targets which enemy ships would present. However, steps were now being taken to re-vitalize and modernize training and in this, records *The History of the Royal Artillery*, 'probably the most potent factor . . . was the introduction of the moving target'.

The first of such targets took the water in either Cork or Hong Kong, in 1882, and the idea 'took on at once'.

It was not, however, taken on universally and fixed targets continued to be used. For instance, it was not until 1895 that the Norfolk Artillery first fired at a moving target, this exciting event being watched by the Prince of Wales, who was afterwards entertained to dinner by the officers. After this, it was reported that firing at towed targets became more general, though as late as 1897 *Garrison Artillery Drill* contained instructions for the anchoring of targets.

At the outset target-towing duties were very much on an *ad hoc* basis. Naval tugs, torpedo boats, hired vessels (certainly in Tynemouth) and even RA-manned vessels were in use. No doubt, also, RE-operated craft of the Submarine Mining Service would also have been used. The SMS, referred to in Chapter 3 and Appendix II, had been operating a considerable fleet of craft since 1871; by 1898 it numbered sixty-seven, ranging in size from 125 ton steamers to 20 ton launches. It is unlikely, therefore, that the WD Fleet, which had been operating steam launches for nearly twenty years, would not also have been required to help out.

The difficulties of establishing a standard *modus operandi* with so many different agencies must have been considerable and it could therefore only have been a matter of time before some rationalization was seen to be necessary. We may conclude that the WD Fleet had by then given

Sir Redvers Buller, although the first to be built as a target tower, had a dual role as a cargo carrier

sufficient proof of its efficiency and ability to carry on the task alone. Having said that, it must be added that there was some dissatisfaction over the use of vessels which were, after all, not designed for use other than the carriage of rations and stores and for harbour duties, the complaint being that they were too slow, not having been built for speed.

Nevertheless it took another thirteen years, to 1895, before the first custom-built steam target towers joined the Fleet. These were the *Sir Redvers Buller* (570 tons) and the *Osprey*, (288 tons). The former, though classified as a target tower, was based at Woolwich and was used in the winter months as a cargo-carrier. *Osprey*, built at Hull and stationed at Devonport, had a speed of 10 knots and was the fastest built for the Fleet up to that time. In 1897 her effectiveness as a target tower was greatly increased when she became the first vessel to be fitted with winding gear, enabling her to increase considerably the speed of the target across the range. This winding gear soon became standard.

The master of *Osprey*, Mr J.W. Nicholson, suffered an unfortunate accident while the vessel was undergoing steam trials in a gale off Spithead. He fell from the bridge onto the deck, and, from the after-effects of the concussion he suffered, was forced to retire in early 1897. He had served for thirty-one years and it was reported in the ASC journal that 'his skill and judgement was only equalled by the zeal and care shown in carrying out his many and trying duties'.

These two vessels were soon followed by more purpose-built steam target towers, reflecting the speedy growth of the new task. In 1896 *Lord Wolseley*, (also a Woolwich cargo-carrier) *Lansdowne* and *Sir Robert Hay* joined the Fleet. There were already a number of steam launches in service and these also increased in number, no doubt reflecting the parallel commitment for range safety. All these, and subsequent steam towers, had a built-in capacity for general service duties in addition to their designed role.

An early account of a shoot from the Western Forts, Isle of Wight, is given in the *Minutes of Proceedings of the Royal Artillery Institution, Volume XIII*:

A Royal Artillery range party aboard *Sir Robert Hay*; they have the Hong Kong target surrounded

It was originally intended to fire at targets, specially prepared to drift with the strong tides . . . but when a steamer was made available, two old four-oared boats were purchased, and a rough triangular wooden framework, surmounted by a small flag, was lashed upon the gunwales of each. The tow-rope used was 200 yards long; but half that length would have been amply sufficient for safety. The first boat was hit twice, and when she filled, the other, which had been towed close behind the steamer, was allowed to drop astern, and take her place. The steamer's speed was greatly retarded by dragging this water-logged boat until a lucky shot cut her adrift altogether.

It is interesting to note that the minimum length of tow for safety was later to be established as 300 yd. The problem of coping with water-logged boats was obviated by the introduction of the Hong Kong target, a lattice-work structure usually towed in a set of three, the centre one being larger than the other two, to simulate a warship. Although other

Steam target tower *Sir Desmond O'Callaghan* with three Hong Kong targets in simulated warship formation

types, such as the Splash target, were introduced very much later, the Hong Kong remained in use throughout almost the whole period of target towing. Why 'Hong Kong' targets is not certainly known, but one may make an educated guess.

Having now accepted this new commitment, the WD Fleet was the only logical contender for yet another task which, ninety years later, is still being carried out around the coasts of Britain, albeit by contract.

Target practice seawards, by both the Royal Navy and the Royal Artillery, was creating safety problems in the crowded estuaries and harbours of Britain and Ireland. Very many complaints were reaching MPs and the Government of danger to life and restrictions in commerce and fishing being caused by allegedly reckless firing. Passenger vessels reported being straddled, fishermen complained of being prevented from going about their business and of guns frightening the fish away and even damaging their nets. At Plymouth a local person said he had been in danger on several occasions from shooting from Bovisand and on 1 August 1891, while the Prince of Naples was visiting the battery, 'wild firing was indulged in' and a shot from one of the big guns landed in the water 400 yd away and ricocheted to within 20 yd of his yacht.

In another recorded instance, the Devon Militia Artillery bracketed a Saltash boat during a practice, giving the irate owner a 64 pounder bath. In his complaint he alleged that visibility was only 50 yd; the battery commander, who was obviously on a hiding to nothing, claimed that, on the contrary, visibility had been good, probably reasoning that poor shooting would be accounted a less heinous offence than faulty judgement in continuing the shoot. He was severely censured.

There were, of course, two sides to the problem. Thus *The History of the Royal Artillery, Volume I* states:

> The very fact that coast batteries were built to protect the entrance to important harbours implied that the water before them would usually be crowded with shipping. And with the increase in the power of guns, and the consequent enlargement of the danger zone for ricochets, the trouble grew ever greater. It had been bad enough in the days of the moored barrel, for the constant delays took the hearts out of all ranks and induced a general lassitude which was hard to eradicate. But when the moving target appeared on the scene the conditions became hopeless – almost ridiculous. All that

could be looked for was an occasional shot, and officers and men, wearied out with waiting, lost all interest.

According to *The Times* newspaper reports, it would seem that the Royal Navy's gunnery practice seaward was equally perilous, if not more so, for local civilian interests. The rather inappropriately named gunboat HMS *Plucky* accidentally sank a fishing boat, killing one of the crew. In another incident, put down to an accidental discharge, the missile somehow flew ashore and destroyed a greenhouse.

The volume of complaints from fishermen, from commercial interests and from yachtsmen had grown apace with every incident, and eventually, following the *Plucky* incident, the Government was forced to act. In 1892, under the auspices of the Board of Trade, an inter-departmental committee was set up to enquire into the system of target practice seawards 'now carried on from ships and forts and the conditions under which it may most suitably be carried out in future'. The Board appointed Sir Charles Hall, KCMG, QC, MP as chairman, with two representatives each from the Admiralty and the War Office (both Royal Artillery Colonels) and two MPs to represent the fishermen and shipowners.

The committee first met in March 1892 and periodically thereafter took evidence in London, Portsmouth and Plymouth, from members of the aggrieved public as well as from naval and artillery officers. Many of the latter pointed out the frustration experienced when they had to stop firing, sometimes for many valuable hours of daylight because of traffic in the danger area. The MP for the Totnes Division said that the fishermen and yachtsmen who had complained to him had not exaggerated, and were very angry at the suggestion that they sometimes placed themselves in the line of fire in order to obtain a new sail or some other compensation.

The officer commanding at Cork raised a laugh when he said that at Cork the fishermen voluntarily got out of the way because they were not quite sure whether the military possessed the right to send a shot into them or not. He did make the point that what was wanted was a steam launch, by means of which warning might be given to those in danger, and this, indeed, was to be the tenor of one of the committee's recommendations.

The report of the committee was presented to both Houses of

Parliament early in 1893. It commented at length on the various types of complaint, and on the hindrance to practice, showing in this regard a commendable appreciation of the effect on the gunners of long delays caused when boats and small vessels remained in the line of fire for long periods. The most important recommendation of the several made, was that for the purpose of preventing vessels anchoring or remaining within the danger area during target practice, power should be given to the military and naval authorities to tow boats away. For this purpose, steam tugs, in addition to those required for the towing of targets, should be placed by the War Department at the disposal of the officer in command of the forts.

The report was duly tabled but the last available reference to it was in Hansard on 12 May 1893, when Campbell-Bannerman, the Secretary of State for War, said, in answer to a question, that the report had been sent to the GOCs of the Districts and that their recommendations were awaited. It has not been possible to trace any further action, or formal direction or authority which would enable us to put a date to the Fleet's assumption of what became known as range safety or range clearance duties. There is no evidence, however, that power was given to the naval and military authorities to tow offending vessels willy-nilly out of danger areas. Instead, in many areas by-laws were passed under the Military Lands Acts and enforcement became a legal business.

As we shall see, this range safety task out-lasted target-towing, passing from the civilian fleet to the Navy and from the Navy to civilian contractors.

5
NINETEENTH-CENTURY SHIPS AND SEAMEN

The silent self-effacing way in which the Fleet carried out its duties through the nineteenth century was only occasionally broken. So while we know in general what its duties were, it is not very often before the arrival of the ASC journal in 1892 that we find reports of specific activities or incidents.

Naval and military matters were given daily coverage in the 'quality' newspapers . . . troop and warship movements, manoeuvres, weapons developments, promotions and appointments, accidents and incidents. Through these media the veil was sometimes twitched aside. The *Morning Post* occasionally carried brief reports of the movement of WD vessels in and out of Chatham dockyard, carrying such items as shot and shell and Armstrong 20 and 40 pounder guns to and from Woolwich, and *The Times*, in an 1838 issue, mentions the movement of Board of Ordnance hoys on the Thames. These barely newsworthy items merely serve to underline the 'bread and butter' nature of the Fleet's work. The biggest story, at least in terms of space, was that of the move of the 81 ton gun referred to in Chapter 2. This article contained what was almost certainly the first published illustration of an actual, named, Fleet vessel. Later, in 1895, artists' impressions of the WD vessels *Petrel* and *Collingwood Dickson* appeared in the press with accompanying stories.

The *Petrel* incident is described below. The steam launch *Collingwood Dickson* made news in April 1895 when, according to a report in the *Daily Graphic* she was instrumental in towing a stranded Training Brig, *Martin*, off the Shingles Bank near Yarmouth, Isle of Wight. *Martin* was apparently grounded at high tide and it was 24 hours before the WD vessel succeeded in freeing her.

From histories of York (Revd C. Caine and C.B. Knight) we learn that improvements to navigation in the River Ouse enabled the War Department to land stores from Woolwich directly into a newly-constructed Ordnance depot. For this purpose a jetty and hand-operated crane were built in 1888. In spite of the navigational improvements, however, direct coastal traffic into York was almost entirely confined to two 'Government Schooners', *Celestine* and *Princess*.

There is no trace of these vessels in available military records and it is therefore thought they were hired vessels, probably operated by Messrs W. France & Co., whose shipping served Yorkshire and the north-east from London. It is of course possible that they may have been crewed by WD Fleet personnel. The practice was not unknown. By the 1930s, however, WD vessels were off-loading downriver at Selby into rail and road transport.

There was an interesting parliamentary question, clearly relating to a Fleet vessel, in September 1893, when the member for Peterborough asked the Civil Lord of the Admiralty for information on the steam launch

> said to have been given to the Duke of Connaught for use while Commander of the Army Corps at Portsmouth and whether Parliamentary authority had been given and was it necessary for him to carry out his public duties as Commander of the Land Forces at Portsmouth.

This question having nothing at all to do with the Admiralty, the Secretary of State for War replied that the steam launch had been supplied to enable the GOC of the Southern District to visit the numerous forts and posts in his command without delay or difficulty. He added that the necessity had been recognized before the Duke of Connaught's appointment.

The scarcity of reported incident beyond the trivial round and common task must be due more to a lack of interest in chronicling Fleet history by its controllers and officers rather than to extraordinary good fortune. So it is that we have certain knowledge of only a few major happenings, and in two of these the details are virtually non-existent. It is stretching belief to accept that these were the only untoward events worthy of record to have been visited upon the Fleet in a century, but no others have so far been traced.

The earliest, to which reference has already been made, was the loss of the *Balaclava* in 1865, off the Wexford coast. The second was the loss of the steam launch *Ethel*, built at Devonport, which broke from her tow and foundered off Dover in October 1889. This was stated in the ASC journal to be the first War Department loss since *Balaclava*.

In between these two losses, the screw steamer *Lord Panmure* had a narrow escape on 20 March 1869, when, as reported by the *Kentish Independent* she was run into by a collier off Greenhithe. She sustained an 8 ft long gash in her hull and had to be run ashore to save her from sinking in deep water. *Lord Panmure* was on passage to Bull's Point with Armstrong guns and, unfortunately for him, the household effects of one of Woolwich Arsenal's deputy storekeepers, a Mr Holloway, who was taking up a new appointment there. In addition to the ship's stores and fittings, his furniture was reported to be 'entirely spoiled'. With the assistance of the WD vessel *Earl de Grey & Ripon* and two barges, the stricken steamer was patched up with tarpaulin and taken back to the Arsenal for repair. She subsequently served the Fleet for over thirty years.

Another incident which had a happy outcome, at least for the WD vessel, involved the *Marquess of Hartington* and was appropriately reported in full in an ASC journal of 1896:

The WDV *Marquess of Hartington* arrived here (Portsmouth) on 11th July, on passage to Woolwich, and reported that on the 9th inst., when about 26 miles from Cork signals of distress were observed flying from a ketch – the *United Friends* of Plymouth, bound from Newport (Mon.) to Cork with coals. On the previous day a gale of wind had blown her sails away, and the heavy seas had strained the little vessel, causing her to leak badly. Signals had been flying all day, and the crew were extremely exhausted with incessant pumping and exposure. The steamer boarded her and took them on board, where they were supplied with fresh clothing and food, and generally well-cared for. The *Hartington* called at Plymouth to land them and the Master (A. Hooper) handed them over to the Ship-wrecked Mariners Society. The ketch – the deck of which at the time of rescue was being continually swept by heavy seas – foundered soon after the crew had left her, so that they had good cause to be thankful that their signals were at last seen and acted upon by some passing vessel.

The most tragic peacetime incident, however, had happened in the Thames the previous year. On 23 January 1895 the sailing barge *Petrel* ran aground below Gravesend at Lower Hope Reach. Explosives reports showed that she had left Woolwich for Purfleet with a mixed cargo of explosives and other stores properly separated by wadmiltilts (coarse woollen cloth covers).

She arrived at Purfleet and discharged and loaded cargo, then left for Shoeburyness at 10.45 a.m. The weather was very rough and soon after leaving Purfleet *Petrel* was seen drifting on to Hope Point. The master declined assistance offered by the coastguard and soon after noon it was seen that the barge was on fire. There was an explosion, followed at intervals by others until, at 7 p.m., she was completely wrecked and burnt out.

The two ABs, J. Hoare and Tom Greensmith, took to the ship's dinghy and the boy Luttrel jumped overboard and was picked up by them, all later reaching Woolwich safely. The master, who was seen to jump overboard with his clothes on fire, perished. It transpired that he had apparently been in a state of temporary insanity at the time.

Petrel, though operated by the Royal Gunpowder factory at Waltham Abbey, was a WD vessel. The 1887 sailing barge *Sallie*, re-named *Georgina*, was purchased by the ASC to replace her, and Mr J. Jackson, from *Collingwood Dickson*, was appointed master. This factory had always operated its own small fleet of sailing and towing (horse-drawn) barges, the latter for work on the Grand Junction Canal. There were also a number of small boats (no less than thirty-one in 1869) for local work within the factory area. The sailing barges were also used for the carriage of stores, as in the case of the ill-fated *Petrel*, on the requisition of the Commissary-General at Woolwich.

It is obvious from the answer to a parliamentary question of 14 March 1893, that the Waltham Abbey fleet was considered a separate service. Colonel Hughes of Woolwich asked why crews of WD vessels at the Arsenal 'are compelled to wear uniforms marked with the broad arrow and pay for it a sum of £1.16.9d. each out of their wages, while at Waltham Abbey uniform to the value of £3 each is supplied free to crews of WD vessels'.

The Financial Secretary to the War Office replied to the effect that as the seamen were paid good wages, there was no hardship involved in requiring them, for purposes of discipline, to provide themselves with suitable clothing. He added:

The barges carrying gunpowder and explosives constitute a separate and peculiar service. There are only about a dozen men employed and for the last half-century and probably for a much longer time it has been the practice to supply each man yearly with a uniform costing about £2.14s. There is really no analogy between the two cases and it is not proposed to make any alterations.

This separate fleet, outside the control of the ADMT, was remarkable in that it does not seem to have ever employed anything other than towing and sailing barges. Even as late as 1931 two replacement wooden sailing barges, *Lady of the Lea* and *King Edward VII*, were commissioned under the supervision of the WD Fleet's Superintending Engineer and Constructor of Shipping. David Wood, in his *Powderbarge WD*, says that *Lady of the Lea* had the distinction of being the last wooden sailing barge built on the Thames. The builders were Messrs Hyams Oliver & Co., Rotherhithe. The Waltham Abbey factory closed in 1945 after over a century and a half of operation and the last vessels were sold into private hands. *Lady of the Lea* still survives at Faversham, itself once the location of an important powder works.

The WD Fleet proper and the powder barges must have carried thousands of tons of powder and explosives, but the *Petrel* incident is the only known example of a loss of a WD-crewed vessel, and even that appeared to have been the result of arson. Hired vessels were extensively used, and one of these, a Grand Junction Canal Company barge, was lost in 1874 when its cargo of five tons of powder exploded in Regent's Park, killing the crew of four and destroying a bridge.

The implication in the answer to the parliamentary question mentioned above was that the Waltham Abbey powder bargemen were not as well paid as WD crewmen, and so were compensated by the free issue of a somewhat more expensive suit of clothes. However, Mr Wood states that the bargeman would be entitled to sick pay, he had a hospital service available and could look forward to a pension or gratuity on retirement.

If this were so then bargemen were rather luckier than one of their predecessors in the same employment a few decades earlier. After serving five years in the Faversham gunpowder factory, John Banks became mate of the powder vessel *Lord Howe*, serving in that capacity from 1803 to 1822. He was 'reduced', i.e., made redundant, when the vessel was sold.

In 1824 he petitioned the Duke of Wellington for half-pay, if not for some employment suitable to his age of 53, on the grounds of a

> severe hurt upon his breast in lifting a barrel of powder which fell on him when on duty in the vessel in 1806 of which he still feels the effects as it has rendered him totally incapable of hard labour.

The duke passed the petition to the Board of Ordnance with the recommendation that it be dealt with in accordance with the regulations. The latter granted Banks 'a sum equal to one month's pay from the date of his discharge' and told him that the regulations did not permit of a pension to mates of Board of Ordnance vessels on reduction.

Had Banks not put in a further sixteen years' service in *Lord Howe* after his accident, he might have been luckier. In 1828, Edward Williams, referred to earlier, got a £16 pension after losing his arm while firing a salute, and Thomas Walker, who served twenty-six years, and was a cripple, got a pension of 9d. a day. In Ordnance Estimates for various subsequent years, there are references to masters of Board of Ordnance vessels being granted pensions after long service. Superintendent of Shipping Thomas Dickinson was an exceptional case, being given a pension of $^{11}/_{12}$ of his former salary after forty-five years' service. His £660 would represent over £25,000 at today's values. He retired at 72 'due to age and infirmities' and one hopes he lived long to enjoy it.

But pensions were not easy to come by. In 1908 there were only three men serving who would be entitled to pensions. A Cox'n Horgan, of No. 1 Local Boat's Crew, serving at Queenstown, Co. Cork, was not one of these three. When he retired in 1912 after forty-seven years he was, however, convinced that he was so entitled, and OC ASC Cork was endeavouring to confirm his claim. It is not known if he was successful. The dismayed Horgan was also surprised to find that he had no entitlement to fourteen days' leave before discharge, but his OC treated 'this veteran, white of beard and hoary of countenance' with compassion and guaranteed his last fourteen days' pay. Incidentally, his vacancy was nepotistically filled by his brother, who remarked that he had waited thirty-nine and a half years for his promotion!

Apparently apprentices on a long service scheme qualified for pensions but there is evidence to suggest that pensions policy had been changed to the disadvantage of Fleet members. According to the Heath Report (see

Chapter 7), 'present crews were in hope of getting them again', which in fact they did. A modified pension scheme had been proposed for the Inspector of Shipping, his assistant, and for masters and first engineers.

Loyalty, as exemplified by long service, seems always to have been the main characteristic of the Fleet. All ranks seem to take to heart the injunction, contained in the 1859 and 1897 Regulations and continued, in more or less the same wording, in all subsequent Regulations:

> Every man or boy employed in this service will devote himself exclusively to it.

Although WD seamen of all ranks were classified as 'civilian subordinates' (the class of employee we now know as civil servants), their special status required them to be bound by Articles of Agreement – then on Woolwich Form 140 – in which each agreed to serve on any sea-going or coastal vessel and 'to use his best endeavours for the service and safety of HM Ships and vessels . . .'. This agreement provided for only three days' notice. Seamen continued in the twentieth century to be bound by articles on an ADMT form from which, however, the original injunction had been dropped for a rather less exhortatory undertaking to work by day and night if necessary and 'obey the lawful commands of all my superior officers . . .'.

With the exception of engine-room staff, all crews were engaged in the first instance as boys, between the ages of 14 and 16, preference being given to sons of soldiers and of men who were or who had been, serving in WD vessels. Herein, perhaps, lies a clue to that characteristic loyalty. Army ex-boys have always tended to make a long-service career of the service: as in the Army, so in the Fleet. Boys wishing to join the Fleet had to be physically sound, of good character, and possess a certificate of education not below the 5th standard. Their names and recommendations were registered at Woolwich.

Typical of long-serving seamen in the nineteenth century were Mr T.N. Moors and Mr A. Hooper. The former joined the sloop *Wellington* as a boy in 1853 and after many years of service afloat he was appointed Inspector of Shipping in 1902, retiring after fifty-three years' service in 1906. It is recorded that on his retirement he was presented by Col. R.A. Nugent, CB, the then ADMT, with a silver tea and coffee service, a barometer and, for his wife, a dressing bag. He was evidently not content to sit back and rusticate as shortly after retirement he was elected a member of the Metropolitan Borough Council of Woolwich. His successor as Inspector of Shipping was Mr Hooper, erstwhile master of the *Marquess*, whose service, again as a boy, dated back to 1866. Hooper had accompanied Moors as mate of the *Stanley* when, as mentioned in Chapter 3, she took a cargo to the Mediterranean. The following year he had taken the same vessel to Gibraltar when Moors was ill.

There were many other boys of nineteenth-century vintage whose careers spanned a generation and beyond. W.C. Young joined the Fleet in 1899 at the age of 14 and served for fifty years. F. Rhodes joined at 16 in 1894, and was appointed Inspector of Shipping in 1939. H. Petty joined in 1882 at the age of 14 and served for forty-five years and at Woolwich, in 1902, Mr J. Oliver was in his fiftieth year of service to the Fleet. Then there were two holders of the Bronze Medal and Certificate of the Royal Humane Society, Francis Reynolds and Edward Greensmith.

The former, while mate of the WD vessel *General Peel*, according to the citation, 'at great personal risk, rescued Wm. James from drowning in Pembroke Dock, on the 2nd March, 1886'. Reynolds went on to serve

Capt. Francis Reynolds served from sail to steam and earned the nickname 'Nelson' during the Second World War

with distinction as a master during the 1914–18 War when he was engaged in the cross-channel service carrying munitions. His daughter recalled that

> On one occasion he called for members of his crew to go with him to tow a live mine out of the path of a troopship. The effort was successful and he and five members of the crew returned safely to the ship in their small boat.

His obituary credited him with many thrilling experiences, and adds that 'his calm contempt of danger earned him the name of "Nelson" among his shipmates'.

When serving at Shoeburyness in 1902, Stoker Edward Greensmith went swimming with Ordinary Seaman Harfield. Harfield was seized with cramp and, being unable to reach the lifebuoy thrown to him, disappeared below the surface. Greensmith dived in fully-clothed and after great difficulty managed to get Harfield to the surface, but lost him again in the struggle. He persisted and eventually got him up again and managed to keep his head above water until help came. Harfield recovered after artificial respiration. The awards were presented to Greensmith by the Commandant of the School of Gunnery after church parade in the presence of a general parade.

Greensmith seemed to make a habit of this activity as six years earlier, when he would have been about 14, he had saved two children at the same station. One of three brothers who served in the Fleet (Tom of the *Petrel* incident, recorded above, was another), Greensmith had joined the Fleet in 1901 and went on to serve in no less than twenty-nine different vessels. Always a most cheerful individual, he insisted that no-one should live over the age of 60. This he proved to his own satisfaction by dying at that age while serving as an acting 2nd Engineer in 1942.

6
THE ARMY SERVICE CORPS IN CONTROL

By the end of the century, military control of the Fleet by the Army Service Corps was well established. It is clear from the tone of an 1894 article by a Lt. W.H. Foster in the ASC journal that responsibility for all aspects of Fleet operation was taken seriously:

> Every effort should be made to promote good feeling between the men of this Department and those of the ASC; as far as my experience goes, this should be a very easy matter as it would be difficult to find any body of men with whom it is a greater pleasure to deal, and I am glad of this opportunity to testify to their steadfastness, sobriety, willingness and zeal, frequently under the most arduous and trying circumstances.

There is evidence that these were no empty words. Two years later, at a special smoking concert held in the sergeants' mess at Portsmouth, Capt. Foster presented binoculars to Messrs Mountifield, of the barge *John Adye*, and Pelton, recently of *Falcon*. He congratulated them on the respect in which they were held by officers, comrades, friends and subordinates. The binoculars had been subscribed by 'Royal Naval Ordnance and our Transport Departments, the two branches having originally been one and now work hand in hand together'.

Mountifield was retiring after thirty-six years and eight months' service with a pension of £95 6s. 8d., 'his 4 years' service in the Revenue Cruisers and Navy being ignored by the Treasury'. Pelton was awarded £85 16s. for thirty-three years' service but on further representations this was increased to £93 12s. for thirty-six years.

In his article, Foster goes on to quote extensively from notes made by Lt.-Col. F.E. Stevens. Lt.-Col. (later Brevet Colonel) Stevens was the then Deputy Assistant Adjutant General for Transport at Woolwich Arsenal and, therefore, the Head of the Fleet. His notes were published the following year as *Notes and Information regarding the Conveyance of War Office Stores, Explosives and Supplies by Rail, War Department Vessels, and Hired Water Transport.* Col. Stevens did full justice to this lengthy title in sixty-three pages and sixteen appendices, covering every aspect of the movement of stores by water and rail, including personnel administration. So it was that, for the first time, a detailed picture of Fleet operation and administration emerges.

Col. Stevens shows that at this time the Fleet establishment at home consisted of:

Station	Vessels	Boats
Portsmouth	10	17
Devonport	5	36
Chatham	3	12
Dover	–	1
Harwich	1	4
Channel Isles	–	2
Cork and District	3	15
Woolwich	10	–

and abroad:

Station	Vessels	Boats
Barbados and St Lucia	–	6
Bermuda	2	30
Ceylon	–	3
Gibraltar	–	6
Hong Kong	3	15
Jamaica	2	5
Mauritius	–	4
Malta	1	1
Nova Scotia	1	19
Sierra Leone	–	1
Singapore	2	1

This gave a total of 43 vessels and 178 boats. The dumb barges do not appear to have been taken into account.

Stevens gives an interesting, but, alas, not exhaustive list of the 'War

Department Vessels of the Transport Service'. It contains 12 steamers, 16 steam launches and 7 sailing vessels, but there are a number of known omissions, apart from such dumb barges as the celebrated *Gog* and *Magog*. A listing is given at Appendix V.

The oldest steam vessel in the Fleet was the *Lord Panmure*, (1859), referred to in Chapter 3, now nearing the end of her service life. *Panmure* apart, the average age of the steamer fleet was just over six years. With three building, including *Sir Evelyn Wood*, the Fleet was well up-to-date. The steam launch fleet, ranging from the 80 ton *Satellite* and *Stanhope* to the 25 ton *Ida*, had an average age of 9 years, the doyenne being the aptly named *Grand Duchess*, built in 1874.

But even in this modern fleet, as already mentioned in Chapter 3, there was still room for wind power. The sailing hoys *Sebastopol* (1857), *Lord Vivian* (1862), and *Emily* (1867), though not named by Stevens, were known to be still operating in the Fleet at this time, though the 1874 *Alice* is the oldest listed as part of this still economic, wonderland. *Lord Vivian* continued in the service at least till 1914, her life having been prolonged by conversion from a hoy to a dumb barge.

These vessels and boats were manned by 183 civilians and 169 military personnel at home, and 164 and 58 respectively abroad. This is the first time any reference to the employment of soldiers in the Fleet has been traced. Unfortunately, Col. Stevens does not enlarge on this employment, merely stating that 'soldiers are employed at many stations, for vessels and boats, and are given extra duty pay at rates varying from 4d. to 1s. per diem.' Instructions for the handling of gigs are, however, contained in some Royal Garrison Artillery training manuals and it may well be that such boats were on the strength of the Fleet. It is therefore possible that soldiers crewed the small craft used on various minor harbour duties.

From the statistics given it is not possible to discern any particular pattern which might assist in determining the policy. At home, only Woolwich employed no soldiers; civilian crew strength there was seventy-six. No soldiers were employed in Hong Kong, Jamaica and Mauritius, but in Gibraltar there were seventeen military and one solitary civilian. The largest contingent was at Devonport, where soldiers outnumbered civilians by eighty-one to twenty-five. Portsmouth employed the largest contingent of fifty-two civilian crew outside Woolwich, with thirty-four soldiers. Whatever may have been the policy for the employment of soldiers, however, it is clear from the absence of any further reference in Col. Stevens' very detailed notes on administration of the Fleet, that military personnel were not part of it, and would therefore have been locally detached from their parent units for temporary duty.

The duties of the Fleet are specified in the following terms:

> The work carried out by the different vessels and boats at home is various, and consists of the conveyance of stores of all descriptions between stations and districts in the United Kingdom; transport of troops locally, distribution of rations to forts, etc; towage of targets; visits of staff and other officers to outlying forts, etc.

Special War Office approval was required for the use of vessels for private purposes and 'such applications should be very special and very few'. The days of 'recreational' transport were still a long way off!

The qualifications for entry into the Fleet have been referred to in Chapter 5. Promotion qualifications up to boatswain all included mandatory periods of service in a Woolwich coasting steamer, from four months for boy to ordinary seaman, six months from OS to AB, and twelve months from AB to boatswain. Ordinary seamen had to pass an examination to the satisfaction of the Inspector of Shipping, while boatswains and mates had, of course, to get the appropriate Board of Trade certificate (home) to secure advancement. It was also noted that special consideration would be given, when opportunities occurred, to masters of WD vessels who obtained 'foreign' Board of Trade certificates.

Below decks, the qualifications for first and second engineer required, respectively, possession of the Board of Trade 1st and 2nd Class certificates. First appointments were subject to the recommendation of the Superintending Engineer and Constructor of Shipping, who 'will be responsible for their competency for their several posts'. No doubt all engineers would have taken to heart the admonition in paragraph thirteen of *Regulations for WD General Service Vessels*:

> All repairs and adjustments will, as far as practicable, be executed by the engineers on board; and that engineer will show himself the most efficient who works his engines with the least expenditure of coal and other stores, or cost for repairs.

Engine-room staff were exempt from the requirements to wear the uniform of the Fleet, being provided, free of cost, with two canvas suits of working clothing annually, issued from the clothing centre of the Services at Pimlico. All other crew members were required to provide their own, which would differ only in detail from that worn by their successors of the twentieth century. A full description of the dress is given in Appendix III. ABs, ordinary seamen and boys could obtain their clothing from Pimlico on repayment, but the officers were expected to go to Messrs Scarrott & Sons of 70 Queen Street, Portsea who held the sealed patterns. Scarrotts undertook to supply cap, badge, jacket, waistcoat and trousers at £3 5s. for a master, £3 1s. for a mate and £2 17s. for a boatswain. We know from the answer to a parliamentary question in 1893 (see Chapter 5) that crew clothing cost £1 16s. 9d., which would have made a considerable hole in an ordinary seaman's first pay packet of £3 15s. a month sea-going, or £3 10s. harbour. Boys got a pound less a month.

Rates of pay in force at this time had been set in 1891. The pay of masters started at £14 a month for sea-going, rising to £17 after six years' service as such. Masters of harbour vessels got £10 on appointment, rising to £13 after fifteen years. This latter figure was the starting point for masters of the larger *Osprey* and *Sir Robert Hay*, steam target towers, and the Woolwich steamer, *Katharine,* but they received no subsequent increases.

The pay of mates in charge of small vessels and steam launches rose from £6 15s. to £7 10s. after two years, but sea-going mates and those in charge of vessels for which a master's certificate was required, started at £8, going to £9 after two years. Below decks, pay ranged from the stoker's £5 to the first engineer's £12, rising to £14 after six years' service as such.

In addition to their base pay, crews of harbour vessels at Woolwich, Chatham, Portsmouth and Devonport were allowed extra pay ranging from 5s. a month for an ordinary seaman or boy to £2 for a senior seaman when acting mate employed on coasting service. It may be borne in mind, as a guide only, that the 1890 pound would be worth about thirty-six times as much today.

The *Notes* indicate that only a few officers and men serving in the Fleet were entitled to superannuation. Under the Superannuation Act of 1887, however, those who had served for not less than seven years and had been made redundant could get a compassionate gratuity from the

Treasury of £1, or one week's salary, whichever was the greater, for each year of service.

Similarly, retirement caused by permanent incapacitation resulting from infirmity of mind or body, after not less than fifteen years of service, could also attract the same rate of payment. There is no mention of an upper age limit for service, but as seamen were subject to the same rules for pay as civilian subordinates in general, it is fair to assume they would have had a retiring age of 60.

Eventually, however, all long-serving 'established' seamen became entitled to pensions, and during the Second World War the rules for establishment were eased by the Treasury for some late entries into the Fleet. They authorized the establishment of sea-going mates and second engineers up to the age of 55, provided, however, that they were able to complete ten years' reckonable service for pension at the age of 60.

In spite of what to the modern eye seems to be an adequate fleet to handle the movement of stores within the United Kingdom, it is clear from the *Notes* that there was a considerable amount of movement by contract hire. Stevens lists five modes of transport and the arrangements for them:

> Steam freight – to all Districts by agreements with steamship companies;
>
> WD vessels – to all Districts by Officer in responsible charge;
>
> Coastwise freight (sailing) – to all Districts by contract;
>
> Lighterage – to Thames, Eastern, South-Eastern, Woolwich and Aldershot;
>
> Canal – chiefly to Aldershot by WD barges, and to Weedon, Aldershot, Enfield, and Birmingham.

Very urgent or urgent stores were to be sent by steam freight if WD vessels were not available. Otherwise, the order of priority for ordinary traffic was:

> War Department vessels
> Sailing freight
> Lighterage
> Canal

Stevens goes on to list fourteen shipping companies dealing with coastwise trade, covering every part of the country. It is interesting to recall that in the early days of the Government Fleet water transport had been the safest, and the most practicable, means of transporting freight. Now, nearly a century later, despite intense railway competition, it had also become the most economic. Stevens produced figures to show that dispatch by rail from Woolwich cost twice as much to York and Dublin, three times as much to Devonport and Leith and four times as much to Newcastle. So all but the most urgent of traffic was still consigned by water. Stevens says,

> By far the most economical mode of transit is by War Department vessels and while there is a vacant foot of space in these vessels hired freight should never be resorted to.

Thirteen years later, his successor was able successfully to prove that nothing had changed.

7
INTO THE TWENTIETH CENTURY

The beginning of the twentieth century would have found the Fleet in very good heart. It was under efficient and firm but sympathetic military control; it was up-to-date, and had displayed its versatility in quickly developing the techniques and practices necessary to carry out its new target-towing and range safety duties, and was still expanding to meet those commitments. Above all it was, as a 1908 investigation was to find, a sound economic proposition; then, as today, that was the supreme test.

The Fleet's versatility was well demonstrated at Sheerness, where the Fleet vessels were largely engaged on duties in support of the School of Gunnery at Shoeburyness and the Thames defences. These duties often went beyond the straightforward target-towing and general administrative tasks. In August 1900, for instance, headed by the 1898 steam launch *Sir Henry Alderson*, whose 10 knot capability made her one of the fastest vessels in the Fleet, the small flotilla took part in a full-scale exercise to test the Thames District Mobilization Scheme. This lasted eight days and involved over four thousand troops and boom defence ships, and even a number of destroyers. The WD craft filled the role of attacking vessels.

This was an exciting time for local residents. According to a contemporary newspaper report, at Shoeburyness they were treated to 'a spectacle of dazzling splendour' from the three searchlights, 'flashes of lightning, intermingling with the beams of the electric lights, made up a picture of weird brilliance'. When *Sir Henry*, at the head of a flotilla of steam cutters, endeavoured to effect an entrance to the harbour the troops were called out and 'a heavy cannonade opened on the vessel until she steamed out of range'.

The following day Lord Wolseley, Commander-in-Chief of the Army, accompanied by Sir Evelyn Wood (the General, not the vessel) and 'a brilliant staff, including a Prince of Siam', arrived from Chatham in the submarine mining vessel *Sir Howard Elphinstone*. That night the august party were entertained by watching the night operations, when once again *Sir Henry* steamed in, and once again, at ten minutes to nine, drew the fire of the guns.

As in 1818 and 1886 (and, no doubt, on other undiscovered occasions), so in 1908 the question of the very existence of an Army Fleet was once again addressed, this time by a committee under the chairmanship of the Director of Transport and Remounts, Maj.-Gen. C.E. Heath, CVO.

His terms of reference were:

To consider the general policy of maintaining a War Department Fleet and whether it is desirable to extend the hire of vessels for water transport services and target towing.

He was assisted in his task by the ADMT Woolwich Arsenal, then Col. R.A. Nugent, CB, and representatives of the Royal Artillery, Royal Engineers, the Admiralty and the War Office. The Royal Engineers' representative was from the School of Electric Lighting, his specific sphere of interest being submarine mining vessels.

This report is valuable in that for the first time, we are given a complete picture of the Fleet's vessels throughout the world. At home there were:

    2   freight ships
   10   steam launches
    5   sail barges
    7   dumb barges
   19   target towers
    3   special craft
           (*Katharine*, *Gog* and *Magog*)
   82   small craft
    1   oil motor launch (76 MT Coy, ASC)

The last vessel is the military forerunner of the RASC Fleet; it was stationed at Shoeburyness for range clearance and gunnery observation duties for the School of Gunnery and was crewed by a corporal and a private. Built in 1902, and powered by a 24 hp 4-cylinder Daimler engine, it appears to have been the first motor launch introduced into the service. 76 Company ASC was stationed at Chatham. It was probably no coincidence that, nearly fifty years later, 76 Company became the first LCT (Landing Craft Tank) Company. Although never described as such in official lists, the launch is believed to have been named 'Camel'.

The overseas list included:

    7   high speed steamships
    8   steam launches
    2   sailing cutters
    1   schooner
    1   powder vessel
    4   lighters
    4   barges
    62 small craft

The complete list of vessels and their locations is given in Appendix VI.

In addition there were eleven steam vessels and a few small boats, formerly part of the now defunct RE submarine mining fleet, and to which the Corps had managed to cling. It was found that most of these were duplicating the harbour work of the WD Fleet.

As in 1895, so at the time of this report the Fleet could be regarded as well up-to-date. Remarkably, there was only one steam vessel older than the *Marquess of Hartington*, (1886). This was the *Katharine*, whose task was to tow the gun barges *Gog* and *Magog* up and down the Thames. The report recommended the retention of the *Marquess* and *Sir Evelyn Wood* and

when worn out they might be replaced by vessels of a larger type (with same crew) about 15 feet longer than the *Wood*, 2½ feet more beam and large enough hatches to take 9.2 inch guns without dipping.

They estimated that they (the Department) would get £2,000 for each ship after forty years, thereby considerably underestimating their durability. The *Marquess* had actually cost £10,000 to build, or about £330,000 in today's money. *Sir Evelyn* cost a little more at £10,850.

A financial sub-committee met to consider the economics of Fleet operation and came to the satisfactory conclusion that vessels on charge to the ASC all paid their way, with the exception of the steam launches *Sir Lintorn Simmons* at Malta, and *Quadroon* at Gibraltar. GOC Malta pointed out that if the WD vessels were reduced, local boat-owners would immediately put up their prices, and this was accepted. As *Quadroon* was HE The Governor's launch, however, no justification appears to have been given or sought. Indeed, all overseas stations seem to have come out of the review with honours. Tiny Bermuda, with a flotilla which out-numbered all the others, but only had enough seamen to crew half of their four major vessels (steamship, steam launch and two cutters) pleaded 'essential for defence' and 'costs higher to use civilian ships' to hold their own. Other colonies pleaded the latter justification, also with success.

The Director of Accounts, though agreeing the recommendations of the committee, was less than impressed with the computations of this sub-committee, describing them as the 'most extraordinary he had ever seen'. Among the figures that he choked upon were the daily costs of the Woolwich freight ships (figures in brackets are the very approximate prices today):

> *Marquess of Hartington* – £5 14s. 6d. (£146)
> *Sir Evelyn Wood* – £6 7s. 6d. (£162)

The sub-committee stated that a contractor charged £10 (£250) a day for hire.

Other figures quoted concerned target-towing and compared the average cost of a vessel fitted for target-towing as £5,610 (£142,000) plus £1,761 (£44,000) for maintenance. Pointing out that speed was necessary and that a mean 25 knots was achieved with special winching gear, the conclusion was that it was not practicable to hire for this activity. Only one firm had offered an estimate: £85 (£2,000) or £98 a week.

The committee looked at the cost of maintenance of the Fleet and reported an enviable record of only thirteen cases of damage in five years, with *Sir Redvers Buller* being involved in the two incurring the highest costs. The amounts concerned in the first incident were £35 (£890) in repairs to bulwarks and £115 (£2,900) in payment to the private yacht owner with whose vessel the ship had collided. In the other case, *Sir Redvers* had cost the taxpayer £50 (£1,250) in damage to stem and bow plating when it struck the quay at Guernsey. Fortunately there was no damage to the quay. In eight cases, the committee reported, repair costs to the War Department were nil. Col. Nugent, the ADMT, concluded:

Our comparative immunity is due to the efficiency of our labour under the apprentice long service scheme.

The Royal Navy, in a change of heart and policy, had taken over responsibility for torpedo and submarine mining from the Royal Engineers. Eleven steam vessels and a few small boats used for 'electric light work' and transport of RE personnel and stores remained, and the committee thought that these should be handed over to ASC control. They also noted that artillery practice had come into prominence and it was necessary to provide high-speed target towers at considerable expense. These had greatly increased water transport facilities, especially in the Thames, at Perth, Plymouth, and in Ireland, Malta and Hong Kong.

In its final report, the committee considered the role of the Fleet in three contexts – crisis, war and civil disturbance. They thought, however, that these might be considered 'such remote contingencies as to be outside the terms of reference', but, somewhat apologetically one feels, pointed out that without such things, however remote, there would be no War Office, no Army Service Corps and no WD Fleet. 'We must not omit them, as they go to the very root of the matter'. It may seem passing strange to the present-day reader, to whom none of the three conditions is remote, that such circumstances should not have been taken into account as a matter of course.

The committee argued that although trade may or may not be cheaper in peacetime, if it failed to answer at a crisis it could not be said to be cheaper all round. They termed the costs as annual peace insurance against 'those contingencies to meet which we are agents of the community'. In case of war, when the Navy would be fully occupied and 'the trade too timid', it would be an advantage to have our own ship to carry explosives to Ireland, Gibraltar and Malta. It could be argued that its peace earnings would in fact be an appropriation in aid.

This argument does not seem very potent, but does underline how preoccupation with the economics of Fleet operation tended to over-ride more serious consideration of its military value. But if this argument seems thin, the justification in case of civil disturbance seems even thinner. This contingency they linked to what they described as the important aspect of pensions, which they held were important to security, inferring that WD Fleet employees with pensionable service could be relied upon against civilian strikers who would not have this benefit. There was obviously more in this than met the eye; the Navy had objected but it was noted that the matter would be raised again. Col. Nugent thought the Fleet would lose its national and commercial advantage if the 'present apprentice long service pension system is not adhered to. He is apprehensive that if pensions were withdrawn a different situation would be created for his successors'. Gen. Heath, in presenting the report reiterated these views. The Fleet was to prove its loyalty eighteen years later during the General Strike, but it cannot be said with any certainty that pensionable service was a factor!

The committee finally summed up their conclusions by saying that they had satisfied themselves that the WD vessels effect a financial saving as compared with the cost of hiring, besides being conducive to military efficiency. They recommended the retention in the service of the vessels now on ASC charge, the transfer to ASC charge of the RE vessels, and finally, that the system of hiring vessels should be continued as necessity arose.

The report was now submitted to the appropriate War Office directors for their approval, a process which took nearly nine months. Gen. Heath started the ball rolling by paying a handsome tribute to Col. Nugent, upon whom most of the work in producing the report fell, (and whose diligence in his own cause undoubtedly saved his department from a mauling).

The financiers got very busy on the figures quoted by the committee in its deliberations. The view of the Director of Accounts has already been recorded. He was supported by the QMG's Finance branch (QMGF), who, inevitably, did a lot of figure-crunching themselves before they pronounced themselves satisfied. Among the figures produced they reported that in one year, nine ships had conveyed to Woolwich 83 tons of miscellaneous 'produce' (the Ordnance term for unserviceable stores with a residual or repair value) and 12,000 tons of all other stores.

After more leisurely discussion, Gen. Heath waxed somewhat impatient and, in November 1908, asked for a decision, and finally got unqualified approval for the continued existence of the Fleet, as well as approval to take over the RE vessels. Shortly after, however, the Master General of the Ordnance pointed out that there would be RE personnel involved, and asked what was to happen to them? There were seven military coxswains, one warrant officer and six senior NCOs. The coxswains appeared to have been quartermaster sergeants. A proposal that they should all be transferred to the ASC met with no favour and eventually it was agreed that they be attached to the Army Service Corps until they had completed their current military engagements. They would then be absorbed as civilians.

In the event, the RE fought a successful rearguard action and managed to retain most of the personnel. One, however, QMS Wilkinson, took his discharge after seventeen years' service and was appointed mate in charge of his vessel, the *Emerald* launch, at Gravesend. Ten of the eleven vessels were finally transferred, *Collingwood Dickson*, which had already seen previous service in the Fleet, being condemned as unfit. Apart from 76 Company's launch crew, there is no other mention in the report of any military personnel in the Fleet.

So, once again, the Fleet had sailed through a review with flying colours. They could congratulate themselves, but would have to ascribe their success not to their seamanship, not to their reliability, not even wholly to their efficiency, but to the amalgam of these qualities which made them, in the modern financial idiom, cost-effective.

8
THE FIRST WORLD WAR AND AFTER

The operations of the Fleet in the years following the Heath Report, even up to the end of the First World War, were once more but sparsely recorded. Strangely, the many histories of the Great War do not even acknowledge the existence of the Fleet, let alone its operations. This hiatus inexplicably extends to the otherwise comprehensive post-war history of the Army Service Corps.

At the outbreak of the First World War, the following was the strength of the Fleet throughout the world:

> 53 steam vessels
> 2 motor barges
> 1 motor launch
> 2 sailing hoys
> 7 sailing barges
> 29 dumb barges and lighters
> 3 tongkangs

This represented an increase of six steam vessels since 1908, only three of which were newly-built, the others being the remaining ex-submarine miners. This small increase in vessel strength contrasts with the thirty-two which joined the Fleet between 1900 and 1908. About half the vessels were less than 15 years old; *Katharine* (1882) and *Marquess of Hartington* (1886) were the veterans of the steamer fleet. Oldest of all was the Woolwich tow barge *Lord Vivian*, referred in Chapter 6, which had entered the service in 1862.

Of the seven sailing barges still in service, three were abroad, three at Portsmouth, and one at Chatham. *Seagull II* and *Thalia* were the last hoys: the former was at Pembroke Dock and the latter serving as a floating magazine at Woolwich. A complete list of the 1914 Fleet, from the *Naval Service Pocket Book*, 1915, is at Appendix VII.

Strangely enough, there does not seem to have been any building programmes for the Fleet during the First World War; indeed, no vessels were built between 1913 and 1926. It must therefore be assumed that the whole of the additional wartime commitments of the Fleet were met by requisitioning and hiring.

Conversely, the Fleet seems to have suffered little from the enemy's attentions during the war. Apart from the steam launch *Swale*, damaged during an airplane air raid on Shoeburyness on 28 January 1918, no other reports have come to notice. *Swale* does not seem to have been the main target; the single bomb dropped hit an explosives store on the gunwharf when she was lying alongside.

Fourteen vessels were stationed at Woolwich, reflecting the continuing importance of the Arsenal in the Fleet's activities. From here, the *Marquess of Hartington*, *Sir Evelyn Wood*, *Sir Redvers Buller* and *Lord Wolseley*, the Fleet's four major sea-going vessels, carried supplies, guns and ammunition to the Continent, around the British Isles, to Alexandria, Gibraltar and Malta, and once to Chanak, in the Dardanelles, when the Greco–Turkish war of 1921–2 and its aftermath caught the army of occupation in the middle of an explosive situation. The major task, however, was in support of the armies in France; a cross-channel service was maintained throughout the war.

This latter task continued after the war for the British Army of the Rhine. The *Sir Redvers* had her masts shortened and her funnel adapted to enable it to be lowered to allow passage under bridges. This enabled her to operate up the Rhine to Cologne. The *Sir Evelyn* and *Marquess* transferred their cargoes into barges and lighters at Rotterdam; *Katharine* and *Sir Stafford Northcote* then carried the freight forward to Cologne and Wiesbaden.

This cross-channel service appears to have been maintained throughout the war uninterrupted by hostile action though there must of course have been many unpublicized incidents, similar to that which involved Capt. Francis Reynolds (see Chapter 5). Otherwise, it seems very much to have been a case of business as usual.

The ever-restive situation in Ireland also provided much work for the sea-going vessels. Garrisons were located at Buncrana on Lough Swilly, right round to Bantry Bay. Troops required supplies at Londonderry, Carrickfergus, Dublin, Kingston (Dun Laoghaire), Queenstown (Cobh) and Bere Island. Three WD vessels were permanently stationed at

Queenstown to support the fortifications at Temple Breedy, Carlisle, Camden and Spike Island. They were employed on a 24-hour basis, for which purpose each had two crews. The Irish connection is, however, dealt with more fully in the next chapter.

Elsewhere in the United Kingdom, the smaller vessels continued to carry out local duties. The largest contingent was based on Portsmouth gunwharf, *Lansdowne*, *Moore*, *Haldane* and *Hurst* all engaged on target-towing duties, and the conveyance of personnel, supplies, equipment and stores, supported by several minor craft, barges, horse boats, cutters, etc. The pattern was the same at Plymouth, with seven steam vessels, headed by *Osprey* and *Sir Frederick Walker* based on Devonport dockyard. The Fleet ensign also flew at smaller stations: Dover, Leith, Grimsby, Harwich, Falmouth, Isle of Wight, Weymouth, Pembroke Dock, and Sheerness.

Target-towing for coastal defences carried on uninterrupted by the air attacks that made it such a hazardous occupation in the Second World War. This activity must have been a considerable factor not only in maintaining coastal defences at the peak of readiness, but also in making life a little more interesting for gunners who waited in vain for a chance to test their undoubted skill and expertise in earnest. Such, however, was the Navy's superiority that, after the naval raids on the north-east coast in December 1914, the coastal guns were not again called upon to speak in anger.

Overseas, too, at Gibraltar, Malta, Singapore, Hong Kong, Jamaica and Bermuda, the daily round would have continued, far and remote from the scenes of war. Vessels in these stations were manned by locally-engaged crews under a United Kingdom-based civilian Fleet officer. It was only in the Middle East that water transport was used in support of operations. An ASC-manned motor boat company operated in the Dardanelles and, following the collapse of the Gallipoli campaign, shifted its operations to the Canal Zone, providing detachments for duties on the Dead Sea, Sea of Galilee, Haifa and at Tripoli in Syria. Ten steamers operated between Alexandria and Mersa Matruh, and, commanded by a lieutenant, ASC, an armed section patrolled Lakes Besnik and Langaza in Bulgaria with infantry support. Meanwhile, the Inland Water Transport organization of the Royal Engineers was heavily engaged in the Mesopotamian theatre. In this latter campaign the IWT Directorate operated a heterogeneous fleet of nearly 750 vessels.

This sister water transport service was set up in December 1914, fell a casualty to the Geddes Axe ten years later, but was resuscitated in 1939. It was absorbed into the Royal Corps of Transport on its formation from the Royal Army Service Corps in 1965. Although outside the scope of this history, it is worthy of more than a passing reference if only to establish the *raison d'etre* for two water transport services in the same Army. A brief account of the organization is therefore given in Appendix IV.

There was a close parallel between the Fleet's duties immediately after the war and its task a hundred years earlier at the close of the Napoleonic Wars. Just as the Board of Ordnance Fleet had been heavily engaged in the withdrawal of war *matériel* from the Navy and coast defences, so the WD Fleet became heavily involved in the return of stores and armament to Woolwich, and also in the major new and potentially dangerous task of ammunition dumping. And less than thirty years later, this latter task started all over again.

Cargoes of high explosives, glass mustard gas bombs and barrels of picric acid and other chemicals were loaded chiefly from the magazines at the Royal Arsenal and Purfleet and were dumped in the Hurd Deeps off Alderney in the Channel Islands. The chemicals were, of course, the most dangerous. These had to be carried as deck cargo. The wooden picric acid barrels were often in a parlous condition and such was their state that they often burst open on hitting the water, staining the sea yellow. Calcium carbide was another hazardous cargo. Capt. Jack Cains, then an AB, remembers his apprehension when, carrying carbide in badly rusted steel barrels on deck, his vessel was shipping green water in a heavy head sea.

> The barrels gave off a nasty smell, and I realised that the lot could go up in a sheet of flame. I seemed to be the only one of the crew to be aware of the danger. A few years earlier I had seen a barrel, washed ashore at Fort Victoria, which had ignited and burned through two tides.

Unlike the vessels used for ammunition dumping after the Second World War, the shipping used for the task could not be properly adapted for the purpose. To dump deck cargo, a stack was built up level with the hatch coaming and the bulwarks, and the barrels then rolled off. The hold cargo, usually high explosive shell, was hoisted with the ship's

Loading a 9.2 in gun from the Humber Forts into the *Marquess of Hartington* at Grimsby in September 1933

derrick. Soldiers were usually embarked at Alderney to assist the crews in dumping but as they were mostly seasick they were of little use and eventually this practice was abandoned. Thereafter the ship's crew did the job and were paid a very welcome 9d. an hour during the actual handling and dumping. One crew member was lost overboard from *Sir Evelyn Wood* while employed on this work.

Tough and dangerous though this job was, there were compensations beside the 9d. an hour. The crews were always made welcome in Alderney, and some had hit on a somewhat hazardous way of obtaining their 'beer money'. When laden with 9.2 in shell from the Western Front, they would knock off the driving bands of this high explosive ammunition in the hold, working with an oil lamp. The bands weighed 3½ lb of pure copper. This initiative was well-rewarded at the local pub.

In some cases, withdrawal of armament from coast defences proved also to be hazardous. Jack Cains describes what was involved:

A party of Royal Garrison Artillery specialised in this work. In one instance, two 9.2-inch guns in barbettes were withdrawn from Spurn Point, at the entrance to the Humber. The heavy gun barge, *Gog*, towed by *Katharine*, was brought from Woolwich for the task. The barrels weighed 29 tons each and were accompanied by heavy and cumbersome shields and racers, etc. The work was carried out as the tide permitted and a keen eye on the weather had to be kept, as if the wind came from the east in any force the whole operation would have become quite dangerous.

When the guns were loaded into *Gog*, she was towed to Grimsby and her cargo transferred into the *Marquess*. This operation was somewhat complicated as the RGA team was employed elsewhere and only sheerlegs were available and as they work only from the upright position, the ship had to be moved back and forth as necessary. Pulley tackles and snatch blocks were necessary to position the barrels securely in the hold, and when all was loaded it had to be shored off and tommed down in order to be kept quiet and secure during heavy weather for passage to Woolwich.

The Grimsby station was established to serve the north-east. The *Sir Herbert Miles* doubled as a target tower and support vessel for the outforts at Bull, Hale Sands and Spurn Point in the Humber. The *Lord Wolseley* had water tanks fitted to supply water to these outstations and, from 1918 to the end of 1919, after their closure, served as a carrier for maintenance personnel. By the 1950s Grimsby was the last port with facilities for the refit of coal-burning steamers and so maintained a connection with the Fleet almost to the end.

During 1919 the *Lord Wolseley* made some sort of Fleet history when she made an interesting voyage to Gloucester, entering the Gloucester Canal at Sharpness. A horse led off with a tow-rope and gave a pluck as necessary to assist steering, while a man rode ahead on a bicycle to open the lock gates and close them afterwards. Following this stately procession the vessel moored well into the city and loaded a cargo of tentage for conveyance to Woolwich Arsenal.

The retrenchment which inevitably follows all wars went well beyond the speedy and far-reaching, even savage, reductions in the Forces. Economy was the watchword, and the 'Geddes Axe' was the weapon. This was named for Sir Eric Geddes, chairman of a committee on national expenditure, who recommended draconian economic measures, the effects of which were felt throughout the nation. As coast defences were withdrawn and guns put into preservation, etc., various target-towing vessels were either disposed of locally or brought to Woolwich, where those not sold were put into reserve and moored in the canal at the Plumstead end of the Arsenal. Two such vessels, the steam launches *Haslar* and *Satellite*, were transferred on the closure of Milford Haven station. Two major casualties were the *Lord Wolseley* (1896) and *Sir Redvers Buller* (1895), sold and replaced by only one vessel, the *Sir Walter Campbell*, in 1928.

Capt. Cains recalls *Sir Redvers* with no great affection, as a cold, wet ship. On a winter voyage to Cologne in 1925 he was given the task of chipping the ice off the white paintwork in order to wash it! The skipper, Capt. Reynolds, reminiscent of Capt. Kettle with his pointed beard and moustache, drove the ship hard in all weathers. She had a tendency to go under water like a submarine in whole gales. It was often preferable to spend the watch 'below' huddled on the boiler casing rather than to risk life and limb making for the forecastle and the comfort of a hammock.

The Geddes Axe not only decimated the vessel strength. Overtime was forbidden or limited to vital services only and Fleet members declared surplus were weeded out, medically examined where necessary, and discharged. A reserve crew was kept on for the care and maintenance of the vessels in the canal, and to provide replacements for the sea-going vessels.

These measures went even further; cuts in pay were imposed throughout the Government service, both military and civilian. At that time, a leading seaman was paid £2 15s. 6d. a week (about £60 at today's prices), rising to £3 0s. 6d. when at sea. Out of this he had to buy his own food. The cooking chores on the sea-going vessels always fell to one of the ordinary seamen. One hand would do the catering for dinners only and would do that at 4s. a head, plus 6d. a head for his trouble. Seven dinners for 4s. 6d. was considered reasonable. With variations, these cooking arrangements, on coal-burning stoves, remained traditional until the end. It was at times an unenviable task. But if cooks had their problems, then so did some masters. Jack Cains recounts one embarrassing experience:

> As ordinary seaman on the *Sir Evelyn*, it was my turn to do the cooking. We had come down the Thames and as we rounded the

northeast buoy we ran into a southerly gale that was working up. I had taken the master's dinner out of the oven and balanced it on the door. It was a nice roast dinner, baked potatoes and a chop. Just then the ship gave an almighty roll; the dinner crashed away and landed in a heap of coaldust. The master came down from the bridge very concerned and asked if I was alright. 'Yes, Sir!' I replied. 'What's that down there?' he asked. 'Your dinner, Sir!' I replied. He wasn't very pleased!

Charles Codner, too, as a boy on the coaster *Sir Walter Campbell*, recalls interpreting the master's instruction to put some winkles over the side as an order to throw them overboard, rather than to lower them in a bucket to keep them fresh!

9
THE INTER-WAR YEARS AND THE IRISH CONNECTION

Wartime duties over, the aftermath cleared and the bitter after-effects of the Geddes Axe absorbed, the Fleet loyally settled down once again to its regular duties. During the General Strike of 1926 crews everywhere remained on duty. The sea-going vessels continued to load stores from the Royal Arsenal and food supplies from the supply reserve depot at Deptford, the crews loading their own cargoes. Jack Cains remembers one detail required the collection of a stand of arms from the West India dock under armed escort, but there were no real dramas. At the end of the strike, all members of the Fleet were congratulated and thanked by the Secretary of State for War.

If the General Strike produced no drama for the Fleet, the continuing commitment to the maintenance of the Irish coastal defences did, from time to time. The Irish Free State, as it was now called, had been given the same constitutional status as that of the Dominion of Canada under the Anglo-Irish Treaty signed in December 1921. Although the treaty provided for the IFS to have its own armed forces, it had nevertheless also been agreed that Britain would remain responsible for coastal defence until the new state was in a position to take over. Provision was made in the treaty for a review at the end of five years. Accordingly, the harbour defences at Berehaven, Queenstown (Cobh) and Lough Swilly remained in British care. All other British troops had left Southern Ireland by the end of 1922.

Irish coastal defences had been in existence for at least 250 years, and possibly longer and had formed an integral part of the defences of the British Isles. By 1783, there were eight forts or garrisons, and two floating batteries in Dublin Bay but by the late war only those named above remained, plus Belfast in the north. The WD Fleet and, undoubtedly, its predecessors, had formed a close association with the forts and the local population over a long period.

Indeed, many members of the Fleet were Irishmen from the Cork area, and some transferred to the Irish Department of Defence when the vessels were handed over in 1938. Visits to Southern Ireland were always popular and those who had the good fortune to be stationed over there with their vessels generally enjoyed the experience. It was, however, deemed advisable to carry an armed guard on vessels running up to Carrickfergus and Buncrana on Lough Swilly, a duty often performed by Royal Marines, who would live on board.

There was, however, an uneasy period following the signing of the Anglo-Irish Treaty, when opponents of the Provisional Government took to the streets and a short, but nasty, civil war followed. British troops, who of course kept aloof from the struggle, must have been disconcerted to find Queenstown, rather close to home, in the hands of the anti-treaty forces. Fortunately, they withdrew after a short period, offering no opposition to an Irish Government force. Earlier in the year, in March 1922, a 'gang of Republican conspirators hostile to the Provisional Government' hijacked the RN steamer *Upnor*. The vessel was carrying a cargo of weapons and ammunition from the naval base at Haulbowline to Devonport. According to a statement by Mr Winston Churchill in the House of Commons, a War Office steamer and other vessels were sent in pursuit and *Upnor* was discovered empty of her cargo. A later statement to Parliament contradicted this, saying that a destroyer and a sloop sent after *Upnor* had prevented the greater part of the cargo from being removed.

There were more serious episodes. The steam launch *Cambridge* which served the Camden and Carlisle forts and Spike Island was approaching Queenstown with Royal Garrison Artillery passengers on 30 August 1922, when a group opened fire on her from the shore. Three soldiers were wounded and the master of the vessel, Mr Bell, was shot in the foot. The soldiers were unarmed and had been employed on mail duties for the garrison at Spike Island. In the worst incident, in March 1924, IRA gunmen dressed in the uniform of Irish National Army officers, opened Lewis gun fire on a WD vessel while landing passengers from Spike Island at Queenstown, murdering Pte. Aspinall, RASC and wounding twenty soldiers. The Irish Government, in exchanges of messages with Prime Minister Ramsay Macdonald, expressed outrage in the strongest terms.

There was an echo of this incident in July 1927, when two brothers were arrested and remanded in custody, accused of the murder of Pte. Aspinall. They were later released for lack of sufficient evidence.

The 1903 steam target tower *Wyndham* was in service for sixty-four years at Cork, her last twenty-nine, from 1938 to 1967, with the Irish Army

This Irish connection came to an end in 1938, when three agreements were signed: defence, economic and commercial. Under the Defence Agreement, articles 6 and 7 of the treaty were abrogated and the Treaty Ports, as they had been termed, were returned to Ireland. The last British troops stationed in Southern Ireland left on 30 September 1938; they handed over Berehaven and embarked for Fishguard, seen off by a large crowd. On 3 October, forts at Lough Swilly were handed over to the Eire Defence Force, the Union Flag being hauled down by two Royal Artillery NCOs. By coincidence, it was reported, that Sgt. O'Flynn, who hauled down, and Sgt. McLaughlin, who hoisted, their respective flags, were brothers-in-law. The final chapter was written on 11 July 1938 when the last troops at Spike Island handed over the garrison, ending 150 years of British occupation of this main defence work and one-time penal settlement.

A number of vessels had always been locally employed on the Irish coastal defence services for harbour and target-towing, etc., duties. In

1892, there were three vessels and fifteen boats recorded, and later, in 1907, there were three steam launches, a hoy, and a barge. This establishment, based on Cork, was later increased to seven vessels: two steamers, four launches and a motor barge. Two of these were stationed at Lough Swilly. There would still, of course, have been a number of small boats but no details of these are available.

In addition to the real estate, the now surplus WD flotilla of seven vessels was handed *in toto* to the Irish Defence Forces, and formed the nucleus of a civilian-manned maritime service which has similar functions to those carried out by the WD Fleet.

The Irish Forces accordingly gained the motor cargo vessel, *John Adams* (98 tons), two steam passenger vessels, *General McHardy* (100 tons) and *Wyndham* (93 tons), three motor passenger vessels, *Jackdaw*, *Raven*, and *Sir Cecil Romer*, and a motor launch, *Wuzzer* (re-named a rather more euphonic and ethnic *Colleen*). There was also a motor oil fuel barge *Chowl*, but this does not appear to have been a Fleet vessel. Apart from the veteran *Sir John Wyndham*, built in 1903, none of the vessels was yet ten years old. *Sir John*, named, as were two of the others, for former Secretaries of State for Ireland, served the Irish Department of Defence

One of the last steam vessels to be built for the Fleet, in 1927, *General McHardy* served the Irish Forts and was handed over to the Irish Army in 1938

until sold for scrap in 1971, at the ripe old age of 68. Others served well into the 1980s.

As mentioned above, some crew members also went over to the Irish service. Two of these ex-Fleet seamen, Jack Stockley and Bill Tobin, recalled *Cambridge* being relieved by *General McHardy*, the exchange being supervised by the ADMT. A visit by the ADMT, they said, was regarded as a very special occasion. This visitation would probably have been by Col. H.M. Caddell, CMG, DSO. In February 1926 Tobin was commended by Gen. McHardy, Director of Movements and Quartering at the War Office, for saving a fellow crewman from drowning while on the *Wyndham*.

The year 1926 saw a resumption of building in the Fleet after a hiatus of thirteen years. The first vessels were the *Sir Noel Birch*, a steam target tower, and *Sir Walter Campbell*, (525 tons), a coaster which, in the summer months, supplemented the target-towing fleet. The *Sir Noel*, at just over 101 ft in length, with a displacement of 191 tons, was, briefly, the largest of its type so far built. It was sent to Gibraltar to share station

Sir Noel Birch was the first vessel to be built for the Fleet after the First World War

duties with the 24-year-old steamer, *May*. *Sir Walter*, with a 525 ton displacement and, like *Sir Noel*, powered by triple-expansion coal-fired engines, joined the Woolwich vessels. The first triple-expansion oil-fired target tower, the *Lord Plumer*, replaced *Sir Noel Birch* as the largest of its type in 1927. Although a fraction shorter, its displacement was 212 tons. *Lord Plumer* spent her working life in the Mediterranean, and was stationed in Malta during the war.

The same period, 1927 and 1928, also saw the last coal-fired vessels, *Sir Desmond O'Callaghan*, and *General McHardy*, referred to above and, in 1928, the introduction of the first diesel motor barge, named *Vawdrey* for Col. G. Vawdrey, CB, CMG, CBE, lately ADMT. Two other diesel motor barges, *Geoffrey Stanley* and *Henry Caddell*, named respectively for ADsMT, joined the Fleet not long after. These three vessels appear to be the only ones named for holders of this appointment, so important for the Fleet. One cannot help but wonder why Col. Stevens and Col. Nugent, both of whom made such great contributions to the administration and efficiency of the Fleet in its earlier military days, were never similarly honoured. Col. Nugent, particularly, must have richly deserved the honour having served from 1903 to 1908, and then again throughout the First World War.

While pondering on the naming of vessels, one might also wonder if the former Quartermaster General, General McHardy, felt at all put out at the vessel chosen to bear his name. His vessel was smaller than his subordinate's *Vawdrey*, she was coal-burning as against diesel, and she was then given to the Irish Government.

And so, throughout the 1930s, until the advent of the high-speed launches, to which reference will be made in another chapter, there was a small but steady influx of shipping to the Fleet, as the older and obsolete vessels were phased out; veterans like the Woolwich coaster and target tower *Sir Redvers Buller* (1886), the steam launch *Louise* (1904), whose entire service was spent in Bermuda, and the steam launch *May*, a familiar sight at Gibraltar for over twenty-five years. The author, in Gibraltar for five years as a child, had a personal affection for the *May*, then skippered by Mr James Day, son of a former Inspector of Shipping, and who served in Gibraltar for twenty-three of his fifty years in the Fleet. The *May* was often used as 'recreational transport' for Mess outings across Algeciras Bay to a beach on the Spanish mainland, and towed a dumb ambulance barge which provided ample accommodation for the large quantities of food and even larger numbers of crates. No formalities were required on landing, beyond offering refreshment to the solitary Spanish gendarme who would appear from nowhere and lay down his carbine.

Then there was the 1882, 250 ton steamer *Katharine*, which had steadily ploughed the Thames, with an occasional foray across the Channel during the late war, towing the heavily-laden gun barges, *Gog* and *Magog*, to and from Shoeburyness. As described in a subsequent chapter, *Gog* had her hour of peril in 1928. *Katharine* was replaced by the motor barge *Katharine II* (295 ton displacement) in 1930 after forty-six years in the Fleet.

Katharine II, whose model is displayed in the Royal Logistic Corps Museum, Dettingen Barracks, Deepcut, Hants, had a comparatively short career of twenty-eight years before falling victim to the general rundown of the Fleet. In that time, however, she, like the *Marquess*, proved worthy of the best traditions of the Fleet. She soon became a familiar sight on the Thames, conveying ammunition and general stores to and from Woolwich, the Isle of Grain and Shoeburyness, as well as, inevitably,

The motor barge *Katharine II* worked for nearly thirty years on the Thames and along the east coast

towing *Gog* and *Magog*. Early in her career she was commissioned to lay a cable from St Margaret's Bay, Kent, to Calais.

During the war years, in No. 5, later No. 632, Company (Water Transport), *Katharine II* was extensively employed along the south-east coast and in the Thames on stores and ammunition carrying, and towing duties in connection with Royal Engineer Mulberry harbour construction in preparation for D-Day. Her multifarious post-war tasks are referred to in Chapter 18.

When replaced, the earlier *Katharine* had been the oldest vessel in the Fleet; others, nearer but not of her vintage, were not yet ready for the scrap-yard. In 1934, the steam vessel *Abercorn*, built as a 145 ton target tower in 1903, made the ocean voyage to Jamaica to continue service there until after the war. Calls had to be made at the Azores and again at St Lucia for coaling and every available inch of space was filled with bags of solid fuel to enable the little vessel to steam the thousands of miles between coaling stations.

Another elderly, but still trim, target tower, the 1902 *Langdon*, had a welcome variation in her routine duties at Dover in 1925 when she was

The handsome *Langdon* (1902) escorted Channel swimmer Lt.-Col. (later Lt.-Gen. Sir) Bernard Freyberg, VC, on his crossing in 1925

detailed to escort a Channel swimmer. But this was no ordinary Channel swimmer; First World War hero Lt.-Col. Bernard C. Freyberg, VC, DSO, MC, was making the attempt, which he completed in 16 hours and 49 minutes. Lt.-Col. Freyberg again distinguished himself in the Second World War as the leader of the New Zealand Forces in the Middle East and, as Lt.-Gen. Sir Bernard Freyberg, became Governor-General of New Zealand. Master of the *Langdon* was Mr F.B. 'Freddy' Wales, later Master Superintendent at Woolwich. Freddy Wales' son, F.J.T., was Master of the *Haig* at Dunkirk and his son Tony joined the Fleet as a boy just after the Second World War.

Meanwhile, the two senior ships, stately in their advancing years and still good for another thirty, were those fine old Woolwich steamers, the *Marquess of Hartington* and *Sir Evelyn Wood*. The former, however, did have a narrow escape from destruction in Liverpool in 1923 in an incident as a result of which the War Department was severely criticized by the Liverpool Dock Board.

The *Marquess* was in the process of loading a 120 ton consignment of picric acid, sent by rail to Liverpool from Shropshire for shipment to Portsmouth, when the axle of the steam crane broke. The crane toppled over and spilled its boiler fire under the rail wagons now awaiting unloading into the *Marquess*. The fire, however, was extinguished by a watchman and three other men, two of whom were awarded £5 and two, £3, by the Dock Board for saving what was described, somewhat extravagantly, as an explosion which would have blown 'the whole side of the county away', in the words of a contemporary report. As nobody had notified the Board of this dangerous cargo, they were not best pleased and did not hesitate to let their views be known.

There was another dramatic incident in 1932, in Plymouth Harbour, when a twin-engined 'Solent' flying-boat collided with a dockyard pinnace. The aircraft was just skimming the water to land when the pilot, suddenly seeing the pinnace in his path, tried to take off again. Several men lost their lives. The steam target tower *Hurst II* was first on the scene with assistance. Charles Codner was a cabin boy on *Hurst II* and, being on deck at the time, actually witnessed the accident.

In 1934, the Fleet mustered 23 steamers and steam launches, 23 motor vessels and launches, 17 barges and tongkangs, etc., and 132 small boats. Apart from the high-speed target towers mentioned above, only five more vessels were built between now and 1940. Among these were the

The steam target tower *Hurst II*, the last vessel to be built before the First World War.
This was Charles Codner's first vessel

last steam target tower, the *Sir Hastings Anderson*, doomed to destruction
in Singapore, and the coaster *Malplaquet*, the last coaster to join the
civilian fleet. In 1939 vessel strength was between 66 and 71, with about
250–60 personnel. A list of vessels which served between 1934 and 1939
is at Appendix VIII.

The conditions of entry into the Fleet in the 1930s remained much
the same as they had been in the previous century. Deck staff still
normally joined as boys with priority given to sons of ex-servicemen and
those whose fathers were serving, or had served, in the Fleet. They were
rated as ordinary seamen on attaining the age of 18 and as able seamen at
24. Advancement beyond this status was, of course, subject to Board of
Trade certification. Engine-room staff grades had now been expanded to
give stokers entry to third engineer status, through leading and chief
stoker grades, all by selection. Some advance had been made in the
matter of pensions since the days of the Heath Report (Chapter 7) as
these were now payable to masters, first engineers and 50 per cent of the
authorized establishment of mates and second engineers. There was
further improvement in 1944 when Treasury authority was given for the
establishment of sea-going mates and second engineers up to the age of

55 provided they were able to complete ten years' reckonable service for pension at 60.

The normal civil service rules for establishment following a period of probation applied. Apart from the permanent members of the Fleet there were a large number of temporary crew employed in the summer months to meet the seasonal target-towing and other Army and Territorial Army training commitments.

Pay had not changed much since the 1891 rates, probably because of the legacy of the Geddes Axe. A sea-going master, now a master first class, was still paid the same £14 (£3.50) a week, rising by 84s. biennially in 3s. 6d. steps to £21 (£4.25). A second class master had fared better, and now started at 12 guineas as against £10. All mates were now paid alike at 49s.(£2.45) a week or £9.80 a month, nearly £3 more than the lowest rate of 1891. Engineers, too, were better off at 14 guineas as against £12. It should be remembered of course that the 1938 pound was worth just over £23 of today's. Even taking that into account, the 1930s sailor was by no means overpaid.

There were, however, a considerable number of allowances which had not been available earlier. There were the extra (sea-going) allowance for Woolwich vessels ranging from 15s. 9d. a week for masters to 1s. 9d. for boys, the Mediterranean allowance for masters, mates and first and second engineers, from 4s. 6d. up to 22s. 6d. a week. Then there were Out-of-Port allowances, exceptional employment allowance, night duty allowance, lodging allowance, hard-lying money, confined-space allowance, dumping allowance (for dumping explosives at sea), pilotage allowance, and allowance for handling cargo. One can well imagine how much midnight lamp oil would have been burnt by masters in seeking to squeeze the last penny out of the system. Most of these allowances had their own special form on which to apply. Regulations for the War Department Fleet 1932 lists 30 Army forms, 14 ADMT forms and 8 books essential for running the Fleet. (Twenty-two years later this documentary mountain had reduced to thirty-eight items, according to a 1954 RASC training pamphlet.)

All members of the Fleet, as hitherto, were still required to sign a form of agreement, expressing willingness to serve on any harbour or sea-going vessel in any capacity for which they might be qualified, and agreeing to work day and night when necessary. Willingness for temporary service for duty in the South Irish Coast Defences required separate agreement.

10
A GUN IS LOST

Several references have been made to the barges *Gog* and *Magog*, which became something of a legend in the Fleet, perhaps because of their association with the mythical giants, perhaps because they were unique, perhaps because they were so long-lived. Built respectively in 1886 and 1900, classified as gun barges, they served on the Thames, and occasionally further afield, until well after the Second World War. They were constructed for the purpose of carrying heavy gun barrels from the Royal Arsenal to the Proof and Experimental Establishment at Shoeburyness and to the similar establishment at Yantlet Creek on the Isle of Grain for proofing. They could handle guns of up to 18 in calibre, weighing over 100 tons. In 1923, *Gog* had carried the 16 in guns for HMS *Nelson* and *Rodney*.

Gog, the larger of the two, was a wooden vessel 105 ft in length, with a beam of 30 ft. Like *Magog*, she was of the straight-stem open lighter type with portable stern gates and a length of standard gauge railway laid in her hold. When a gun was to be loaded the stern gates would be lifted away and connection made with the military railway on shore. The gun would be run in on two bogies and the gates replaced. They would be secured and made watertight by very strong bottle screws. *Gog* had a great 'barn door' rudder, hung slightly to port, and was tiller-steered. As has previously been mentioned, both barges were towed by the twin-screw steamer *Katharine*, built four years before *Gog*, and soon to be replaced.

On 23 November 1928, the *Daily Chronicle*, under the dramatic headline: '£20,000 NAVAL GUN SUNK IN THAMES' reported the story of a WD master's fight to save *Gog* and her cargo from loss in storm conditions in the Thames. The story of the struggle and its aftermath is as told by the skipper, Capt. Freddy Ayles, to the late Mr John Smale and published in a magazine *Coast and Country* (Parrett & Neve Ltd, 1980).

On 16 November 1928 *Gog* loaded a 52 ton gun. Originally a 12 in naval gun it had been converted to 8 in calibre, and was being returned from Shoeburyness to Woolwich after testing, for examination and acceptance into Army service. It was about 47 ft long. At 1 p.m. the gun barge left on the flood tide, towed by *Katharine* and secured by two 5 in manila hawsers of 50 fathoms each. The wind was moderate from the south.

The tide turned a couple of hours later and it was decided to slip the tow and allow *Gog* to anchor on the edge of Blyth Sand a mile or so south of Canvey Island. *Gog* let go her starboard anchor and brought up in 5 fathoms of water a half a mile up river from the sailing barge *Royalty*, which had anchored near the East Blyth buoy. *Gog* always carried a spare anchor but on this occasion it was not shackled onto its chain.

In the fading light the wind began to freshen, first from the south and then, later, veering west. Before long it was gusting to Force 7 or 8 and rapidly increasing in strength, reaching Force 10. In the strong ebb tide, *Gog*'s anchor started to drag. The captain ordered chain to be paid out to 52 fathoms and hailed *Katharine* to take them in tow again. The anchor held for a time but as *Katharine* steamed up it started to drag again. Two tow-ropes were quickly connected and with *Katharine* taking the strain, the dragging was checked and it was possible to shorten cable by 15 fathoms with a view to re-anchoring close to the Blyth Sand.

All the time the gale was increasing in strength and in spite of *Katharine*'s engines running at full power she could only just hold *Gog* which, by then, was in danger of drifting down on to *Royalty*. Then, just after five o'clock, in lashing spray and mountainous waves, a squall of hurricane violence caught *Katharine* on her port bow and blew her round to northward out of position. Ayles was obliged to slip the tow-ropes and once more *Gog* was on her own, depending on a single anchor.

But it was all to no avail. The skipper saw that *Gog* was in imminent danger of drifting helplessly across *Royalty*'s bows. He grabbed the *Gog*'s tiller and by veering and checking the anchor chain managed to sheer *Gog* clear. She came broadside on to *Royalty*.

In an attempt to pick up the tow again *Katharine* backed down with her stern between *Gog*'s starboard bow and *Royalty*'s bow, but almost immediately *Gog*'s starboard fell lightly on to *Royalty*. Fenders were dropped between the two vessels and skipper Ayles, still at the helm, gave *Gog* a sheer, and managed to move the vessels apart.

Gog then paid away cable and dropped below *Royalty*, while *Katharine* shifted position to anchor on her port bow so that with *Royalty* on her starboard bow she was sheltered from the heavy sea, but was still shipping a lot of water. Although *Gog* was fitted with hand pumps, they were worked from the deck. The weather was much too bad for them to be manned; the crew had to stay where they were and hold on for dear life to avoid being blown overboard.

At about 6.35 p.m. a loud crack was heard which could only mean that a cable had parted, and *Royalty* bore down on *Gog* at considerable speed and hit her very hard on her starboard bow. It was later found that her bows had been set by the force of the blow and the stove in her forecastle had shifted a foot or more. The water in the hold began to rise alarmingly which could only mean that the force of the collision had started her stern gates. *Gog* began to settle and was not rising to the seas as she had before, so that more and more water came over her decks.

Conditions became so bad that, in spite of the howling wind and driving spray, Ayles managed to hail *Katharine* to come alongside and take them off. At 7.30 p.m. *Katharine* manoeuvred with great difficulty close enough to the barge's port side to take the crew off, leaving the wallowing *Gog* to her fate.

Gog's anchor was still holding so *Katharine* steamed into a position just ahead of her and started spraying oil on the heaving waves. However, the barge's cable parted shortly afterwards and she drifted away into the night. *Katharine* steamed after her and eventually found her with her riding lights still burning, laying in the vicinity of the West Leigh Middle buoy with her bows in the air and her stern submerged. She disappeared altogether at about 8 p.m. and *Katharine* then went upriver to shelter.

The next morning *Gog* was reported in tow of the Trinity House tender *Alert*. Apparently she had shot her gun through the stern gates, which had been carried away, and then come to the surface and drifted away in her water-logged state.

Alert found her awash close by the Girdler Sands. She was lifted by salvage vessels of the Port of London Authority and taken upriver to the Arsenal where she was berthed on a wooden cradle at the shipwright's shop and hauled out for repairs. These involved the stripping and replacement of her top structure, together with repairs to her stern gates. After that she was used only on rare occasions for carrying guns and spent a great deal of her time as an accommodation vessel until she was sold in 1956.

The search for the missing gun was impeded by strong winds and stronger tides. Retired skipper Jack Cains was one of the crew of the WD sailing barge *Sir Stafford Northcote* at that time, and for several weeks after the loss of the gun his barge, together with other WD craft and the PLA salvage steamer *Yantlet* went sweeping for it. He said:

> Sweeping operations were both arduous and dangerous, particularly when you came foul of something as we soon did, finding an old anchor which must have been there for a century. Then it shut in thick and there we were in a dense fog, having to ring a bell every 30 seconds, being then transferred into a Wreck Marking Vessel off the Chapman Light to get a position and departure. Ugh – it were bloody awful!

They swept in vain and the gun remained undisturbed until July 1929, when it was discovered by accident, a fisherman catching his gear on an underwater object which a PLA diver subsequently identified as the missing gun. It was raised six months later and beached but was found to be only fit for scrap, the long immersion in salt water and the scouring effect of sand having rendered it useless for the service.

The fisherman tried long and hard to get compensation from the War Office for the loss of his nets, but was unlucky. Capt. Freddy Ayles fared no better. When he got back ashore he turned up at his fiancée's house at Bow with just the crumpled, salt-stained clothes that he stood up in. Everything else, including his money, had gone down with the *Gog*. No doubt, says Mr Smale, his claim for compensation survives on a file somewhere. Capt. Ayles came out of the resulting Court of Inquiry without any blame being attached to him, and retired as Inspector of Shipping in 1958 after forty-five years' service.

As for the *Royalty*, her skipper told a different story, reporting that an unknown barge had dragged her anchor and collided with him, breaking *Royalty* adrift and causing her to blow ashore on the Chapman Sand. She refloated and then collided with another vessel at anchor. The barge's crew abandoned her and scrambled aboard. *Royalty* drifted away and was later recovered. She was one of those lost at Dunkirk twelve years later.

Gog must sometimes have had a will of her own. Tony Wales, then a boy seaman, recalls an occasion when, while towing up the narrow and shallow Yantlet Creek, *Katharine II* was suddenly struck a tremendous blow on the stern by the heavily-laden *Gog*, which drove her aground. The steam vessel could only navigate the creek at spring tides so the crew

The motor barge *Katharine II* aground in Yantlet Creek, Isle of Grain

had a race against time to get her free. Fortunately, little damage was caused to either vessel, and this time *Gog*'s 16 in gun barrel cargo arrived safely at its destination.

Gog and *Magog* were not the only special craft closely connected with activities at Shoeburyness. There were two other interesting Fleet vessels with a rather strange, but extremely useful, task, employed on the Shoeburyness ranges. These were the barges *Arctic II* and *Forth*. Both dated from 1931, and both had replaced earlier vessels of the same name, going back to the nineteenth century. There are now no details of *Forth* available, but *Arctic II* is known to have originated as a Thames 'Swimmie' barge.

These two barges, their superstructures strongly reminiscent of Noah's Ark, were used for target-towing, but with a difference. Working in tandem on the ranges at Maplin Sands, latterly with the aid of diesel engines and winches, they hauled Hong Kong targets on wheels between them, for the benefit of courses training on 6 in guns. Thus the *Navy and Army Illustrated* of 6 August 1897 states that:

Not unlike Noah's Ark, *Arctic*, and her sister barge, *Forth*, towed targets to and fro across Maplin Sands, Shoeburyness

Admirably complete arrangements are made for the provision of moving targets, both towed by sea and across the sands to represent the approach of galloping ranks of attacking cavalry and infantry, and otherwise to simulate the incidents of actual warfare.

The barges were normally crewed by Royal Engineers, but had always been borne on the Fleet establishment as WD vessels. *Arctic II* (and, presumably, *Forth*) was released from this unusual task after the war, and served for a time as a floating guardroom at Yarmouth, Isle of Wight. She was eventually sold out of the service in 1981 after a period at Priddy's Hard, Portsmouth, as a sort of floating boat-house for army water activities.

11
LIVERY, ENSIGN AND DRESS

In peacetime, WD Fleet vessels were always easily distinguished in the ports of the United Kingdom and abroad, not only by their livery, and blue ensign, but by an immaculate air of naval smartness, which alone would have set them apart from commercial shipping.

From keel to bulwarks, black varnish was relieved by a white riband immediately above the rubbers. Casings, coamings, ventilators, winch and other deck fittings were finished in dark brown, while skylights, companions and other teak work on deck and bridge were varnished. Outside metal work was of course, white, as were lifebuoys, with the letters WD and broad arrow in black. Internal fittings were nearly always of varnished teak or french polished mahogany, and there was gleaming brasswork everywhere. The funnel was buff, with a black top. Lifeboats were black topsides, with white bottoms. The name of the vessel was often in brass or bronze on the stern only, with the letters WD below in place of a port of registry.

Many of the older steam launches, like the warships' pinnaces and admirals' barges of the pre-Second World War Royal Navy, would have been adorned with brass, rather than painted, funnels. Such a vessel was stationed at Portsmouth in the last decade of the nineteenth century as the Garrison Commander's launch. Whether or not it was established as such, or appropriated, on the principle that rank has its privileges, is not known. However, that personage took a very personal interest in the craft; according to George Thomas, who was mate in charge, the Garrison Commander would 'play hell' if he could not see his own reflection in the polished funnel. At Plymouth, too, the high-speed 'Bird' class launch *Eagle* was used personally by GOC, Western Command, and on that account was distinguished by a smart black hull, but deviated from the standard in having pale blue roof tops; she was always kept immaculate. There were other deviations at overseas stations, where the white-painted hulls of launches lent an extra touch of class in the blue waters of tropical harbours.

Of course, all this finery disappeared under a universal coat of drab grey when war broke out, much to the delight of those seamen whose daily tasks were thereby lightened. Charles Codner was one of these but, some years later, as second mate, he took an equal delight in supervising the restoration of *Sir Evelyn* to her pre-war condition, burning off layers of grey paint, uncovering varnish and brass work. He 'found' this work for the crew during a period of enforced idleness and reports that 'she came up beautifully' – so much so as to attract wondering admiration when re-fitting in a Clyde shipyard and to be chosen, at Cairnryan, to be inspected by a visiting general.

To complete the picture of a smart workmanlike vessel, the Fleet's Blue Ensign with crossed swords confirmed its status. The Fleet and its predecessor under the Board of Ordnance had always had its own ensign, but was originally red. The Red, White and Blue Ensigns, broadly speaking, originated through the division of the Navy into three coloured squadrons, each of which flew an ensign according to its colour. This system was abolished in 1864 as it had been found very inconvenient. The Red had been the senior colour, having been adopted in the seventeenth century as the national colour, the flag of St George.

After 1864, it was ordained that the Navy should use the White Ensign, together with the Royal Yacht Squadron and Trinity House Vessels when escorting Royal Yachts. The Blue Ensign was for the RNR and the Red adopted as the national ensign by all other ships. The wearing of the Blue Ensign was later extended to vessels other than ships of war in Admiralty service, British merchant ships commanded by officers of the RN on the retired list or of the RNR, and by vessels belonging to public offices, dominions and colonies, etc.

The first ensign believed to have been adopted by the Board of Ordnance was authorized in a Royal Proclamation of 1694 (William and Mary), which authorized vessels of various public offices, including Their Majesties' Ordnance, to wear a Red Jack with the Union Jack in the upper canton, with the Seal of the Office. As, however, the Board of Ordnance did not operate its own fleet at that time, this authority is more likely to have applied to hired storeships. No information is available as to the design of the seal with which the Jack was defaced. It is known, however, that at some time, the Board adopted a seal which had the now familiar shield-shaped device with three cannons and three cannon balls.

While this gradually came to be accepted as the Arms of the Board, it was not registered at the College of Arms until 1806.

Five years earlier, a Royal Proclamation of 1801 (George III) ordained that:

For the better distinct of ships or vessels which may be employed by the Principal Officers of Our Ordnance Our Royal Will and Pleasure is that such ships and vessels as shall be employed for Our Service by the Principal Officers of Our Ordnance shall wear a red Jack with a Union Jack in a canton at the upper corner thereof next to the staff and in the other part of the said Jack shall be described the Seal used in such of the respective Officers aforesaid, by which the ships and vessels shall be employed.

This proclamation varies from that of 1694 only in that it is specific to the Board of Ordnance.

The Board of Ordnance disappeared in 1855, and in 1864, following the introduction of the Blue Ensign (see above) the Ordnance Ensign was changed to that colour. WD vessels accordingly hoisted the blue Ordnance flag. The last change, which reflected the Fleet's transfer from civilian to military control, was made on 3 October 1890, when the 'Blue Ensign of Her Majesty's Fleet with the Badge of such other Military Services, on the Fly thereof, namely two crossed swords' was authorized by the Admiralty. There is evidence to suggest, however, that the Woolwich vessels, being under operational control of the Ordnance Department, continued to wear the Ordnance flag until after the First World War.

So much for the dress and appearance of the ships. The uniform of officers and crew was no less smart and seamanlike in appearance. There had of course been some changes in the rigs from those referred to in Chapter 6 and set out in Appendix III but these mainly reflected, or followed, changes in naval fashion. Ratings and deckhands wore the navy-blue jersey with the letters WD in red across the breast, with a round black sailor's cap with black silk band lettered 'War Department' in gold. White covers were issued for summer wear at home. This type of cap did not impress Mr Eric Kimber, a wartime seaman, who says they 'made us look like First World War U-Boat sailors'.

Charles Codner, a Fleet member of twenty-one years, recalls that

Charles Codner in 1942, with son, Gifford, aged 2

when scrubbing decks, leather sea-boots were worn. These were issued and were kept in good repair through HM Prison contracts. Later, they were superseded by rubber boots. All other footwear, including the white rubber-soled shoes essential for use on high-speed vessels, was provided at expense of the wearer. Oilskins were in use for inclement weather and very welcome indeed in the older vessels where, until bridges were built-in, the only shelter on the bridge was the canvas dodger. Oilskins occasionally needed a dressing of either fish-oil or raw linseed oil to prevent the material sticking together when folded. The elements would dispel the strong smell of these preservatives on deck, but below it was a different matter.

To complete the rating's dress a coat of heavy black material, not unlike the modern donkey jacket, and reaching to the knees, was worn. This was known as a 'pea-flusher' or 'pea-jacket' and derives from the Dutch word, *pij*, for a similar coat. A comparable garment, in blue cloth, was worn by the nineteenth-century seaman. The pea-jackets and leather boots were originally supplied to the School of Gunnery at Shoeburyness and later adopted for the Fleet. They were made at the Pimlico Clothing Depot by military tailors, as were the bridge coats referred to below.

Mr Codner describes the deck officer's uniform as still in a style reminiscent of the Victorian Navy. The cap had the very short peak typically in use up to and after the First World War. This outdated fashion was not to the liking of the wearers, and so the general custom was for officers to have naval tailors fit conventional peaks. The cap badge up to 1941 was a laurel wreath with crossed swords and the letters WD on either side of the hilts. Thereafter, the crossed swords and WD were replaced by the letters RASC. When the Fleet became part of the Royal Corps of Transport (RCT) this lettering was removed and not replaced. The jacket, made of worsted, was also cut in Victorian style, high-buttoned, almost to the neck. Again, it was the practice to have the jacket modified by folding the lapel to have a deeper cut, and to omit to fasten the top button (this latter fashion an idiosyncrasy shared with Battle of Britain fighter pilots). The ensemble was completed by a very smart officer's greatcoat, or bridge coat, based on RN design. This was cut very long, reaching to the tops of the boots. Both jackets and coats were of the best quality and were very popular.

Badges of rank now followed Merchant Navy practice; instead of the two rings worn by the nineteenth-century master, four gold-braided bands were now worn. Chief engineers wore three bands with blue backing. Mates now wore the two bands, and the second and third engineers two bands and one band respectively.

In November 1943, there was a major change in the Fleet's uniform, when authority was given for RASC civilian personnel to wear blue battledress. The officers' pattern continued to be adorned with gold buttons and gold braid badges of rank, as hitherto. There was further welcome variation in August 1944, when approval for the provision and issue of shoulder flashes was given. The design was that of the RASC ensign, and is still in use.

In hot-weather countries, white duck and white drill uniforms were worn, and in some colonies the round cap was replaced in summer by a topi with the 'War Department' ribbon. In common with the Forces as a whole, this head-dress had been discontinued by the end of the Second World War. Officers usually wore white tunics which buttoned up to the neck, but in later years the more comfortable open-necked shirt, white shorts, stockings and shoes were adopted with slip-on shoulder badges. Where the climate required summer and winter wear, the latter followed the home regulations, except that, in Gibraltar for instance, deckhands wore naval pattern flannel vests under reefer jackets, with short-peaked caps with chinstrap and ribbon.

12
TARGET PRACTICE SEAWARDS

Ian V. Hogg, in his *Coastal Defences of England and Wales, 1856–1956*, records that the instructor on a field artillery long gunnery staff course observed that the going rate for anti-aircraft artillery was 1,000 rounds for every aircraft shot down. Field artillery fired ranging shots before getting on target, but coast artillery hit the target with the first shot fired. The next day the instructor's students saw a 6 in gun blow a fast-moving target out of the water with its first shot.

While this must occasionally have happened, the instructor's enthusiasm slightly outranged reality. It would be nearer the truth to say that coast artillery opening rounds would fall within the 50 per cent zone of the gun and in all probability would hit the target thereafter. Thus, the general objects of 'Target Practice Seawards', in which the Fleet played such an important part, were achieved. These objects were stated in early editions of Garrison Artillery Training, and in all subsequent instructions, to be:

> To train units for their duties in war with armament to which they are allotted.
>
> To test the efficiency of the artillery as regards organization, personnel and material, in fulfilling its duties in the defence of the fortress or defended port.

In the furtherance and successful attainment of these objects the Fleet had played its full part, not only by its comparatively recent range work, but by centuries of logistic support. Typically, however, there has never been any public acknowledgement of this contribution to the high standards of efficiency coastal artillery had reached by the 1930s.

The requirements of coastal defences for realistic moving-target practice seawards had changed but little since the need had been recognized in the late 1880s. The slow speed of the first steamers constructed for the task, whose unencumbered maximum speeds of between 8 and 10 knots would have been nearly halved by target drag, was overcome by the fitting of winding gear. The first vessel to be so fitted was the *Osprey*, in 1897. This gear was eventually able to winch targets across the range at up to 20 knots. As *Instructions for Practice Seawards, 1931* states that target speeds should not be less than 12 knots, there was, at that time, an ample margin.

For practice purposes three targets in an arrangement representing a length of 300 ft simulated a battleship, cruiser, blocker or boomsmasher; two targets 150 ft apart represented a destroyer. For a motor torpedo-boat two targets 50 ft apart were used and a submarine was represented by a 150 ft sail-like target 9 ft by 5 ft. The standard target used was the Hong Kong, referred to in Chapter 4, and the centre one of an arrangement of three would usually be larger to simulate the superstructure.

The target tower carried a range officer and a party of military personnel to assist in signalling, recording, and other target duties. Before the advent of wireless, communication between battery and target tower was by morse flag, semaphore or lamp, using a modified commercial code of signals. For wireless use, a simple letter code was later adopted and the radio operators were also required to have a supplementary Aldis lamp. Gunnery instructions issued in 1914 dictated the use of heliograph or codes based on the flying of prisms, spheres, circles and triangles for long-range signalling, when 9.2 in guns were firing. Opening and ceasing fire were controlled by red flags. The range flag on the vessel would be hoisted when she was on course; the hoisting of the battery flag indicated that firing could proceed. Lowering of either flag signified a cease-fire.

Following the introduction of the winch came the invention of the Travis Rake, named for the inventor, Mr Henry Travis, the second Superintending Engineer and Constructor of Shipping to be appointed to the Fleet. This was a device which enabled the range officer in the launch to observe, record and report the fall of shot. It had the appearance of a garden rake, the teeth on a 4 ft movable and pivot-mounted crossbar representing gradations of 10 yd, and the handle calibrated so as to correspond with the distance of the tow line from the target, from 250 to 800 yd. As the distance varied the assistant could slide the crossbar back or forward as necessary, at the same time keeping it parallel to the line of fire, the range officer taking sightings through a window sight. For distances over 800 yd, the represented scale was halved. Later an automatic rake was introduced which was geared to the vessel's winch and adjusted automatically to the length of the tow as shown on the indicator dial.

Mr P.A. Claydon, a range-finder with coast artillery, describes the use of the rake:

> The floating targets were let out astern as far as possible, then we would wind them in with *Hurst* doing about 7 or 8 knots. The total speed may have been about 30 knots for the three targets skimming along behind. The officer on board would order the open fire to be flashed and would look along the rake centre tine on the targets with the rake coming in at the same relative speed as the cable was being wound in. Boom – the shot hits the sea and the rake would show the officer plus 10 yards (over) or minus 10 yards (under) and I would note on a prepared sheet. The shoot controller at Picklecombe would record error left or right. At a predetermined point, after some ten or twelve shots, my officer would yell 'Cease Fire!' to be flashed by the waiting signaller to the guns. There were some who swore that the officer would wait until the shells fell ahead of the *Hurst* before giving the order to cease fire!

Target practice was not only a daytime occupation; night firing was just as essential to coastal defence training, perhaps even more so. The development of the uses of electricity and its application for defence purposes had led to the establishment of Defence Electric Light, or DEL, units to operate searchlights. Until December 1939, these were manned by Fortress Companies, Royal Engineers, and were an integral part of coast defences, but between December 1939 and June 1940, this responsibility was transferred to coast artillery. There were special instructions for night practices. Orders to the range officer as to hour of attack, course, etc., were to be kept secret. Signals to launches towing targets were if possible, to be avoided entirely. Red lamps performed the function of red flags, and numbers of picquet boats ensured range and target-tower safety, with supplies of green and red rockets and flares. The writer has a vivid recollection of pyrotechnic displays during such practices in Gibraltar in the 1930s involving *Sir Noel Birch* and 29 Battery, R.A. Searchlight practice, without firing, was also a part of coastal defence training.

Yet another form of coastal artillery practice was the throw-off shoot, when the WD launch, untrammelled by targets and free to jink, manoeuvre and vary speed, tested the ability of the gunners to engage. The safety of the launch was ensured by stationing at each gun an officer or responsible NCO with orders to observe the launch through the telescope of the auto-sight and to stop the firing if it should appear to be dangerous. During the Second World War open sights were attached to both sides of gun-shields where practicable, which gave gun safety officers better control of safety, providing a larger field of view.

The Bermuda Militia Artillery engaged in such a shoot at their annual camp, with their two 6 in guns. A RASC warrant officer was tempted from his natural habitat to act as gun safety officer. These guns were not equipped with telescopes, or open sights, and his instructions were to align his graticulated binoculars with the gun-shield and to shout an order to cease fire when the vessel reached the statutory 5 degree angle of safety. Unfortunately, every time the gun was fired, the sudden explosion destroyed his careful alignment and it became a race between re-alignment and re-loading. Fortunately, he managed to keep one step ahead and *Helford* and her master, Alan Houghton, were never seriously threatened. *Helford* belonged to the first generation of post-war fast launches, the 44 ft 6 in 'River' class, built by British Power Boats in 1945 and 1946.

It is a tribute to the discipline of all concerned in Target Practice Seawards that mishaps involving damage to vessels or injury to personnel were very rare under peacetime conditions. Since the free-for-all days described in Chapter 4, only one death had been recorded. This happened during target practice off Wembury Point, Plymouth in the early 1920s, when a stray shot sliced through the engine-room of *Sir Frederick Walker* and killed the engineer.

Capt. Frank Bourne, the last Master Superintendent, recalled the only mishap he had known, which concerned the launch *Albert* at Falmouth. During target practice the boy went below to make a cup of tea and found the floorboards floating in the forecastle. The skipper immediately ditched the targets and beached the vessel. It was found that a shell had gone right through the forecastle below the water-line and out the other side.

Maj. P.J. Lee, a coast artillery officer, was on a launch off Llandudno when rounds fell short and ricocheted over the vessel, the subsequent inquiry showing that a misread dial was the cause. He added that:

it was not all worry as to whether you were going to be hit by a stray shell. I remember on one occasion we were towing Hong Kong targets and a large radar screen for a counter-bombardment radar shoot, which had been damaged. The targets were brought alongside. The No. 1 of the target party jumped onto the target, only to disappear through a hole made by an unrecorded 9.2 in hit. We got him out of the sea alright, using boathooks, wet but amused.

There was one occasion when firing came to an abrupt halt through a quite unconnected incident. *Sir Robert Hay* was towing for a Militia shoot off Southsea when a signal to stop firing was given. When the master inquired the cause he received the message: 'No more practice. Troops gone to fire at South Parade Pier!' Whether to fight it or watch it was not made clear.

Sir Robert Hay was one of the earliest steam target towers and had in fact joined the Fleet as a paddle-steamer, being eventually converted. Like her successors, right up to the mid-1930s, she had a speed of less than 10 knots, relying on winching to bring target speeds up to practice requirements which had changed not at all since the beginning of the century – indeed almost since the beginning of target-towing. *Sir Desmond O'Callaghan*, in 1927 the penultimate steam target tower to join the Fleet, could barely achieve 8 knots against the tide, when towing off Shoeburyness. For 9.2 in shoots, when a 1,200 yd tow was required, winding-in to attain a realistic target speed often resulted in a broken cable. In 1936, however, two new connected developments were to render these old target towers obsolete.

It will be recalled that one of the reasons for the introduction of moving target practice was to counter a new threat seen as coming from fast-moving motor torpedo-boats (MTBs). History now repeated itself as a new generation of much speedier MTBs and faster destroyers demanded improved counter-measures. So these developments generated a requirement for improved armament and target speeds which, at 40 knots, were practically double what could be achieved by winch-towing. So far as the former was concerned, the anti-MTB 6 pdr twin gun was introduced to replace the 12 pdr QF for close defence. To meet the concomitant requirement, two possibilities, towing by airship and towing by torpedo-boat, were examined by the Senior Engineer and Constructor of Shipping, Rear Admiral R.C. Boddie.

The first proposal was nothing if not imaginative, and so the War

Office approached the RAF for assistance. Plans were drawn up for an airship to be built at Cardington for a sum of £500. However, after further thought, the project was abandoned. The vulnerability of the conventional towing vessel to air attack, amply demonstrated a few years later, shows this to have been a very wise decision. It was concluded that future target-towing commitments could best be met by the development of a new generation of high-speed launches.

Accordingly trials were run with fast motor launches built by the leading boatbuilders, Thornycroft, Samuel White, Vosper and British Power Boats. The last-named were successful, and very soon afterwards the first of these beautiful 57 ft craft, built of mahogany and teak, powered by twin 500 hp Napier Lions, were brought into service. The vessels were named for military commanders, *Haig*, *Allenby*, *Kitchener*, *Raglan*, etc. It was clearly established at the time that these boats would continue to be operated and maintained by the Army.

The same year, 1937, saw the advent of the first custom-built fast range-clearance launches. These, too, were built by British Power Boats. Smaller than the target towers, they were 45 ft long and were powered by three 100 hp Power-Meadows engines, giving a speed of about 25 knots. Eighteen of these vessels, the 'Bird' class, were built.

The advent of these high-powered vessels, a complete list of which is at Appendix VIII, did much to improve practice facilities for the gunners; apart from increased speeds, the time taken to get on range and to prepare targets was shortened considerably. However, for the 6 pdr twin equipments, designed to counter high-speed craft that could manoeuvre and jink, the straight across-the-range-and-back operation, however speedy, still did not give the gunners sufficient practice.

So, to improve still further the practice facilities for these equipments, a radio-controlled target boat, the 'Queen Gull', was commissioned by the coastal branch in 1940 and built by the British Power Boats Company. This was a 12 ft 6 in boat powered by a Ford 10 engine that could travel at 20 knots and jink about to simulate a MTB. The advent of this aid to coastal gunnery provided the Fleet with the additional task of towing the 'Queen Gull' to the target area, providing communications, and recovering the 'Gull' after practice. The provision and maintenance of these craft also became a RASC responsibility, though the wireless equipment was maintained with the assistance of REME. Between 1941 and the end of the war 161 'Queen Gulls' were built.

The 48 ft 'Derby Winner' class inshore target tower *Isinglass* carried Field-Marshal Earl Wavell's coffin from Tower Pier to Westminster en route to the Abbey

Following the highly-successful 'Bird' class launches came the twenty-four 'Derby Winners' class, named evocatively for such famous Derby winners as *Hyperion*, *Call Boy* and *Blue Peter*. These were somewhat larger, at 48 ft, but with much the same performance. Several other increasingly large and powerful target-towing classes and acquisitions from the other services joined the Fleet during the next few years (*vide* Chapter 18 and Appendix IX).

Mr E.A. 'Ted' Cowdry, a boy seaman in 1937, recalls target-towing duties in various vessels, including the *Marquess*, surprisingly used as a range safety vessel for anti-aircraft practice off Manorbier. The target was a sleeve towed by a manned aircraft; later, off Watchet, the vessel was performing a similar function for the radio-controlled 'Queen Bee', which also towed a sleeve.

In 1939, Ted Cowdry was fortunate in being selected to join the new 'General' class target tower, *Haig*. The master was George E. Ansell, a future Master Superintendent. This vessel, together with the 'Bird' class

Recreational use of a Hong Kong target; crew members of the target tower *Haig* take time off in Lagos

range-clearance launch *Swallow*, was dispatched, with crews of six and three respectively, by the Elder Dempster steamer *Apapa*, to Freetown, Sierra Leone, to practice the 6 in shore battery there. His lasting impression of the tour was the heat; the crews found it impossible to sleep on the vessels and were accommodated in barracks. The task lasted four months, and they had a very pleasant return voyage, this time on the Elder Dempster *Accra*.

Following leave, he rejoined *Haig* to continue target-towing duties. Like many employed on this task, he was to face far greater hazards than those, more apparent than real, hitherto met in fifty years.

13
THE FLEET GOES TO WAR AGAIN

In the immediate and frantic pre-war period the pressures of rearmament and expansion of the Army saw the Fleet's traditional tasks at home multiply and take on a new urgency. Coasting vessels plied between the main UK ports, carrying War Department cargoes and moving Royal Naval and Royal Artillery gun equipment from the Royal Arsenal to ship-building yards and emplacements. Other craft ferried personnel and carried fresh water to outlying sea forts. Steam and high-speed target-towing vessels were meeting the increasing training requirements of the fixed defences, assisted by range safety launches.

Charles Codner, a boy seaman in 1931, recalled the earlier, quieter, daily routine of the steam target tower *Hurst II* at Plymouth. These vessels, when not employed on target-towing duties, were fully employed as harbour launches. Each morning, Monday to Friday, *Hurst II* would take six to eight passengers, usually civilian maintenance workers, and deliver them to the various coastal defence batteries in Plymouth Sound. The vessel, towing a small boat for landing workmen at batteries where they could not come alongside, would call first at Picklecombe Fort, thence to Drake's Island, Elphinstone Steps below the Hoe, and on via Drake's Island to Bovisand and, occasionally, to Penlee Point. From Bovisand and Drake's Island, *Hurst II* would embark the caretakers' wives for shopping expeditions, dropping them at Millbay Docks. The afternoon schedule mirrored the morning's activities. The summer routine was varied by weekend target-towing for the TA off Bovisand Fort and occasionally at Falmouth.

There were other welcome changes in the life of a WD seaman; an occasional visit to Weymouth or Portsmouth for repairs by civilian contractors, and the annual visit of the ADMT Woolwich, into whose arms it was cabin-boy Codner's duty to thrust the standard cork lifebelt during the demonstration of lifeboat drill.

Later, on the sea-going *Sir Walter Campbell*, based at Woolwich,

Charles Codner remembers carrying a considerable variety of stores for both Army and Navy. The Navy could always find freight for the WD vessels when space was available, and so *Sir Walter*, in addition to ammunition, oils, paints, blankets and bedding, time-expired bully beef and Mills bombs for dumping, and miscellaneous Ordnance stores, also carried the Navy's spirit ration for the Spithead Review, a mast for the Royal Yacht *Victoria and Albert* and an anchor chain for the mighty but ill-fated HMS *Hood*. There would still have been many serving in the Fleet at this time able to remind their younger shipmates of the days, forty years earlier in the 1890s, when these latter cargoes had been commonplace.

Only a few craft were maintained overseas, in such peacetime Commands as Gibraltar, Malta, the Middle East, Hong Kong, Singapore, Bermuda and the Caribbean. These were mainly steam target towers, range launches and one or two specially built Governors' Barges. They were crewed by locally-employed civilians, usually under a United Kingdom-based master.

It had been foreseen that in the event of war, training and administrative commitments would be vastly increased to the extent that some reorganization of the overall control and administration of the Fleet would be essential. It would be necessary to decentralize the control of existing craft to formations and commands. Hitherto, local administration and control had been in the hands of the local officer in charge of transport, under the Assistant Director of Military Transport (ADMT) at Woolwich.

In pursuance of this policy it was decided to appoint suitably qualified officers to take over the general administration and maintenance of the craft. For this purpose they would be required to establish small Water Transport Companies under War Office control. No time was lost; Nos 1 to 5 Water Transport Companies were set up in January 1940, respectively at Leith, Portsmouth, Barry Docks, Singapore and Woolwich. Later in August of the same year, it was also decided that the ADMT's organization would be disbanded, and absorbed into the Supply and Transport Branch of the War Office as ST1 with an Assistant Director (a lieutenant colonel) in charge. Thus, after four centuries, ended the Royal Arsenal's direct control of the Fleet and its predecessors, though of course it was to continue for several years as one of the main centres of Army shipping activity.

During this period, the important decision was taken to form military water transport units, to allow the inclusion of such companies in future orders of battle. Volunteers, such as yachtsmen, longshoremen, fishermen and deep sea sailors, were sought from all arms of the service and transferred to the new unit, No. 1 Motor Boat Company, RASC, at Salcombe, Devon, which became the training unit. No. 2 Motor Boat Company followed and was soon operational, and so, for the first time since the days of 76 Company's solitary range safety launch at Shoeburyness, before the First World War, there were soldiers in the Fleet. There is good reason to mark this development as the beginning of the end of the civilian fleet.

The continued manning of military vessels by civilians during the war years appears from contemporary documents to have been considered a necessity forced upon the War Office by the severe restrictions in manpower rather than an acknowledgement that they were the best fitted and suited for the tasks. It was probably felt, however, that an all-military fleet would provide a flexibility in training and employment, particularly where services of a hazardous or security nature were required, which a mixed force would lack. But, as we shall see, the civilians had their full share of the hazards of wartime service. In any event, although approval was given in 1943 for military to replace civilians up to a limit of thirty-four officers and 400 other ranks (a good indication of the size of the civilian establishment at home at that time) it was never possible to make more than a few such replacements until after the war. Then, however, the circumstances, both military and financial, were different, and restricted approval for only 25 per cent militarization was given. Nevertheless, the writing was now indelibly on the wall.

There were two types of non-operational Water Transport Company into which the civilian fleet had been organized. One type was designed to administer 32 to 71 vessels, and a smaller to administer 12 to 31. Officers were allowed on a sliding scale of one for every eight vessels, covering all but the Officer Commanding, and in the larger units an administrative officer was allowed. There was also a small military shore staff. Otherwise, the crews, administrative and workshop personnel were all civilians. Later in the war, however, a shortage of civilian artificers led to the employment of low medical category soldier technicians in some cases. A new post, Master Superintendent, was created to act as adviser to

The Marquess of Hartington in wartime rig, with Carley Floats spoiling her looks

the OC on navigational matters and on the administration of the crews. This was welcomed in the Fleet as an important new step on the promotion ladder. Hitherto, the only further advancement available to the many aspiring deck officers had led only to the posts of Inspector or Assistant Inspector of Shipping.

The war did not start very quickly for the 'Queen' of the Fleet. The *Marquess of Hartington* was based in the north-east after having, in the words of Charles Codner, 'rushed' a cargo of 4.7 AA guns and ammunition to Scapa Flow a few months earlier. (Somehow, 'rushed' is not a word one would associate with this dear old lady's 9 knot progress!) Her subsequent part in the opening period of the National Emergency was to remain at Hartlepool with steam up, a role which evoked the curiosity of the townspeople and several enquiries from Naval authorities as to her availability for minesweeping. It also gave Mr Codner time to drop his matrimonial anchor. The *Marquess* finally left in January 1940 for Woolwich, where she joined the newest and last vessel to join the old Fleet, the coaster *Malplaquet*.

After Dunkirk, implementation of the concept of Britain as an Island Fortress made urgent and heavy demands on the Fleet. Expansion proceeded apace, in step with ever-increasing commitments. By the end of 1941 the number of vessels had increased to 200 and, two years later, to 1,110 worldwide. In the United Kingdom the vast increase in vessels was in response to heavy demands from all Commands. The formation of many new coastal artillery regiments created an urgent need for many more high-speed target towers. The fortification of hitherto unprotected islands such as Flat Holm and Steep Holm in the Bristol Channel involving the conveyance of thousands of tons of defence stores and building materials, the establishment of new seaward forts, echoing the measures taken during the Napoleonic Wars, launches for security officers at ports, all added up to a scale of activity not experienced since 1815.

The original four United Kingdom Water Transport Companies had been formed to serve Scotland from Leith, Southern Command from Portsmouth, Western Command from Barry (later Bangor) and the whole of the east and south-east coast from Chichester to the Scottish border from Woolwich, the latter Company being spread over twenty-two stations. Following a reorganization which started early in 1943, the spread of Water Transport Companies eventually became as follows:

> 614 Company Leith
> 615 Company Portsmouth
> 616 Company Bangor
> 629 Company Grimsby
> 630 Company Ipswich
> 631 Company Woolwich
> 632 Company Sheerness
> 644 Company Plymouth
> 647 Company Sandbank (Clyde)

It is a measure of the size of Woolwich's responsibilities that no less than four of these companies, 629 to 632, were formed from 5 Company. A contemporary report in the RASC journal describes the work of the RASC Water Transport Companies from 1940 to 1942:

Another Branch of the (Supplies and Transport) Directorate administers the War Department Fleet, probably the least known of all the calls of the sea. It is today a substantial and growing fleet which includes over 250 steam and motor vessels, craft ranging from small cutters to ocean-going cargo steamers, from dumb barges, which can carry 16 inch guns, to 57 foot high-speed motor launches, with a pair of aero-type 500 hp marine engines tucked away in their hard chine hulls.

It carries out a variety of military duties around the coasts of these islands as well as in defended harbours of the Empire. Marine target towing for the Royal Artillery is one of the Fleet's most important tasks, and for this purpose the fastest and most powerful motor launches are used. At need, these target-towers are used under naval control for air rescue work and a good many RAF pilots owe their lives to them.

The carriage of troops, supplies, water, ammunition and stores to islands and sea forts around our coasts and in harbours at stations overseas employs a considerable number of vessels; employs them fully, too, because it is not uncommon for masters and crews to be on duty for eighteen or twenty hours a day, sometimes for months on end. It is hard and often hazardous work for there is an uncomfortably good chance of striking an uncharted mine, or arousing the interest of enemy aircraft.

Recently four of the Army's cargo vessels, the largest of them 500 tons burthen, between them carried 15,000 tons of heavy cargo between the mainland and a fortified island in the course of a single month. The feat was the more remarkable because practically every ton of this cumbrous freight had to be manhandled ashore at improvised jetties. In the same period a 30 foot launch carried 2,000 troops and 26,000 gallons of water to sea forts, making 530 trips to do it. A thousand passengers in a week is the best record so far set for a 'taxi-boat.'

Not long ago the master of one vessel lying alongside waiting to discharge his urgently required and highly explosive cargo got under way single-handed during a heavy enemy air attack and in pitch darkness took his ship straight across a minefield to an alternative gun site on the coast. There are stout hearts in the WD Fleet.

Maj. Jim Goodrick was a Royal Artillery officer commanding two batteries established in the re-activated Bull Fort in the Humber Estuary. He remembers with admiration the unfailing support of the civilian fleet vessel based in Grimsby and the high standard of seamanship the crew always displayed. Coming alongside the fort's small jetty in bad weather when the rise and fall of the sea could be as much as 15 ft, was very often a quite hazardous manoeuvre. Another hazard was mines. The Humber Estuary was a collecting area for Murmansk convoys and mining by air was an almost nightly occurrence, often interfering with the launch's night runs for searchlight practice.

Everything was carried by the WD launch – personnel, stores, ammunition, mail, rations and, before a spring supply was found, water. Maj. Goodrick recalls that the launch once brought out a piano which, however, did not quite make the jetty and sank without a trace. The only other mishap he remembers was a mistimed jump by a NCO, too anxious, perhaps to start his leave. He was fished out laughing!

So varied were the Fleet's activities that it would be difficult to describe any personal experiences as typical, but Mr Codner's brief account of the early voyages and tasks of the *Malplaquet* in 1940 and 1941 capture the essence of the Fleet's wartime work in home waters. *Malplaquet*'s first passage was to Hull to load coke and Nissen huts for the

The 1940 coaster *Malplaquet* (528 tons) was the last cargo-carrying sea-going vessel built for the civilian fleet

Orkneys. For personal defence the crew were issued with rifles, from which, however, they did not derive any great sense of security, no ammunition having been provided. From Hull the vessel sailed in convoy to Scapa, delivering the coke to various islands. The ship then took up station at Stromness and was engaged in supplying various fortified islands with stores and supplies. Prior to the Norway campaign, many warships had to be supplied with anti-freeze for their guns. Codner reports that they were trying to deliver this while the ships were preparing for sea; many were too busy to accept it!

Other tasks included troops and lorries to the Shetlands, GPO telephone cable from Lerwick to Scapa for discharge into a cable-layer, ferry duties from Scrabster to the islands. Just after Dunkirk the vessel's cargo of troops and baggage also included strawberries from the Channel Islands!

Enemy activity was not a great problem that far north. Once their trawler escort dropped a number of depth-charges and evidently shook the *Malplaquet* far more than anything beneath them. The occasional air raid was met by a box-barrage, but apart from being splattered with mud from a near miss, there was never any damage or casualties. One barrage was so fierce that *Malplaquet* was promptly dispatched to Aberdeen for urgent replenishment of ammunition.

The vessel was not quite defenceless; she had been armed with twin machine-guns either side of the bridge, together with an old Lewis gun. Little instruction was available at this time and Codner says they never got this armament working satisfactorily. Much later they were removed and replaced by Oerlikons and a contraption that fired a rocket and suspended a wire by parachute. Two RN gunners were then attached to the ship, and the crew were also trained as gunners. Additional protection was provided in the form of concrete blocks round the wheelhouse. Later, while on the Faröes run, *Malplaquet* was adorned first with a box-kite, then with a balloon which was 'towed' from the foremast-head down to a reel fixed on a winch. When streamed out at a good height it was steady, but Codner recalls that on bringing it down to the mast 'it used to go berserk, charging down at the ship and then leaping skywards again'.

This, then, was part of one vessel's war and gives an insight into the mundane, routine nature of the sea-going duties of the Fleet in home waters. The type of task was still much the same as in peacetime. A cargo was still a cargo, 8 knots was still 8 knots; only the ports of call and the perils multiplied. Numerically, of course, the sea-going vessels formed only a small part of the Fleet. Hundreds of small vessels, fast launches, steam launches, pinnaces, trawlers, motorized fishing vessels, workboats, barges, etc., thronged Britain's harbours, wearing the blue Fleet ensign and carrying out a multiplicity of tasks. Target-towing, range safety, passenger-carrying, water-carrying, port security, a hundred-and-one chores came their way; mostly routine, unexciting and rarely the stirring stuff of history, though some would have their moments.

14
THE FLEET UNDER FIRE

The WD Fleet did not have long to wait for its baptism of fire, indirect though it was. An unnamed target tower, having completed a run for the Dover defences, was passing through St Margaret's Bay when its targets were straddled by what the skipper thought were shells from a 6 in battery. He quickly found that they were coming from a German vessel which was taking the opportunity of some practice at the British taxpayer's expense; even more quickly he removed his vessel from the area at a speed which he had thought beyond the vessel's power.

From May 1940 the German sea and air forces were able to intensify operations in and over the coastal waters of southern and eastern England. Target towers were especially vulnerable. Although high-speed launches were employed almost exclusively now, their predictable target-towing courses and necessarily slow turnround while winching in targets made them sitting ducks, particularly for air attack. Equally vulnerable, of course, were the larger coasters and other steam and motor vessels.

Consequently, and for the first time, WD vessels were armed for defence. At first .300 American pattern Lewis guns were fitted; these were later replaced by twin Bren light machine-guns (LMGs) on straddle mountings. As indicated in Chapter 13, certain of the larger vessels were fitted with Oerlikons. And, of course, as opportunity permitted, Fleet crewmen received training in anti-aircraft defence.

The distinction of being the first WD vessel ever to come under direct unfriendly fire and to be able to fight back, fell to the target-towing vessel *Marlborough* one evening in May 1940.

Capt. E.L. 'Winkle' Beard's 'General' class launch had been lying at anchor south of Dungeness awaiting darkness for a night shoot to begin after target-towing for the coast batteries during the day. The weather, however, was deteriorating and further firing had to be cancelled. As she was raising anchor to return to base, she was suddenly attacked by two Messerschmidt fighters. The first opened fire with machine-guns and cannon, a shell exploding in the engine-room and bullets punching a row of holes along the starboard side of the hull.

Mr Spencer, the deckhand who was working with the winch, saw the attack coming and made for the Lewis gun, but was hit twice in the arm before reaching it. Capt. Beard, then at the controls in the wheel-house, rushed on deck to see the second fighter approaching from over the beach. He seized the Lewis gun and with the RA gunner and his Bren gun, held fire while the attacking aircraft straddled the vessel with cannon shell. When the range closed he ordered fire to be opened, with such accurate effect that both fighters broke off the engagement.

Mr Rose, the engineer, was badly cut in the cheek by a flying splinter, but refused any medical aid until he had repaired the oil and water coolers damaged in the attack. He got the engines going again and, with the assistance of all hands, plugged the bullet holes in the hull. The launch then headed for Dover, where the master received a dressing down from the Royal Naval harbour headquarters for unwittingly discharging casualties at the wrong berth!

Although *Marlborough* was badly mauled in her first encounter with

One of the first generation of high speed towers, the 'General' class *Marlborough* was the first to come under enemy fire in the Second World War. Note the Lewis gun aft

enemy forces, she was back in action the following month when, with other vessels of the Fleet, she played her full part in the Dunkirk evacuation.

Here nine of the fastest launches in the Fleet, the 45 ft 'Bird' class *Grouse*, *Kestrel*, *Pigeon*, *Swallow*, *Teal* and *Vulture*, and the 'General' class *Wolfe*, *Haig* and *Marlborough* played a full and courageous part in the evacuation. *Haig* (F.J. Wales, master) rescued over 900 personnel, mainly French troops; she also escorted the destroyer *Ivanhoe*, which was on fire, and, steaming at 30 knots, maintaining a continous fire with her two Lewis guns, rendered innocuous a half-hour air attack by three waves each of twenty-one bombers. Her exploits ended when she was accidentally rammed twice in quick succession by French motor vessels and sank in Dunkirk Harbour. *Haig* was raised by the RAF the following day and sailed to Ramsgate.

Teal became a total loss and *Swallow* was badly damaged, but working on only one of her three propellers, remained continuously in service for 24 hours, ferrying between 700 and 800 men from the beaches to waiting destroyers. The master, Mr W.R. Clark, was later to be killed in the sister launch *Falcon* when she was destroyed by an enemy bomb while lying alongside Harwich Pier in April 1941. Capt. Beard's *Marlborough* was again in the thick of the action, saving 132 men in four trips before being towed into Dover with her rudder and propellers lost. *Wolfe* made two trips and *Vulture* three before being put out of action, having between them saved 164 lives. *Kestrel* was leaking badly when she limped back to Ramsgate, after four passages and the rescue of fifty-five men. Mr R. Walter of *Haig* and Messrs F. Cherry and H.C.H. Hay of *Swallow* were mentioned in dispatches for their services.

Haig ran into trouble again. Mr Ted Cowdry was aboard in November 1940 when the vessel left Sheerness for Great Yarmouth for a target-towing stint. Leaving Harwich after refuelling, she was attacked by a dive-bomber and sprayed with machine-gun fire. Both the chief engineer, Mr Reg Walter, and Cowdry, were seriously wounded; Walter, who had distinguished himself at Dunkirk, died later. Cowdry spent six months in hospital, and after a short while at Woolwich, resigned and joined the Merchant Navy; his first ship was torpedoed and sunk!

Apart from these craft, the venerable old coasting vessel *Sir Evelyn Wood* evacuated many more from the beach-head of St Valery. In the process she rescued the beachmaster and his party after their small craft had been damaged by shell-fire from a German tank.

The 'Bird' class range clearance *Kestrel* was another of the 1937 generation. She was one
of several WD vessels that distinguished themselves at Dunkirk

Sir Evelyn had a good share of the Fleet's fortunes of war. For some
time she was employed in carrying cargoes of bombs to Northern
Ireland, and on one occasion a serious fire broke out in one of the holds
while loading was in progress. The master, chief engineer and crew
immediately entered the hold and fought the blaze, and their courage and
initiative in so doing averted a serious explosion and loss of life. Some
time later, in 1944, the ship again narrowly escaped destruction when
carrying a cargo of explosives and rockets for the Normandy beach-head.
A V1 just missed her mainmast.

Gen. Sir Walter Venning, the Quartermaster-General, sent the
following message to all the masters concerned in the Dunkirk operation:

> I wish to thank you, your engineer and crew for the very fine part
> which you played in the recent evacuation of the BEF.
>
> In particular I wish to convey my admiration for the way in
> which the personnel of the WD vessels participating volunteered to
> perform a dangerous task quite outside their normal duties.
>
> To have been successful in saving the lives of over 1,200 British
> and Allied soldiers is a feat of which all of you concerned may well

feel proud. The damage done to so many of the craft engaged is a testimony to the dangers which you and those serving under you faced with cheerfulness and gallantry.

I am proud to think that, as Quartermaster-General to the Forces, the War Department Fleet comes within my sphere.

The damage sustained by the launches, none of which came out of the operation unscathed, reduced the subsequent availability of vessels by some 60 per cent and seriously interrupted target-towing and searchlight training duties for some months.

Later, the Fleet received further setbacks when seven urgently required 48 ft launches of the new 'Derby Winners' class nearing completion in contractors' yards, were destroyed by enemy air attack. Three others were badly damaged. At another time, during the blitz, ST1, the 'Admiralty' and administrative centre of the Fleet, suffered considerable inconvenience when its War Office premises in Whitehall Place were destroyed.

In the same year, AB-in-charge R.E. Davey of the launch *Pauletta* was awarded the BEM (Civil Division) and the Lloyd's Medal for bravery at sea. Davey and other Fleet members were sleeping on the depot ship at Shoreham when they were awakened by air-raid alarms and the sound of falling incendiary bombs. Davey takes up the story:

We rushed on deck and saw several burning on the wharf, and then noticed a hole in the top of *Eagle*'s engine-room [the fast launch moored alongside]. Looking into the engine-room, we saw the incendiary bomb resting near the port engine; it had broken some of the fuel pipes. I got down into the engine-room and carefully lifted it clear, quickly got back into the cockpit and threw the bomb onto the wharf.

Mr Davey omits to say that he was fully aware that the vessel had on board a large quantity of high octane petrol already leaking through the broken fuel lines. Ironically, *Eagle* was accidentally destroyed by fire in March 1946, in South East Asia.

Although there was a clear distinction between the operational Motor Boat Companies and the non-operational Water Transport Companies, these incidents show that there was certainly no distinction in the perils to which they were exposed. There was of course very close co-operation between the two, and a co-ordination of effort. A good example of the way in which both worked together was reported in *The Story of the RASC 1939–45.*

The first deployment into a theatre of war of the Motor Boat Companies occurred in November 1942, when No. 2 Company, now re-numbered No. 247, was shipped to Algeria in support of Operation Torch, the North Africa landings. In addition to their own vessel complement, the company requisitioned or otherwise acquired a variety of local boats and did invaluable work running coastal re-supply services in support of the overloaded road and rail lines of communication.

Additional craft were urgently needed from the United Kingdom and two Yarmouth drifters, the 100 ft *Ocean Breeze* and the 90 ft *Boy Phillip* (the former a Dunkirk veteran), were refitted and prepared for sailing. To give them sufficient steaming range for the voyage it was necessary to fill their fish holds with coal. When required, the coal had to be loaded by the crew into baskets, dragged along the deck and shot down into the bunkers – a most difficult and risky business in bad weather, for there was always the danger of flooding the hold. Manned by civilian crews of the Fleet under the Inspector of Shipping, Mr G. Sparshatt (later made a MBE for his distinguished services) they joined a convoy of some 340 ships sailing from Milford Haven on 4 December 1943.

They reached Gibraltar on 13 December, meeting heavy seas and strong head winds for the last four days of the voyage. After a few days' stay, they sailed for Oran, where they assisted in the rescue of an 8,000 ton Greek ship which had broken her moorings in a heavy gale. For this they received a signal of appreciation from the commander of the USN forces at that port. A British hospital ship arrived while they were there, and on hearing that there was a lack of cigarettes on board, the civilian crews sent them a case. Much to their surprise and delight, they received not only the thanks of the wounded but also a large turkey and Christmas cake from the OC troops. These were enjoyed at sea on Christmas Day while bound for Algiers in a full gale. The two vessels were delivered safely to the Motor Boat Company the next day. Subsequently, the *Lucien Gougy* and *Elizabeth Therese* were delivered in like manner, and the 500 ton *Malplaquet*, with its civilian crew, was also diverted from the United Kingdom for duty in the Mediterranean.

In the early days of hostilities, the peacetime routine of the Fleet's vessels in such permanent overseas stations as Gibraltar, Bermuda and the Caribbean had been but little affected. As in the United Kingdom, however, garrison strengths increased, old commitments multiplied and new tasks allotted. For instance, when the Chief Inspector of Water Transport arrived in Gibraltar in September 1943, he found vessels carrying out two services peculiar to the Command: anti-sabotage patrols and deep-sea dumping duties. Water Transport Services in Gibraltar were controlled by Mr James Day, who later became the Master Superintendent on the introduction of that appointment. Mr Day had served in Gibraltar since 1922, and eventually completed over fifty years' service in the Fleet, this event being marked by the congratulations of HE The Governor and presentation of a silver table centre-piece.

In the North Caribbean the Fleet had several interesting commitments, like the 650 mile passenger and cargo run between Kingston and Belize. The vessel employed on this service was the 250 ton American fleet auxiliary *Catania* obtained under the Lend-Lease agreement. A civilian fleet crew took delivery of her at Boston, Mass. and sailed her to Jamaica.

Other tasks included the operation of harbour craft for the examination service and the maintenance of local waterborne communications. Fleet activities in this area were centred on historic Port Royal, where now the Jamaica Defence Force's naval service is based.

The oldest vessel on foreign service, the 1903 steam target tower *Abercorn*, referred to in Chapter 9, was heavily engaged in target-towing for the Kingston defences, captained by a Jamaican who, not unnaturally, took tremendous pride in her. After forty-five years in WD service, *Abercorn* was sold and, sadly, went down in a hurricane in August 1951.

In the South Caribbean, a second American fleet auxiliary, *El Alamein*, operated a long-distance service through the area, calling in at British Guiana (Guyana), Barbados, the Windward and Leeward Islands, and Port of Spain, Trinidad. In neither the North nor South Caribbean area, however, were there any reports of enemy action affecting the Fleet.

Bermuda, too, had a very busy, but peaceful war. Its fish-hook shape, many islands and under-developed road system (until the war motor traffic had been prohibited) placed a premium on water transport for cross-harbour communications. In addition there were examination service duties and target-towing for the 6 pdr battery. The launch *Sir John Asser*, under her skipper Mr Alan Houghton, also doubled as both the Governor's and the OC troops' barge, and, at least in the latter's case, not

The motor launch *Sir John Asser* in Hamilton Harbour, Bermuda. Alan Houghton is at the wheel and son, Micky, in the bow

only for official duties. The presence of Royal and US Naval establishments, as well as the US Air Force, brought heavy social burdens in the interests of Anglo–American amity. The fishing was also very good.

Mr Houghton was very popular and highly respected, not only as a seaman, but as a member of the local community. He had been in charge of local WD launches since 1915, and had served no fewer than eight governors. He retired in the 1950s when the garrison was finally withdrawn.

In stark contrast to Bermuda's war was the Malta experience, for the greater part of the war, and the brief but terminal experiences in Hong Kong and Singapore.

In Hong Kong the WD vessels were mostly crewed by locally-enrolled Chinese seamen, who subsequently behaved in the best traditions of the Fleet. The Japanese attack started on 8 December 1941 and immediately after, RASC water transport was fully engaged in evacuating the military hospital from Kowloon to the island. The next day the target tower *Oudenarde*, under continuous shellfire, delivered a load of mules to the RASC camber by lighter. On 11 December all available vessels in the harbour commenced evacuation of the mainland. During these operations the target tower *Victoria* was sunk while evacuating Indian troops, the only casualty being one soldier who broke his leg when he fell into a monsoon drain. In all twelve vessels were lost.

Oudenarde also did heroic work during this evacuation, carrying most of the Indian and Canadian troops across to the island. She then made three trips to the Stanley Peninsula on the south of the island and was finally scuttled on the instructions of Capt. (later Lt.-Col.) G.C.E. Crew. Two other WD vessels, the fast launch *French* and the veteran 1905 steam launch *Omphale*, were also heavily engaged. *French* was commanded by a civilian master, Mr Holden, who was later killed in action. *Omphale* was detailed to take some RN and civilian explosives experts to recover explosives from a Public Works Department store. On the way back, however, she received a direct hit from shellfire and blew up. Throughout the operations the work of the Chinese crews was described as

The handsome *Sir Hastings Anderson* was the last steam target tower to be built for the Fleet. She was lost at Singapore

magnificent. Indeed, in August 1945, three of the survivors immediately reported to Capt. Crew for duty.

At Singapore, a small (No. 4) Water Transport Company was formed in 1940, and was considerably increased in size with the purchase of new and requisitioned vessels. However, there was considerable difficulty in obtaining local crews because of difficulties over rates of pay. In contrast to the behaviour in Hong Kong, towards the end of the Malayan campaign, all the crews left, and the vessels were taken over by military personnel of the Combined MT Depot. These included the *Sir Hastings Anderson*, previously described as one of the most handsome vessels built for the Fleet, *Sir Theodore Frazer*, *Martin* and several launches. They were engaged in destroying ammunition dumps on the islands and left Singapore the day before the Japanese army arrived, but were all either captured or destroyed. Total losses were thirty vessels of all types.

There was a much more praiseworthy and satisfactory outcome to the Fleet's activities in the remaining war zone, Malta. Here, under daily attack, the civilian-manned vessels saw more continuous action than did their confreres, military or civilian, in any other part of the globe.

15
THE MALTA EXPERIENCE

Until the entry of Italy into the war in June 1940, and the fall of France, Malta's part in the war had been small; life had continued at a peacetime tempo. The small water transport section consisted of five vessels, the 250 ton steam target tower, *Lord Plumer*, (named, incidentally, for the First World War general, and one of Malta's most popular and successful Governors) and the launches, *Sir Leslie Rundle*, (the Governor's barge), *Thrush*, *Clive* and *Snipe*. All were under the control of the RASC officer in charge of transport and were manned by civilians, mainly Maltese, though later in the war, some difficulties were experienced in getting additional crews, and some soldiers were pressed into service.

During these first peaceful months *Lord Plumer*, *Clive* and *Snipe* were taken over by the Royal Navy and carried out inshore patrol duties. The crews were given local temporary RNVR ranks. This arrangement lasted for about six months, when the vessels were returned to Army control.

The changed war situation soon plunged Malta into the ordeal of constant and intense enemy air attack which is now a matter of history. During this siege, which lasted for over two years, the WD Fleet, now doubled in size, played its full part, often on tasks not usually associated with a non-operational role. In the course of the siege, several vessels were either sunk or seriously damaged through enemy action and some casualties were sustained by civilian seamen.

In January 1942 *Lord Plumer* was returning from the north-west of the island with a load of sand for airfield repair when she was attacked by a Messerschmidt. The machine-gunner was killed and the chief engineer, Mr Long, was badly wounded and died later. The vessel made port safely, however, and for his gallant part in this action the master, Mr E.W. Elson, was made a MBE. Later *Lord Plumer*, affectionately known as 'Plum-plum', proceeded with a military crew to North Africa, where she remained until the end of the war. The other vessels to suffer from enemy attentions were the launches *Thrush*, *Pike*, *Snipe*, *Trout* and *Clive*. *Thrush* had the ill-luck to receive a direct hit at her moorings in the first air raid,

Affectionately known as 'Plum, plum', the stately steam target tower *Lord Plumer* distinguished herself during the siege of Malta

though fortunately at 7 a.m., before the crew had arrived aboard. *Pike* was damaged beyond repair while slipped, an accidental fire accounted for *Snipe* and *Trout* was sunk at her moorings, but later raised, refitted and put back into service.

The 'General' class high-speed launch *Clive*, whose adventures became something of a legend under her skipper Capt. Jack Cains, was twice attacked and damaged. On the first occasion Cains had his launch, with targets astern, ready to go out on a night shoot when the alarm sounded. He got his crew ashore and had to watch, powerless, while first his targets and then his launch were raked by enemy fire. He saw his lights shot off and considerable damage done to the wheel-house and to both port and starboard petrol tanks. Shortly after, having got the two repaired tanks back from REME workshops, and the centre tank removed in order to replace them, his vessel again came under attack. Again he was able to get the crew on shore and this time, under shelter of a slipway, watched while all three tanks were shot up and three large holes punched in the launch's bows.

At one time *Clive* went through a number of breakdowns and mishaps, among them a mysterious fire, loosened rudders, and three or four broken mainshafts. These latter were due to disregard by the engineer of the correct magneto and coil starting procedures and resulted in his dismissal. For a while *Clive* was dubbed 'The Gremlin Castle', the title being commemorated by the AB, who painted 'two wicked-looking devils with incendiary devices on the front of the wheel-house'.

Plumer was engaged mainly on carrying defence stores, her load often consisting of sand for airfield repairs, running between Gozo and Grand Harbour. The RASC launches were mainly engaged in ship-to-shore work with convoys and troopships, inspection of beach defence posts, ferrying and other harbour duties. The work-load was heavy and continuous; during one period of six months, for example, 7,150 passengers were carried in RASC craft. There was also the inevitable target-towing.

Target-towing for the Malta fixed defences and for the Royal Navy was *Clive*'s main task, but there was one occasion when she earned an official commendation from the Lords Commissioners of the Admiralty in a rather unusual way. She inadvertently became a minesweeper. Capt. Cains explains:

> I was doing a shoot for a 9.2 battery. At the end of each run backwards and forwards across the target area, when I made a right-hand turn the wire stayed on the surface and I could see it cutting the top of the sea. But when I made a left-hand turn, the wire went down and well under, and started cutting the cables securing mines which, unknown to us, Jerry had laid during the night! I had mines popping up all round me, and that wasn't very funny. Following my report a startled Port Minesweeping Officer sent out a minesweeper which cleared a further 28 mines. My Army gunner had tried to destroy some of the mines with our twin Brownings, but hadn't succeeded.

The History of the RASC 1939–1945 records that the work of the Fleet's one and only (unofficial) minesweeper is laconically recorded thus in an Admiralty letter to the War Office:

> Their Lordships note with interest this occasion of a War Department vessel co-operating in mine-clearance operations.

In addition to target-towing for fixed defences and incidental minesweeping, *Clive* also assisted naval vessels, and towed targets for Free French, Yugoslav, Greek and US naval vessels. The French had a cruiser, the Yugoslavs some fast armed launches, the Greeks a destroyer, and the Americans the battleship *Pennsylvania* and the light cruiser *Savannah*. Capt. Cains recalls that the *Pennsylvania* had an 'unlucky' shoot; instead of achieving the aim of straddling the targets, she destroyed them completely with the first salvo.

Clive was nothing if not versatile and from July 1942 to August 1943 was lent to the RAF Air-Sea Rescue Unit. She remained under command of Capt. Cains, but with an RAF crew. During that period she put to sea on twenty-two occasions. Her most notable rescue occurred on Christmas Day 1942, when she went over 50 miles westward and picked up the observer of a Beaufighter. The weather was bad at the time but *Clive* made port in spite of the fact that one engine was giving trouble.

On another occasion she was sent out to pick up a shot-down pilot. While going to the designated area, the vessel passed the wreckage of an

Capt. Cains' target tower, the 'General' class *Clive*, seen here on loan to the RAF as an air-sea rescue craft

Italian E-boat, the crew of which were standing up to their waists in water on the bottom boards. The boat had been completely destroyed by Hurricane machine-gunfire, and all the upper works were missing. Cains took this badly shot-up crew aboard and dressed their wounds. The search was resumed and shortly afterwards *Clive* closed with another E-boat, on which there was only one man visible, waving an Italian flag. As the vessel had all its armament intact, and *Clive* was unarmed (her Lewis gun being unmanned), Cains felt it wisest to request permission to return to harbour and bring out an armed escort. It transpired that the flag-waving 'Italian' was the RAF pilot he had been sent out to collect. He had killed everybody on board before being shot down himself. *Clive*'s crew rued this lost opportunity to bring in a prize!

Shortly afterwards, the busy *Clive* was urgently despatched 36 miles to the north to take possession of another E-boat believed to be in that vicinity. The search, conducted without air cover or escort, was unsuccessful, but she sighted and closed to investigate an Italian schooner carrying German troops, and, later, a British hospital ship coming at high speed out of the Straits of Messina.

At the end of the loan period it was reported that *Clive* had completed 341 hours' duty, of which 115 hours were at sea on rescue work, 172 hours on target-towing and 54 hours going to and from base for repairs and engine trials. The RAF paid tribute to the sterling work she did, adding that 'the loan was very much appreciated at a time when the RAF was sadly lacking in air-sea rescue craft'.

On another occasion *Clive* was chosen for a secret 'cloak and dagger' mission which came to a disappointing end. The intention was to take some French Army officers to Hammamet in Tunisia prior to Operation Torch (the North Africa landings), to make contact with the Vichy French. For the purpose of the run *Clive* was armed with a Breda gun removed from an Italian E-boat, and two Vickers K guns, one each side of the wheel-house. The French officers would man the Vickers if necessity arose, and a rather villainous Czech, known as Ambrose the Thug, was to man the Breda. Ambrose's forte was landing behind enemy lines and slitting sentries' throats.

Unfortunately, as they were passing the island of Linosa, just north of Lampedusa, and half-way to their destination, the engineer, Mr Montgomery, reported a severe oil leak, sufficiently serious to abort the mission. Capt. Cains remembers that the senior French officer, a colonel, did not take kindly to the abandonment; at one time he thought he was about to be ordered to continue at gunpoint. However, 'I told him in no uncertain terms that I was very sorry but my duty is first and foremost to my ship; after that would come my passengers and then the crew. My engineer tells me the ship is no longer serviceable and must return to Malta'.

The unheralded return to Malta posed problems, too. Cains had had orders to maintain radio silence throughout the whole operation, so could not request permission to enter harbour to land his passengers. He therefore lay under Gozo waiting for daylight, at the same time trying to make visual signal contact with Fort Campbell by Aldis lamp. These attempts were interpreted and reported by people in Gozo as 'strange lights' and consequently the Navy sent out an armed trawler to investigate. Coincidentally, this vessel was commanded by an ex-RASC Fleet officer. The trawler circled *Clive* keeping her 4 in gun trained on her, while Capt. Cains was calling frantically, 'Don't shoot, I am Clive!'

Not long before the end of the war, following a visit by the Inspector, RASC, it was decided that Malta needed a Water Transport Company to administer and control the fleet, now numbering some eight vessels. Accordingly, in July 1945, 80 Company RASC (Water Transport) was set up. As mentioned earlier, difficulties had been experienced in maintaining a fully civilian complement and it was now necessary partially to militarize the service. This was good news for Capt. Cains, as he was offered and accepted the newly-established post of Master Superintendent. Cains had arrived in Malta in 1938, and spent the rest of his service in the island, retiring in 1963 after forty-five years' service. He was made a MBE in 1958 for his outstanding service to the Fleet.

Unfortunately, his launch suffered an indifferent fate. At a different time, in a different place, someone might have thought her worth preserving, but she was sentenced to be sold out of the service locally. The Master Superintendent, unwilling to see her operating in local waters as he had known her, had her stripped to a bare hulk. She was sold to an RAF officer for £100.

Now partly civilian-, partly military-manned, 80 Company soon had a considerable number of vessels under command. Coasters and Landing Ships (Tank), at 2,300 tons the largest to be operated by the Fleet, were employed transporting stores and refrigerated cargoes throughout the Mediterranean. The Company was also reinforced by the arrival of the

Capt. J.F. Cains, MBE, one of the heroes of
the siege of Malta

Dunkirk veteran fast launch *Haig*, the new 'Dickens' class craft, *Scrooge*,
Brownlow and *MacStinger* and the 'River' class fast launch *Eden*, the latter
replacing the *Sir Leslie Rundle* as Governor's barge.

One vessel, the ex-Admiralty 160 ft steam trawler *Prospect*,
commanded by Mr J.J. Bailey, was on voyage from Malta to Tripoli on
the night of 18 June 1958 when she was diverted at the request of the
Commander-in-Chief to go to the assistance of the Italian motor vessel
San Raimondo. After a search assisted by US and RAF aircraft the vessel
was located off the Kerkenah Islands. With some difficulty it was taken in
tow by *Prospect* to Tripoli, some 120 miles distant. During the passage the
tow broke and had to be taken up again, but the *San Raimondo* arrived
safely in Tripoli on 21 June. The master and crew were later awarded
salvage money for their exploit.

The Company's commitments eventually waned until only small
vessels remained for harbour and target-towing work; they were also in
demand by infantry units for beaching and night exercises. All, with the
exception of the 'Dickens' class launch *Scrooge,* had reverted to civilian
manning.

16
SOME WARTIME TASKS AND VESSELS

Back in home waters, wartime Fleet experiences were not always as hair-raising as those of *Clive* and *Marlborough*. Nor were they always routine. Early in 1942, the 400 ton *Sir Walter Campbell* was relieved of her cargo-carrying tasks and sent to Iceland for target-towing duties, operating around that coast in often arduous and gruelling weather conditions for six months, earning the thanks and respect of the coastal artillery batteries she served.

Mr C.W. Nevill, a wartime member of the Fleet, recalled some interesting variations in routine when serving in the steam vessel *Sir Desmond O'Callaghan*. This was the only armed vessel in which he served; she had four Lee-Enfield rifles clipped to the back of the wheel-house. Later she was fitted with an Oerlikon on her stern well-deck, and Nevill was sent to the Navy's Gunnery School at Whale Island to learn how to use it. He describes his subsequent experience:

> The gun was installed and we went out for practice – the pride of the Fleet sailing out as an armed man-o'-war, going at a great rate of knots as the tide was ebbing. When we got outside we found we had a slight problem; when firing we could not swing the gun right round otherwise we would have blown our own funnel and wheel-house away. So we came in and a qualified gunnery bloke turned up as an expert to look into the problem. For some unknown reason the large compressed shock spring that is underneath the gun had somehow got released and it ended up with the gun just about showing up out of the water at low tide in the middle of the gunwharf. We managed to get it out and hushed up because in those days it was still WD Fleet and the army was not so strong in control.

It was then decided to install a fast retrieve steam-winch in the well-deck from which the Oerlikon had been evicted. The vessel now embarked on a series of practices with batteries on the Isle of Grain and Sheppey, which proved successful. Mr Nevill continues:

Flushed with success we decided to try a night exercise. We chose a night that was excessively dark; out we went, going like the clappers at something like four knots, paid out the target to the required length, still steaming full ahead with full retrieve on the winch. The army bloke on board called out on the radio for them to commence firing. We saw the flashes, heard the shells and marked off where they were landing, then as the marker came up on the winch wire to indicate the end of the length of run, there was a further curt radio command to cease fire. Pregnant pause, but shells were still coming over, each one plopping a little bit closer to us. A slightly more hurried message over the radio to cease fire, repeated a couple of dozen times, and then finally a scream which was that loud he didn't need the radio, to the effect of what they could do with their guns and shells.

By this time our skipper could see the possibility of going on record as the only skipper to lose his ship in the Thames Estuary, sunk by his own side with dummy shells, and although those shells are not loaded with explosives they can still create havoc, and this was highlighted finally by one hitting just under our stern and the mad scramble by all of us heroes to find out where the life jackets were. Anyway, the skipper, throwing caution to the winds, put on all the navigation lights, lit up the bridge searchlight, dropped the blackout covers, while we uncovered all the porthole lights, and we ended up like a miniature version of the *Queen Mary* sailing fully lit up in peacetime. Luckily the blokes on shore must have got the message, or they stopped firing in sheer amazement to see a ship fully lit up in midstream.

Mr Nevill joined the Fleet on an impulse. After leaving school he had become a Post Office telegram boy and one day happened to deliver a telegram to the WD vessel *Dulcie Bella* lying at Sheerness gunwharf. While waiting for a reply, he found that the skipper had a vacancy for a cabin boy, so went straightaway to the Fleet office on the gunwharf and signed on. He then handed in his bicycle and telegram pouch to the Post

Office and went home to tell his mother, 'who immediately threw a fit', and joined the *Dulcie Bella* the next day. The *Dulcie Bella* was a requisitioned harbour vessel, serving the forts in the Thames Estuary. She was later converted to an ambulance boat.

Nevill later also served on an interesting craft, the luxury launch *Aeromarine*. She was powered by three Napier aeromarine engines, and was very lightly built and faster than any of the high-speed launches in use at that time. He reports that she was so designed for speed as to be useless in estuarial waters. Built more for prestige than for work, her previous owner had been band leader Harry Roy. *Aeromarine* was relegated to quieter Thames waters; Eric Kimber, a wartime member of the Fleet, recalls her being used for day trips for senior officers from Westminster to Richmond. Her skipper, 'Buddy' Olsen, once had the whole crew diving for an expensive watch he had dropped overboard, having offered a £5 reward for its recovery. It was never found.

Another interesting vessel to be requisitioned was the yacht *Sundowner*. This was owned by Commander Charles Lightoller, the senior surviving officer of the *Titanic*. He took *Sundowner* to Dunkirk, accompanied by his son Roger, rescued the crew of another little ship and took on board 120 troops on a boat designed to sleep eight. The vessel was returned to its owner after the war and is now owned by the East Kent Maritime Trust, Ramsgate. This now historic craft was sailed to the fiftieth anniversary celebrations of the operation by another member of the family, Commander Timothy Lightoller.

Maj. A.H. Larsen, RASC (Retd) believed *Sundowner* originally to have been a 52 ft naval steam pinnace which had been extended to conceal the transom stern. Commander Lightoller Senior once told him that boats only needed one engine. Twin installations only meant that there were twice as many things to go wrong! *Sundowner* was requisitioned and stationed on the Clyde at Sandbank after Dunkirk, carrying out the multifarious duties that fell to harbour launches in those busy waters.

Sandbank, on Holy Loch, near Dunoon, was a particularly busy station for harbour craft. Charles Codner was sent there in 1941, taking a requisitioned yacht, converted into an ambulance boat, through the Forth and Clyde Canal from Leith to Glasgow to join 647 Water Transport Company. Duties on the Clyde were typical of harbour work throughout the British Isles. Embarkation staff officers used the vessels to travel to and from the great liners, now troop transports, that slipped in and out of the Clyde; the two *Queens*, the *Aquitania*, the Canadian Pacific 'Duchess' liners, and many others. There were frequent dashes to vessels on the point of sailing, sometimes taking out last-minute passengers, sometimes bringing back personnel recalled. One wonders who were the happier!

One class of passenger would not have been too happy. One vessel on the Clyde station was allocated to the Military Police for the collection and delivery of military deserters and other delinquents.

Types of vessels were almost as numerous as the duties they performed. Codner remembers one craft, belonging to the distillers of Teacher's whisky, that had been requisitioned along with her crew. This was not an infrequent practice; another vessel, a Scottish seine-netter, *Embrace*, brought her crew of fishermen with her. There were many fishing boats, fast launches, river boats, ex-RAF crash tenders, and a number of very uncomfortable open launches, the crews of which had to live and eat aboard. One suspects Codner of understatement when he comments, 'They were not handy boats'.

One vessel, the requisitioned yacht *Tarifa*, was lost through a rather bizarre accident. Having been fully bunkered, she was placed alongside a pier for maintenance. However, the sea-bed sloped at this point and at low tide she leaned outward, causing her petrol tanks to spill into the bilges. When righted by the tide it had been intended to move her to a better berth, but when the engines were started she blew up, seriously burning two members of the crew. *Tarifa* was a total loss.

There were variations in the routine wrought as much through frequent changes in crews as well as in duties. Codner was moved frequently from one vessel to another. This practice would not astonish anyone familiar with the ways of service life. As soon as a mate or AB in charge felt he had mastered the idiosyncrasies of his vessel, his masters would invite him to test his seamanship on another. But there were also changes of scenery. Once in a while, usually for a week at a time, one boat would be sent to Rothesay to operate a ferry service to Tighnabruaich in the Kyles of Bute. This service included returning naval and military personnel after the strains of the last waltz had died away in the dance halls of Rothesay. On a pitch-dark night, with no navigational aids, this trip was not without hazards of which the weary revellers would have been mercifully unaware.

A service much more appreciated by both passengers and crew members was an occasional unscheduled Saturday night run to Fairley on

Charles Codner was mate in charge of the 'Dickens' class II general service launch *Newman Noggs*

the mainland with the ENSA concert party doing a show at Rothesay. It gave the party a chance to get to Glasgow for a quiet Sunday, and earned the crew free tickets.

Charles Codner has given an account of a typical day in the life of a vessel and its crew at Sandbank. The craft lay to buoys at Sandbank and officially two members of each crew were on duty each night. Codner was fortunate in living with his wife in a cottage and, like others ashore, would hide a dinghy under the pier so as to get out to his boat quickly. Normally, however, it was the practice for the first craft to be operational to act as a ferry.

The vessels then proceeded to Gourock pier and reported to the small Water Transport Company control office to be detailed for various duties. Often the instructions were to go to *South Deep*, a dredger, brought from the Thames and moored bow on to the quay. There would usually be in excess of fifty craft awaiting orders to be received by telephone. The Clyde anchorage was divided into designated areas, and a vessel would be

The 50 ft 'Dickens' class I general service launch *Quilp*, one of the highly successful class introduced in 1943

detailed to pick up a party and take it to a named ship in, say, 'B.3'. Duty completed, it was back to *South Deep* and a wait for the next job.

In addition to the duties outlined above, Fleet vessels were much in demand by the Navy for ferrying naval boarding officers out to incoming shipping for examination duties, a task which fell to the Fleet in many other major United Kingdom harbours. A very large number of the craft used for this type of work were requisitioned yachts which, not constructed for the purpose of coming alongside ships in rough seaways or rivers, took quite a lot of damage. This factor, and the mounting repair bills, brought the realization that a purpose-built craft would be an economic proposition.

In 1943, therefore, a new class of general service launch was introduced into the Fleet, and proved both popular and successful. This was the 'Dickens' class, all named for Dickensian characters. Extremely seaworthy and robust, 50 ft in length, they were powered by twin Ailsa Craig 34 hp engines. Twenty-two of this first series, distinguished by a sloping wheel-house and throttle-operated engines, were built. They were followed by a second series of thirty, with box-shaped wheel-houses and telegraph-operated engines. Some are still going strong; three are known to have been taken over for RNR training as recently as 1986, and others, sold out of the service, were converted to yachts.

Codner had a close acquaintance with the 'Dickens' class and at one time or another was mate in charge of five of the craft. His first was *Buzfuz* which he joined in Belfast and operated out of Bangor under orders of the Senior Naval Officer Northern Ireland, actually performing the very tasks for which the vessel had been designed. *Buzfuz* was destroyed by fire after the war.

Meanwhile, at the other end of the country, all along the south coast, the Fleet was fully engaged in the feverish activities building up to D-Day. Capt. Vernon Webber joined 615 Water Transport Company, Portsmouth, and recalled his surprise to find all the vessels crewed by civilians. He found them very adaptable and efficient, all with practical sea-going experience and a great asset in a service where individuality and decision were often required. There were now ten such units in the United Kingdom, deploying 520 vessels and with a personnel strength of well over 1,400, most of whom were civilians. As at Sandbank, so at Portsmouth and elsewhere, WT Companies operated an heterogeneous collection of small craft.

The craft of 615 Company included a Dutch coaster equipped to carry arms and explosives (and, later, coffins), two high-speed planing craft, and two 'Grey' class seaplane tenders with open cockpits. There were the standard WD fast launches of the 'Derby Winner' and other classes, and a new generation of high-speed target towers, with distinctive observation turrets. One of these vessels was detailed to convey Gen. Sir Alan Brooke on an inspection of the Mulberry Harbour at Peel Bay. ('Mulberry' was the codeword for a prefabricated harbour assembled at Marchwood, Southampton, and towed across the Channel on D-Day to protect the beaches and provide port facilities for landing stores. There were two, one for the American Sector and one for the British.)

In addition there was an ex-Navy prototype MTB (Motor Torpedo Boat) stripped of its torpedo tubes. This was the 68 ft No. 102 built by Vosper in 1938 and subsequently handed over to the Fleet in January 1943 and named *Vimy*. No. 102 was powered by three 1,000 bhp Italian Isotta Fraschini engines giving a top speed unloaded of 45 knots. This

The historic vessel *Vimy*, formerly the RN MTB No. 102. She was the 1937 prototype Motor Torpedo Boat and was converted to target-towing. She is still in commission with the Norfolk Sea Scouts

very interesting vessel had taken part in the Dunkirk operation and not only survived the war, but is still in commission with the Norfolk Sea Scouts. A few years ago she had the distinction of appearing in the film *The Eagle has Landed*, for which she had the benefit of a complete refit at company expense. She has one other unusual distinction, being the only Fleet vessel ever to be featured on cigarette cards; in 1938 in a Wills' 'Speed' series and the following year in a Players' set.

Two other similarly powered 60 ft vessels, Nos. 71 and 72, originally built for the Norwegian Navy, were also transferred to the Fleet, allegedly because being of Italian origin, engine spares were no longer available. This problem, if problem it was, appears to have been overcome by the Fleet's workshop support. These latter two vessels were subsequently also named after battles, *Gheluvelt* and *Villefranche*. Seventeen further ex-RN MTBs and MGBs (Motor Gun Boats) were transferred between 1943 and 1946 (see Chapter 18).

One target-towing detail, carried out at East Wittering for a squadron of tanks, not long before D-Day, earned the Navy's displeasure yet, conversely, the thanks of a Brigade Commander. The latter had asked for three targets to be towed at high speed about a mile off shore. Capt. Webber remembers that 'it was a beautiful morning for this operation, to see the squadron lined up on the beach, but rather alarming as the shells ricocheted out to sea, with vessels on the skyline'.

After the tanks had demolished two targets, the Royal Navy arrived on the scene and put a stop to the proceedings. The commander had neglected to inform them of the practice. Unabashed, the brigadier called at 615 Company HQ next morning to thank the unit. The practice, he said, had given his men great confidence, and that had been the main object!

In general, however, duties consisted mainly in supporting Mulberry and Pluto (Pipeline Under The Ocean) assembly activities, commando landing exercises, and ferrying officers and troops hither and yon. There were of course occasional hazards to be overcome, some natural, some artificial. These small craft, when operating outside harbour limits, did so at their peril in heavy weather. Capt. Webber rightly comments that when the black cones were up, the Solent could be as vicious as the North Sea. Two vessels from Portsmouth were swamped and lost in stormy weather, and many others completed ferrying tasks with very queasy passengers.

The boom defences proved to be an artificial hazard for one absent-minded skipper at a south coast port. He came across the boom at full speed and lost his three propellers. To his surprise, however, he was commended by the Boom Defence Officer for having found a loophole (if that is the right word) in his port protective measures! The view taken by the skipper's commanding officer is not known, but was probably somewhat less commendatory.

The south-east coast was covered by 632 Company (Water Transport), which was similarly heavily engaged. This Company was one of four formed from the disbandment of 5 Company at Woolwich and was initially based at Dover, with detachments at Shoreham and Sheerness. Following a visit by the Quartermaster-General later in the year the headquarters was moved to Sheerness and eventually found a home at HM Gunwharf.

The duties of 632 Company, as listed in the unit's historical notes were:

Servicing forts
Target-towing
Searchlight practice
Gun laying
Ferry services
Queen Gull shoots
Port Security duties
Mine disposal
Special duties in connection with
    pontoons and bridge building
    equipment for RE
Towing vessels
Administrative trips (high-ranking
    officers)
Repair facilities for Motor Boat
    and IWT Companies
Servicing Mulberry Harbour

Vessels employed on the latter task had to be refitted on return to normal duties because of the high incidence of damage caused primarily by operating in bad weather.

Servicing the Maunsell Forts in the Thames Estuary, a task in which *Katharine II* was fully engaged, *vide* Chapter 9, was a top priority task from February 1944. These forts provided effective defence against enemy aircraft which made use of the breadth of the Thames as a protective measure against AA batteries on the north and south banks. They were also most effective as a defence against surface attack by E-boats and U-boats. Daily visits were made by the RASC vessels in all types of weather and the unit was proud to be able to say that the supplies were never lacking where they were most urgently required.

The use of target-towing facilities for tank gunnery practice became a regular feature of the Company's commitments, two ranges being opened near Worthing and Black Rock, Brighton. These were heavily used by the Guards Armoured Division and other units in the south coast concentration area.

It is unlikely that civilian fleet members were used on mine disposal work as it was the policy to use military crews for operational and militarily hazardous tasks. However, for the Beach Mine Clearing

Scheme, fifteen Landing Craft Vehicle (LCVs, renamed BMCs) were attached to Water Transport Companies and operated under the supervision of Royal Engineers' Bomb Disposal Units.

From March 1944 to June 1945, this Company was operating an average vessel strength of seventy, more than double the strength of thirty-two for which its officer and clerical strength was established to cope. But this was an all-too-familiar state of affairs, by no means peculiar to water transport services!

Not long after D-Day, the civilian fleet was allotted a new, and very welcome task. They had long enjoyed a close and happy relationship with the Channel Islands and so it was with pleasure they learned of the formation of 841 Company (Water Transport) to form part of Force 135. This force was to accompany the liberating forces and, with twelve civilian-manned vessels, to provide inter-island services. No doubt those selected for 841 Company would have thought it a good way to end the war.

17
SOME FLEET PERSONALITIES

Although the WD Fleet and its successor RASC Fleet had built up a reputation for steady and unremarkable service throughout its life, it was no dull collection of unremarkable seamen. For want of a chronicler, however, we have very little insight into the characters of the nineteenth century crews who handed on its traditions. In contemplating the amount of anecdote which has been recorded or remembered within only the past 70 years, one can only sadly and fruitlessly speculate on the vast fund of stories, of incident and of accident, which time has buried.

Jack Cains, whose remarkable memory remained undimmed up to his death at the age of 89, is one of those who has been able to put flesh on the sometimes bare bones of history. In so doing he has offered a frank glimpse at both sides of the Fleet coin; not all his contemporaries were cast in his mould, but all, whatever their personal qualities and failings, made their mark in the Fleet, one way or another.

Cains joined the steamer *Lord Wolseley* as a boy in 1918, when the vessel was stationed at Grimsby. The master was that same Tom Greensmith whose escape from the blazing *Petrel* is recorded in Chapter 5. First mate of the vessel was Mr F. Luttrel, the boy who fled the burning deck of *Petrel*. Tom Greensmith was known as 'Old Prussian' by the crew but Cains records that he was a kind man and ran a very happy ship.

The third member of the ill-fated *Petrel*, Mr J. Hoare, was master of the *Sir Evelyn Wood* and in later years Cains and his brothers Frank, Fred and Jim all served under him in various capacities. One master Cains described as a big, bombastic man; not over competent, and quite a figure of fun. At sea he dressed in fantastic bad weather gear never envisaged by clothing regulations. He wore a civilian Norfolk jacket over several woollen jerseys, all secured by a thick leather belt, thigh length seaboots, and a huge woollen scarf. This ensemble was topped off by an airman's leather helmet.

This skipper saw sailing days at Woolwich Arsenal as an opportunity to demonstrate his seamanlike qualities to an invited audience of the ADMT's staff. He would mount up to the bridge, clasp the siren lanyard by the hand grip with both hands and give several long blasts, which he then repeated with the whistle. He would then seize the engine-room telegraph and clang it over from Full Ahead to Full Astern several times, all with a flourish of the four gold rings on his sleeve. Next he would shout casting-off instructions to the hands on the forecastle head and on the after quarter, all of which had to be repeated by the mates on duty. The whole procedure often bordered on pantomime, and the office staff of both sexes always enjoyed it immensely.

There was another performance when coming to anchor. AB George Bonner had a very deep voice and manned the lead line. He had to give the soundings, 'By the mark 20', 'By the deep 16', 'Tell me when the line is up and down' (the way being off the vessel), 'Sing out when she comes astern' – every order being repeated in Bonner's deep, sepulchral, voice, mimicked by a humorous cockney named Ted Cogger. It was Cogger who said to Cains one day, while coming down the Manchester Ship Canal and passing a cemetery, 'You and I will be there one day, Jack.'

'Yes, Ted.'

'Never mind, old boy, it's a job ashore!'

It was a hard life; rigid economy was practised and at this particular time ships were being driven unnecessarily hard by sea-going masters who had an eye on a forthcoming vacancy for an Assistant Inspector of Shipping.

The same master often boasted, rather embarrassingly, about his crew, describing them as men of iron. 'Toughest men going to sea.' Then the ship would be in bad weather loaded deep and perhaps carrying a deck cargo of vehicles and howitzers, etc. To get forward from the bridge crew members would have to clamber over these obstructions and the men would wait on the poop for a chance to get forward on change of watch. 'There they go, like rats to their holes!' he would yell. When loading or unloading cargo, particularly at Woolwich, it would be necessary to haul the ship ahead or astern by hand in order to achieve the correct plumb of the crane or transporter. The crew would snatch any spare moment to dive down to the forecastle to eat their meal. Along the deck he would stamp and roar down the entrance, 'Come up, you skunks! Come up!' The ship carried four small sails, a forestay, foresail, mainstay and a mainsail. When clearing the South Foreland and bound to the westward he would order the canvas to be set. 'Clap every stitch on her Mr Mate. Set every stitch! She'll go down the Channel like a thing alive!'

Peacetime losses of vessels were of course very rare, and losses while moored alongside even rarer. But this was the fate of the 50 ft steam vessel *Crystal*, based at Sheerness. One night the vessel was allowed to settle on some stone steps in the Camber at Sheerness on a receding tide. The engineer had come on board at high tide and pulled her in and left her, where she lodged by the bow. As the tide ebbed *Crystal* tilted inward and the mast and funnel were torn out, the vessel filling as the water came in over the stern. Jack Cains and the engineer were aboard at the time and managed to jump ashore. *Crystal* was subsequently considered to be beyond economic repair and sold. At the Court of Inquiry the 17-year-old ordinary seaman Cains rather unfairly got the blame! He always felt that the verdict had something to do with the fact that the skipper was the son of the Inspector of Shipping and the AB was the skipper's son!

Jack Cains then moved to the Royal Arsenal and transferred to the *Katharine*, then commanded by Mr J. Donovan. His duties, now as an ordinary seaman, consisted of cooking for the crew of nine and cabin duties for the master, engineer and mate. These involved lighting five fires each morning, cleaning the cabin stoves and brass funnels. On Monday mornings all five stoves had to swept clean of soot and debris.

Skipper Jim Donovan was quite a good shot, and had two guns, a 12-bore shotgun and a .22 rifle. When proceeding down Sea Reach, and close to the Kent shore he would shoot at wild duck and, for practice, would fire the .22 at a 2 in nail placed on its head on the stern rail. On one occasion *Katharine* lay on one side of the barge pier and the WD barge *Henry* lay on the other. Donovan was practising snap shooting with the rifle when the Master of the *Henry*, Bob Smith, poked his head up from the cabin hatchway. He was wearing a bowler hat, as did most bargees, and said 'Are you shooting, Jim? You couldn't . . . !' and just then his hat flew off and Bob smartly disappeared down the hatch!

One skipper once got into trouble with a naval officer who saw him, rather the worse for wear, being wheeled back to his ship in a wheelbarrow from the sergeants' mess at Shoeburyness. Unfortunately, he was wearing uniform at the time and the scandalized officer promptly reported him to the ADMT. He was suspended from duty but survived the subsequent inquiry.

Following his period in *Katharine*, Cains was transferred to the steamer *Sir Robert Hay*, under a skipper he described as a 'miserly bullying type', who was notorious for having had eight cabin boys in eight weeks at one period. On one occasion, when the crew had finished scrubbing the decks and were enjoying a smoke below, Cains hopped ashore to fill his galley kettles and then jumped back on board without using the gangplank, as the vessel's bulwark rail was level with the quayside. On seeing this, the skipper ordered the mate to turn the hands to and scrub the decks again. When the *Sir Robert* was taken out of service, Cains thankfully moved to the *Marquess of Hartington* under her master, F.C. Rhodes.

Capt. Rhodes joined the Fleet at the age of 15 in 1894, became a first class master (Foreign-going) in 1914, and was appointed Assistant Inspector of Shipping in 1925. He was a fine seaman who impressed with his skill as a navigator. Cains recalls an occasion when they left Belfast for Woolwich and travelled down the Irish Sea in fog. A large vessel followed and fog signals were exchanged all the way. On approaching Land's End the fog lifted a little and they got a glimpse of the land. Mr. Rhodes measured three horizontal angles with his sextant and transferred them to his station pointer and then to his chart. He thus ensured his safe clearance to round the 'Land'. The fog shut down again almost immediately, but the vessel was now round and set course up channel to round the Lizard. The following ship was now blowing her whistle continuously.

Rhodes then said he thought the vessel was ashore on the Runnel Stone (two isolated rocks 4.5 miles south-east of the Longships Light); if she blew again he would turn back to see if she needed assistance. She was not heard again, but Rhodes was right. The vessel was the *City of Westminster* and became a total loss in a severe gale within 24 hours. Cains was then studying for his Master's Certificate, and a few years later Capt. Rhodes presented him with his sextant.

Under him, a volunteer crew sailed in the steam vessel *Lansdowne* to Malta, to bring back the *Sir Edwin Markham*. The vessel took on bunkers at Plymouth, Vigo and Lisbon, and proceeded to Gibraltar. Gibraltar was a very popular port among all naval and merchant seamen in those days; everything was cheap ashore and there were no restrictions on crossing the Spanish border, where, among other distractions, there was often a corrida at the La Linea bullring. It was the practice for the *Lansdowne*

hands to go to market early each morning, where rum and coffee were to
be had for as little as 1d. or 2d. a cup. The hands rarely returned on
board sober, much to the sorrow of Mr Rhodes.

Mr Rhodes often used to preach at the Mission to Seamen and was a
great favourite. He persuaded Cains and the other ordinary seaman to go
there one Sunday. They had arranged to go to La Linea but the master
had waylaid them, and so they spent a long morning at the Mission, a
long session in the afternoon followed by a break for tea and then a
session of hymn singing until the evening service, which lasted until 8.00
p.m. They were then invited to remain for supper but enough was
enough and the two ordinary seamen both ran 'full tilt' for the Alameda
Gardens where they managed to obtain a much needed pint just before
closing time at 9.00 p.m.

The master was not the only religious man aboard. There was a
conversion, every bit as sudden as Saul's, though perhaps somewhat more
physically uncomfortable. A rather unpleasant and often drunken stoker
went too far following a run ashore and was badly beaten up by an AB.
This salutary lesson completely changed his nature. The next morning he
knelt down in the forecastle and said his prayers, and this he proceeded to
do night and morning from then on. He went to church at every
opportunity, never drank nor used foul language again and was even
reconciled with his estranged wife.

Lansdowne completed her mission to Malta; *Sir Edwin Markham* was
prepared for the voyage home with a crew of two ordinary seamen, the
master, mate and engineers. The vessel ran into bad weather off Cape
Bon and ran into Bone for shelter. The master was then asked to go out
and assist some fishing vessels which were reported to be in trouble. One
small boat, with a one-man crew, was located and taken in tow. The
fisherman made the tow-rope fast to the mast and when the *Sir Edwin*
took the strain the fishing vessel capsized. The unfortunate fisherman was
hauled on board, his boat righted and towed into Bone amid much
acclaim by a vast crowd. For this maritime exploit the master was later
awarded a medal by the French Marine Authority.

The voyage was not without further incident. At Gibraltar, Mr
Rhodes' labours on behalf of the Seamen's Mission were rewarded by the
presentation of two black and white kittens, presumably as apprentice
rodent operatives, reflecting, no doubt, the Fleet's long tradition of boy
entry. In the Bay of Biscay, the vessel met severe weather conditions and

was forced to seek shelter under Cape Ortegal after being pooped several times. In preparing *Lansdowne* for return to the United Kingdom the Malta dockyard had left the awnings stanchions in place, making the launching of lifeboats extremely difficult, so that abandonment, the possibility of which came under consideration at one time, would not have been possible.

Capt. Rhodes' appointment as Assistant Inspector of Shipping in 1925 led to his promotion to Inspector in 1939. It is not known when he retired, but he was then 61, having joined the Fleet in 1894 at the age of 16. By 1942, however, Mr George Sparshatt (under whose command two vessels had been sailed to North Africa in support of Operation Torch), had been appointed Inspector. At about this time, the third of the Greensmith brothers, George, was apparently an Assistant Inspector.

Other well-known personalities followed in the top posts of the Fleet; Freddy Ayles, whose struggle to save *Gog* and its gun is related in Chapter 10, and Arthur Turp, considered by Cains to be a fine man and an excellent seaman with whom he had an excellent official relationship. These were followed in 1956 by an exceptional seaman with an outstanding record of service in peace and war, Captain E.L. 'Winkle' Beard.

'Winkle' Beard's exploits in *Marlborough* in 1940, off the east coast and at Dunkirk (for which he received a commendation) are recounted in Chapter 14. He is described by Maj. 'Bill' Wynn-Werninck as of short and stocky stature, with a great sense of humour and a great love of the sea. Unlike the majority of his contemporaries, he came into the Fleet from the Merchant Navy which he had joined as an officer during the 1920s, finally serving with the Eagle Star Tanker Line before transferring to the Fleet during the shipping slump of the 1930s. As during this period the Fleet's fortunes, still suffering from the effects of the Geddes Axe, were still at a low ebb, and recruitment slow, Beard must have been able to produce impressive credentials to the ADMT, not the least being a Master's (Foreign-going) Certificate.

He was 29 when he joined in February 1937 as a temporary mate and between then and July 1944 commanded twelve vessels, the majority of which were target towers. After the collapse of Italy in 1944, he was sent to GHQ Middle East Land Forces as Master Superintendent, where he was responsible for the requisitioning of Italian schooners for the Water Transport Companies. He also carried out a monumental task in the dumping of large quantities of Italian ammunition at sea. A very tight time limit had been placed on the completion of this task but by drive, persuasion and personality he coerced local craft, US and RN Landing Craft, and many other types of vessel into finishing the dumping in time. He was made an MBE for this work.

This experience stood him in good stead when he was transferred to Cairnryan, a major ammunition dumping port, as Master Superintendent in July 1953. He became Inspector of Vessels, as the post was now designated, in 1956, following a tour of duty in Hong Kong, and retired as Fleet Superintendent in 1973. He died in Weymouth in 1978, his ashes being scattered at sea in Weymouth Bay.

Another Master Superintendent who had a distinguished career in the Fleet was George Ansell, MBE, who completed fifty years in the service in 1957, having joined as a boy, seeing service in both world wars. In 1926, he was commended for prompt and seamanlike action in going to the assistance of HMS *Sea Wolf* when that vessel dragged her anchor in Lawrence Cove, Eire, during a squall. He was one of the first Master Superintendents to be appointed, in 1940, and after the war was posted to the Caribbean. He was made a MBE in 1952. His fiftieth anniversary was greeted by a congratulatory message from Maj.-Gen. W.G. Roe, CB, CBE, the then Director of Supplies and Transport.

It is perhaps easy to overlook the great contribution made by locally-engaged civilian seamen overseas since the majority served in the lower ranks of the Fleet. Nevertheless it would be an unpardonable omission not to recognize the loyal and efficient service of those who proudly served the Crown in the former colonies. Wherever the British forces withdrew on independence, they parted from their locally-employed civilian and military staffs with mutual regret and respect, even affection. This was so in the small stations, like Jamaica, Malta and in Bermuda, where Alan Houghton's services, as described earlier, were recognized by the award of the BEM.

It was equally true of Singapore, where Haji Mansor bin Haji Noor gave outstanding service in 37 Company (Water Transport). Mr Mansor joined the Fleet before the war as a boy and served aboard the 1904 steam launch *Moonstone* and the target tower *Sir Hastings Anderson*. Immediately after the war he rejoined the Fleet and served at Pulau Brani until his retirement in 1969 as the Malay Superintendent of the very smart RASC Fleet Malay personnel who manned most of the Company's launches. Mansor also operated the large Scammell breakdown tractor used as a slipway winch and for heavy lifts on the island. It was his great pride and was always gleaming with polish and fresh paint.

Mansor was a great influence on the Pulau Brani community, and by his example set a pattern of loyalty, kindliness and immaculate bearing which earned the respect of all with whom he came into contact. His local knowledge and close liaison with the islanders proved invaluable to every new OC. He was awarded the BEM in 1956. It was a mark of his loyalty and sincerity that, from his retirement in 1969 until his death in 1981, he maintained contact, mainly through Christmas cards, with very many past members of the RASC with whom he had served.

18
THE RASC FLEET – POST-WAR TASKS

At the end of the war in Europe, the RASC Fleet, as it was now designated, had swollen from its original 71 vessels to over 1,600, of which nearly 1,100 were engaged on non-operational duties at home and abroad in the Water Transport Companies. The majority of the 538 vessels based in the British Isles were manned by civilian fleet personnel; overseas, units were manned by locally-engaged civilians and commanded and administered by RASC officers and NCOs. The small number of vessels in minor stations continued to be similarly crewed under the local OCRASC.

The inevitable reduction of the Fleet was soon well under way, in line with the shedding of wartime tasks on the one hand, and the undertaking of clearing-up operations on the other. By VJ Day in August 1945, 200 vessels had already gone. Three years later, vessel strength was down to 340 and all the purely military units had been disbanded and their crews either demobilized or absorbed into the civilian Water Transport units. There were still five of these at home, in addition to the Training Company, and six were deployed abroad in the major stations.

It is interesting to note that while military strength dropped from 2,646 to 660 in the three years, the civilian establishment actually rose from 1,407 to 2,350, an apparent paradox explained in a contemporary War Office paper by the fact that there was now a considerable proportion of larger vessels in the Fleet; 7 Landing Ships (Tank) (LSTs) alone accounting for 455 crew and around 100 (the exact figure is in some doubt) Landing Craft (Tank) (LCTs) for well over 1,000 civilian seamen. We shall return to these vessels and their duties later.

The main military representation was restricted to the south coast, where three LCTs were engaged on ammunition dumping operations off the Channel Islands. A few warrant officers and NCOs were stationed at Leith on harbour duties and, in the Isle of Wight, the Water Transport Training Company was entirely military-manned until 1959.

In 1946 the higher administration of the Fleet passed from ST1, which had fulfilled its wartime task with outstanding success, to another branch of the Supplies and Transport Directorate, ST3. ST3 exercised its responsibilities through the agency of a new body, the Fleet Administrative Unit, under a Fleet Superintendent. The FAU was located at Kingston upon Thames, together with its sister Fleet Repair Unit, REME (Royal Electrical and Mecanical Engineers).

In the meantime, a long overdue change in designation of the Fleet from War Department to RASC had taken place but appears not to have been marked by any ceremony; indeed it is not even clear when the change was made. Although the histories settle on 1945, there is evidence, even in War Office records, that the vessels were being designated *RASCV* much earlier. Charles Codner remembers having to paint 'RASC' on lifebuoys in 1941, and states that RASC replaced WD on clothing in the same year. However, it is only in February 1944 we find War Office issuing an instruction that the letters RASC would in future be painted directly under the name or number of all RASC vessels and lifebuoys, in place of WD and the WD arrow. A special design for the marking of marine stores had also been evolved, consisting of a diamond in which the letters RASC divided by an anchor were inserted, and, lastly, an article in the Corps journal in the same year made a clear reference to the 'RASC Fleet'.

There would therefore have been no sense of the end of an era that had lasted ninety years. In name only, the old Fleet, like the old soldier, had simply faded away; in substance and in spirit, however, it was unchanged. Under wartime conditions never dreamt of by its worthy predecessors, it had fully maintained its traditions of service by its dedication, courage, determination and versatility. And so, in the immediate post-war period, this civilian RASC Fleet would have been looking forward to a bright new era as it turned to its post-war tasks, side-by-side with what would now be a permanent, if small, military complement. It was to be a short-lived era, alas. In little over a decade, the civilian element of the Fleet would be reduced to not much more than a hundred, echoing, but far surpassing, the effect of the Geddes Axe thirty-five years earlier, though the reasons would be different.

In the aftermath of war, however, there was no hint of this as the military and civilian fleets now girded themselves for their immediate post-war commitments. Thus, for the civilian fleet, history was about to repeat itself as, on a far larger scale, the tasks of dismantling fortifications, disposal and redistribution of stores, and the dumping of massive stocks of ammunition, explosives and chemical warfare weapons, familiar to First World War veterans of the WD Fleet, were tackled once again. No time was therefore lost in equipping the Fleet for its additional peacetime duties.

So far as War Department-owned shipping was concerned, the Fleet was still a mixture of several types of vessel, old and new. Many of the pre-war veterans had survived. Vessels like the nineteenth-century *Marquess of Hartington* and *Sir Evelyn Wood*, both still good for another decade, the 1902 coal-fired target tower *Russell*, and the 1907 *Gordon*, were still good for a few more years. Several others of early twentieth-century vintage, all in their 40s, also survived till the end of the war, their working lives necessarily stretched to the very limit of their usefulness.

Katharine II was having a busy time along the Thames, still towing the gun barge *Gog*, among her many other tasks. The heavy east coast floods of 1953, when the Isle of Sheppey was cut off for fourteen days, saw her playing a vital role in maintaining essential food and medical supplies to the island, including the supply of 2,000 gallons of milk daily, by running a ferry service from Chatham to Sheerness gunwharf. She was later employed on maintenance of the Maunsell Forts in the Nore and made eleven voyages for NATO carrying consignments of ammunition from France to UK ports. She was sold to HR Mitchell and Sons of Woolwich in January 1959 and, renamed *Katharine Mitchell*, continued doing military work under contract.

Wartime additions which proved their worth were motor fishing vessels (MFVs), 36 ft open harbour launches for inshore work, and 125 ft coasters. The MFVs gave invaluable service as passenger and cargo carriers; many were retained in the post-war military Fleet. Over 300 36 ft harbour launches were produced for inshore work, the great majority going to the operational Harbour Launch and Motor Boat Companies at home and overseas. All these vessels, and most others joining the service, were initially accepted either into the boat stores depot or, in most cases, by care and maintenance pools operated by the civilian Water Transport Companies, pending issue to operational units.

There were large numbers of target towers, fast launches and general service (GS) launches only one to three years old which had been designed and built by the War Office (ST1) specifically to meet RASC requirements. Nine seaplane tenders were also transferred to the Fleet from the RAF in 1942. One of these, *Grey Dame*, was lost at sea with all hands from 615 Company, Portsmouth in October 1942, having been pooped in a following sea.

Although only about thirty towing and fast launches were completed between 1940 and the end of 1943, over 170 joined the Fleet in the next three years, many during the rundown period, replacing the large number of requisitioned, purchased and chartered craft disposed of out of the service. Additionally, between 1943 and 1946, twenty RN MTBs and MGBs (including the historic No. 102 referred to in Chapter 16) were to be converted to target towers, and twenty-one ex-RN 45 ft passenger launches named for Shakespearian males were taken over, though all but five of these went to military-manned units.

The list of Fleet craft, taken from ST1 records, is as follows (the detail in brackets indicates whence the names of the vessels were drawn):

1944–6	13	40 ft GS launches (Barracks)
1945–6	40	44½ ft fast launches (British rivers)
1944–6	45	45 ft GS launches (Shakespearian)
1941–5	21	48 ft fast launches (Derby winners)
1943–6	53	50 ft GS launches (Dickens characters)
1944–5	21	68 ft target towers (Battles)
1944–6	14	69 ft target towers (Battles)
1944–6	9	70 ft target towers (ex-MGBs) (Battles)
1943–5	8	72 ft target towers (ex-MTBs) (Battles)

Making up the latter twenty were the three Vosper-built experimental craft with Isotta Fraschini engines, referred to in Chapter 16.

The majority of these vessels and the old Woolwich coasters, augmented by nine 160 ft Admiralty steam trawlers, a number of the ninety MFVs acquired between 1943 and 1945 and ex-RN LCTs, were manned by civilian fleet personnel and soon settled down to a mixture of pre-war routine and the new post-war tasks.

However, the re-distribution and disposal of the vast amounts of military stores in the former Mediterranean and Far East theatres of war was a task which required far larger vessels than were operated by the Fleet. Problems of scarcity and expense ruled out commercial shipping

A military-manned 44½ ft 'River' class launch entering Yarmouth IOW Harbour. These were originally built, in 1945, for DUKW amphibians control but used generally for VIP and general duties

A 68 ft, 26 knot, target tower, one of twenty-one built in 1944–5 by British Power Boats, shows her paces

The 2,310 ton LST *Evan Gibb*. LSTs were the largest vessels to be operated by the civilian fleet

and it was therefore decided in 1946 that the civilian fleet should take over seven LSTs from the Admiralty. These were the largest landing ships to be used during the war, and the largest ever to be operated by the Fleet. At 2,310 tons displacement, and an overall length of 345 ft and beam of 54 ft, they had a cargo capacity of 2,000 tons. They were named for distinguished RASC officers and following adaptation to Board of Trade and Merchant Navy standards, were crewed under special Merchant Navy agreements.

Humfrey Gale and *Evan Gibb* lifted 26,000 tons of vehicles and stores between them during the evacuation of Palestine, making thirty voyages between Haifa and Port Said, and they all provided much needed shipping space throughout the world for over fifteen years. The vessels were handed over to the North Atlantic Steam Navigation Company in 1952 and several provided logistic support during the Korean War, by which time, they were being tasked directly by the War Office. RASC still had an interest, however. What was then described as the smallest unit in the Army, the LST Control Unit, consisting of a Maj. N.H. Vincent and Cpl. P. Robinson, both RASC, was set up in Kure to supervise LST operations. Subsequently, in 1961, the remaining LSTs were taken over by the British India Steam Navigation Company.

The other major task, the disposal of munitions, started immediately the war in Europe ended, when the Admiralty released two LCTs – the first of many – for the disposal at sea of unserviceable ammunition, including high explosive and chemical warfare stocks. The civilian crews were provided by 616 Company, RASC (Water Transport), Menai Bridge, and were instructed to report to the Port Superintendent, No. 2 Military Port, Cairnryan, on 30 April 1945. This was the first, largest and longest of many dumping programmes at home and overseas and is dealt with fully in Chapter 19.

After the end of the Japanese war, further LCTs were taken over by military personnel, and, based on St Helier, Jersey, assisted in the dumping of thousands of tons of German munitions into the Hurd Deep, off Alderney, where countless tons of similar (1914–18) material

Albert, a 69 ft 'Battle' class target tower. This class, built by Thornycrofts, were the largest specially designed craft to enter the Fleet

had rained down some twenty-five years before. Eventually, the total number of Ammunition Dumping Craft working in the United Kingdom reached seventy-six. Elsewhere, at Port Said, whence at least eight LCTs were operating, in Italy, where nine were in use, and in the Far East, similar programmes were under way. About 100 LCTs were taken over.

Nos. 1 and 2 Military Ports (the former at Faslane, on the Gareloch) were operated by the Transportation branch of the Royal Engineers, and were constructed as 'shadow' ports for use in the event that Liverpool and Glasgow were rendered unusable by enemy action. Work at Cairnryan began in January 1941 under direction of the War Office Directorate of Transportation, the port becoming operational the following year; construction was fully completed by July 1943. Both ports played an important part in the preparations for D-Day, handling vast quantities of stores and materials being received from the United States and Canada. Many of the reinforced concrete caissons and pontoons for Mulberry were also built at Cairnryan.

Even before the dumping programmes began, Fleet vessels had been assisting in the dismantling of many emergency coastal defence batteries set up around the coasts of Britain; this task had almost been completed before the war's end. Between 1940 and 1941 148 such batteries had been established, though of course by no means all would have required Fleet support. The introduction of a much reduced scale of armament for permanent batteries in 1947 and again in 1949 made further dismounting and removal of guns necessary. So, in many areas the Fleet was kept busy not only in assisting in removal of armament but also in ferrying workmen, stores and supplies to and from the shore to outlying forts.

Charles Codner was engaged on this latter work for a while in the Mersey, in the 'Dickens' class *Newman Noggs*, where contractors were dismantling the sea forts at the Mersey Bar. He did not always find it plain sailing. He once wrote:

Being on the Mersey with a small boat was no picnic. To get from our berth at West Float, first you had to find out what time high tide was. Then go to the bridge operator to see what rail traffic was due. If you didn't pass over a packet of cigarettes, he said 'No go'. Once this hurdle was over, you got as far as the locking out locks. If a ship was going out, you were lucky. If not, just wait and wait!

Used to take five hours to get out into the river. Even that was with a monetary gift to the dockgate men!

Once in the river and able to go out to the forts, if the tide was suitable you could use a channel out of the shipping lane. But this channel dried out completely so you had to watch the tide tables.

Although Royal Artillery emplacements were now much reduced, there was still plenty of range work to be done by the Fleet, both in target-towing and, for AA batteries, recovery of Queen Bees. These were small radio-controlled aircraft of about 10 ft length and a similar wing-span. They were used in practice shoots seaward, with a Fleet vessel in attendance to recover any which either ran out of fuel or fell into the sea for some other reason. For the former event they had an automatically-opening parachute. Codner's *Newman Noggs* was ordered to report to the CO of the Practice Camp at Towyn for this duty and was able to rescue one. He also recounts that when no AA firing was permissible, for weather or other reasons, he would often be required to run down the range dropping 45 gallon drums for the coastal guns to 'blast them out of the water'. As 45 gallon drums were accountable stores and always had to be returned whence they came, one wonders what official sanction was given to this method of training and to what creative accounting measures the Quartermaster of the Practice Camp was driven.

The versatility of the high-speed target towers was tested, and not found wanting, in a brief series of varied post-war tasks. The Leith Detachment of 99 Company (Water Transport) as the Cairnryan unit was eventually redesignated, not only carried out its normal target-towing duties, but also did joint exercises with the Royal Navy. 2nd Lt. John Roe remembers an exciting occasion when the high-speed launches were being used as MTBs. The Navy was using destroyers, the idea being that if one of the Fleet's vessels managed to keep a destroyer in her sights for twenty seconds it was considered time enough for a real torpedo-boat to have fired a torpedo and, providing she was within reasonable distance, to have sunk the destroyer. Conversely, if a destroyer managed to keep the launch in her sights for the same period, the latter would be deemed to have been sunk. One can appreciate that this must have been much more fun than pulling targets back and forth.

One exercise took place in some very rough weather. The custom-built high-speed target towers, such as the 68 and 69 ft 'Battle' class probably involved, were never intended for high speed in bad conditions, being timber-built and lightly framed. On this occasion, however, one of the launches was pursued by a destroyer at full speed, around 30 knots, and was pounding into a head sea trying to wriggle out of the warship's sights.

Back in harbour at Leith, the skipper was sitting on the break between the forecastle and the galley when he suddenly jumped up and said he'd been bitten. Investigation showed that his bottom had been rather painfully nipped between the step where the vessel was 'working'. The pounding she had received had loosened the forward section to such an extent that she was 'working' even while lying in harbour. In consequence, the rules for these joint exercises were rewritten.

Cairnryan became the main centre of civilian fleet activity from 1945 until its virtual demise in 1958. Here, at the height of its Indian summer, four to five hundred civilian crew members would be employed, mainly on ammunition dumping and associated duties.

19
AMMUNITION DUMPING AT CAIRNRYAN

The port of Cairnryan, on the west coast of Scotland a few miles north of Stranraer on the east side of Loch Ryan, was an ideal, if unattractive, location from which to carry out munition-dumping operations. It was road and rail-served, the A77 running a grenade-throw from the dock area and the railway running along the quay. At the jetty-side there was a depth of over 30 ft, and there was ample cranage. It was also within a comfortable distance of the area selected for dumping, the Beaufort Dyke, a chasm about midway between County Down and the south-west coast of Scotland. This trench was about 7 miles long, 2 miles wide and 144 fathoms at its deepest point.

The dumping activities were carried out by ex-naval LCTs, redesignated Ammunition Dumping Craft (ADC), and four coasters, the long-lived steamers *Marquess of Hartington* and *Sir Evelyn Wood*, the younger *Sir Walter Campbell* and the 1940 motor vessel *Malplaquet*.

Cairnryan had some shortcomings. There were almost constant strong winds, from all directions. Also, in its heyday, jetty capacity was sorely stretched, and ADCs had to dock three abreast. The loch is fairly shallow and during certain low water tides, the outward bound cross-channel steamer from Stranraer set up a stern wave, the wash of which, in Codner's words, 'set all vessels rearing and tearing at their moorings, and ADCs moored three abreast were slamming against one another'. He adds that the ferries were assisted on their way by many a fruity oath!

The landing craft was designed for combined operations over beaches and had taken many forms. The LCT was originally built for landing tanks on enemy beaches but was proved to be extremely versatile, later being used for carrying anything its capacious tank deck could hold. There were also LC Flak for off-shore AA protection, LC Rocket and LC Gun for off-shore bombardment, and many other variants of the same design. In this design no concessions had been made to marine aesthetics. Peter Bull, in his entertaining autobiography, *To Sea in a Sieve*, described his first view of the type of ship in which he was to spend much of the war:

> I could hardly believe my eyes. It (for a long time I could not bring myself to call this box 'she') looked a cross between a coal shovel (large size) and an empty water trough.

The ramped bows of the ex-naval LCTs made them eminently suitable for their new dumping task. Described as good sea-boats, though uncomfortable, they did all that was required of them. Three types were used, the Mk.III, Mk.IV, and Mk.IV★, the Mk.III being the larger, with an overall length of 200 ft and a beam of 30 ft. Cargo capacity was of the order of 300 tons and their twin Paxman-Ricardo 500 bhp engines gave a cruising speed of 9 knots and a range of 1,460 miles. The Mk.IV★ differed in that it had a raised catwalk from bridge to ramp and the hull was strengthened. These vessels required little conversion; the defensive

A former LCT·Mk.III converted to ammunition dumping duties

armament was removed, additional accommodation for dumping crews was provided from the hold space and lifeboats were fitted.

These workaday craft did not merit names, retaining the numerical identities conferred by the Admiralty. However, possibly as a quiet protest, they were allocated names of birds for radio call-signs. Many skippers adorned their funnels with their bird call-sign, which 'personalization' had the advantage of making recognition much easier and quicker. Later, four were given names beginning with A – *Augusta, Arno, Arakan,* and *Akyab*. The latter two, military-manned, were, together with the still anonymous ADC 1111, the last survivors of this large fleet, being sold out of the service in 1961. Incidentally, the later LCTs, Mk.VIII, continued the same naming policy.

At first, much of the labour for loading and dumping, including crane operation, was provided by German and Italian prisoners of war. Later, however, this long-running commitment became a Royal Pioneer Corps responsibility, supplemented from time to time by RAF airmen who, on occasion, were employed on the disposal of 5 ton blockbusters. General supervision was by Royal Army Ordnance Corps ammunition technical officers.

Dumping from ADCs was a simple matter of rolling or shoving the load piecemeal down the lowered ramp as the vessel steamed astern. Simple, that is, unless there was a swell running. Codner recalls that in these circumstances the operation could be hazardous when dealing with these 5 ton bombs. Apart from the possibility of their rolling back, there was the 'added attraction of getting a soaking when the swell ran up the ramp'. Smaller types of ammunition were often put over the side with the aid of gravity rollers.

The coasters were used mainly for dumping anything of a reasonably stable nature, like boxed small arms ammunition and rockets; anything that was not cylindrical. The method of disposal over the side was the tried and tested one used after the First World War. Using derrick and steam-winch, pioneer labour would load a platform which was then swung out to the rail where there was another platform from which the boxes were manhandled into the sea. Depending on weather conditions, this could take anything between five and seven hours. All dumping operations were of course heavily dependent on good weather conditions.

Accurate positioning was absolutely essential before dumping could

An ADC under way with a full load

commence. Fixes were taken from Corsewall Point at the head of Loch Ryan, Port Patrick in Wigtownshire and Donaghadee Island, County Down. In the absence of echo-sounding gear, soundings were taken by somewhat old-fashioned Kelvin-Hughes sounding gear. A 20 lb lead sinker attached to a steel rod 5 or 6 ft long was lowered on a very fine wire rope. This wire was run out from a drum on a hand-operated machine fitted with a tell-tale dial and pointer and gave an idea of how much wire had been paid out. To get a more accurate reading of the depth, a glass tube, coated with chromate of silver, was attached to the steel rod. The tube was open at the bottom and water forced into it according to the depth it had reached. The salt water turned the chemical coating into chloride of silver and when compared with a calibrated scale, indicated the depth to which the tube had descended. However, where the trawler escorts were fitted with echo-sounding gear, station-keeping was maintained by radio warning, a somewhat less tedious and speedier practice.

The small armada of LCTs, numbering about twenty-four at the height of the operations in the early 1950s, were supported by five ex-Naval trawlers, designated as 'Dance' or 'Isles' class, bearing such names as *Foxtrot*, *Tango*, *Inchcolm*, or *Colonsay* accordingly. When on escort duty these vessels carried medical staff in addition to their normal crews. There were also a number of launches and Army Fire Service motor fishing vessels which had been converted to fire floats.

Although practically all dumping was carried out in the Beaufort Dyke, it was occasionally necessary to go further afield with dangerous chemical warfare cargoes. These were dumped beyond the Continental Shelf either by the four coasters or by scuttling. Larger ships, of about 2,000 tons, would be loaded with phosgene gas bombs and other dangerous chemical weapons and would be towed, or steamed, out to the dumping area and scuttled. A destroyer escort brought skeleton crews back. Among the ships sunk in this way, in 1945, was the *Emma Alexander*, the vessel upon which Charlie Chaplin made the film *The Gold Rush*. It was loaded with mustard gas shells. After 1947 there were no other scuttlings on this account until 1955 when, amid great publicity, the 1919 *Empire Claire* (5,600 tons) was sent to a watery grave with what was alleged to be a mystery cargo. After much speculation in the Scottish press, an Air Ministry spokesman said that the mystery 'Cargo X' was an old stock of bombs, some dating from before the war. With that, everyone had to be content, though the use of a comparatively large vessel, with a high scrap value, for this purpose was never explained.

When the coasters were dispatched to the Continental Shelf they travelled in a stately convoy of five, led by their trawler escort. The small bunker capacity of the coal burners meant they had to carry bagged coal on deck, but even with this additional fuel, the bunkers were usually swept clean by the time they got back to port. Consumption was unusually high because they often had to use ordinary house coal, Welsh steam being virtually unobtainable at that time.

Mr John Roe, then a flotilla commander, recalls that as late as 1955, dumps of ammunition were still being found in Normandy, the coasters

Loading an ADC at Cairnryan

making regular runs to and from Caen to bring back their contents. On
these long runs the steam vessels could not carry enough coal for the
round trip. As they were carrying dangerous cargoes, they were not very
welcome in ports for bunkering (Londonderry was a notable exception),
so they had to travel with one hold full of coal and then transfer it by
hand to the bunkers. Sometimes it was necessary to do this at sea.
Transfer was made by basket, skip and with the derrick, the coal being
tipped down the chute that led to the bunkers alongside the engine-
room.

Occasionally an ADC would make the run to Normandy. John Roe
decided to make one of these trips; he, and his OC, were curious as to

why this particular vessel invariably took three days longer than any other ship. On the outward voyage the master reported that the vessel would have to put in to the Mersey. Roe asked why and was told that a bearing was running hot on No. 2 generator, or some other technical excuse. They then put in to Birkenhead and the chief went ashore, later returning with what Roe assumed was the part under his arm. Roe continues:

We steamed out again and going past Holyhead I was on the bridge when they brought up a hot drink and nice piece of fruit cake. On the way back the fruit cake ran out and again, off the Mersey, there was some excuse for going in to Birkenhead, and again the chief came back with a large box under his arm . . . it transpired that he had a sister in Birkenhead who baked these cakes and always had one ready for him!

Since it has been estimated that more than a million tons of explosives and ammunition passed through the port of Cairnryan, it probably says much for the care with which safety regulations were observed that there were very few accidents. Perhaps 'probably' is the operative word. Codner, referring to coaster operations says,

Once the hatches were removed, after the initial loads one threw precautions to the wind and handled the cases and bombs most familiarly, but I never heard of anyone being injured.

However, there were fatalities on two occasions, and one major loss. The latter occurred in bad weather conditions in the Irish Sea, when a Cairnryan ADC, working out of Silloth in Cumberland, and heading north with a load of ammunition, disappeared off the Isle of Man without trace. It was never known whether she foundered or blew up. One other ADC that might have shared this fate, but was luckier, ran into a north-westerly gale in the same area and sought refuge in the Isle of Man, but when the harbour authorities discovered her cargo she was refused entrance and had to ride out the storm for two days.

One of the fatal accidents occurred in an ADC loaded with tins of detonators. A faulty one went off and killed two soldiers. On the other occasion, several years later, a load of rockets arrived for dumping, packed in wooden cases. When the first batch was taken out and dumped it was found that they floated for a considerable time. Most eventually sunk at some distance from the dumping point, but some were washed up on the beach. It was therefore ordered that the boxes were to have holes drilled in them and for this purpose the Pioneer Corps men were issued with braces and bits. Eventually, looking for a short cut they started driving crowbars in and breaking the boxes open. On one occasion, with a complete trainload of these rockets on the pier, one drove a crowbar into a box and into a rocket and exploded it; the whole train went up. At the time there were two laden vessels alongside but fortunately the tide was out and the blast went over the top of them without igniting their cargoes. 'Otherwise,' concluded Mr Roe, 'it was thought the blast would have altered the shape of the west coast of Scotland!'

In addition to British and German ammunition, US munitions from the European Theatre were also being dumped at Cairnryan. Willie Aitchison, the last Senior Engineer of the Fleet, was at Cairnryan in an ADC when a US ammunition vessel had a fire on board. He recalls,

> There were some right scrambles then. We were at the other side of the quay and had to turn round and get out. We managed, but it took a long time. There was a squad of pioneers being marched along the road by a corporal who, when he saw what was happening, jumped on a bus which had stopped, and took off!

Fortunately, the fire was brought under control. Regrettably, Mr Aitchison was unable to ascertain how far the fleeing corporal flew, or the marching pioneers marched, before normality was restored.

An amusing mishap occurred at Stranraer, where the ADCs were often beached for painting. One vessel went too far up the beach and damaged a lamp-post on the promenade. A puzzled policeman wondered what his desk sergeant would make of his report: 'Damaged: one lamp-post; Vehicle involved: ship!'.

The Harbour, or Master, Superintendent at Cairnryan was a former naval officer and WD Fleet master, Commander George Fitzgerald, a very popular and highly respected figure, who controlled the operations of the dumping fleet. Commander Fitzgerald had served well beyond the retiring age and died in office at the age of 72. He left instructions that he was to be buried at sea but stipulated that the burial should take place during normal dumping operations. However, Lt. Roe felt that it would not be proper to commit his body to the deep with a consignment of ammunition and arranged otherwise. Following the church service, therefore, the coffin was taken aboard *Malplaquet*, which steamed out to a point 3 miles west-south-west of Corsewall Point. Following the burial, the vessel circled round and wreaths were dropped in the sea.

There was a macabre sequel. A few days later a policeman approached Mr Roe in his office and asked him to confirm that a funeral had taken place at sea. On doing so, Roe was asked then to proceed to a beach further up the coast and identify a body which had been washed up on the shore. As he had supervised the arrangements, which included having the coffin made in the unit workshops, his first thoughts were not comfortable ones as he feared the worst, contemplating the possibilities that the coffin had not been screwed down, that it had not been properly weighted, or that holes should have been drilled to aid its sinking. He wondered what court-martial charge he would face, but found his knowledge of military law unequal to the task. Accompanied by the constable he trod a nervous 200 yd across the flats to where other police were standing by what was obviously a corpse. To his enormous relief, however, it turned out not to be the late commander's, but that of a suicide.

There was much spare time available when weather conditions prevented dumping and very little in the way of entertainment for the civilian seamen, though the Mission to Seamen was a popular rendezvous. Nonetheless there was a splendid *esprit de corps* and morale was always high. In the absence of outside entertainment many took up woodwork; there was plenty of surplus wood in the dock area. One ingenious, and industrious, ADC master was delighted when magnesium flares arrived for dumping. These were used by pathfinder aircraft on bombing missions and were fitted with a parachute to retard their descent. By removing the parachutes, dissecting the panels, and exercising his skill with the needle, he converted them into curtains, a hobby much appreciated in those days of clothes and fabric rationing. His ingenuity went further: the nylon lines he cut into lengths and made into a bedside mat.

There were no facilities for sport, apart from swimming and rowing. There was one famous occasion when a challenge boat race took place between a crew from the *Marquess of Hartington* plus the OC, Maj. F.C.

Strickland, representing the Dark Blues, and an RAF crew representing the Light Blues. The confident seamen, who had watched the RAF's daily practices with an interest bordering on disdain, won by two lengths. During the following celebrations, a sharp-eyed officer noticed that, although the two lifeboats, both from the *Marquess*, were identical, the one used by the RAF lay much lower in the water. Investigation showed that the generosity of the seamen in lending their lifeboat had extended to filling the water tanks!

The dumping operations continued for upwards of ten years. By 1951, however, the two Cairnryan flotillas had shrunk to twenty vessels, the largest of which were the four coasters, the two escort vessels, *Mull* and *Prospect*, and three ADCs. They were manned by 140 civilians. In all there were 167 crew and a further thirty-five employed on maintaining vessels in reserve laid up at Sandbank (then the Company HQ location) and Leith. The remaining 27 crew were operating launches, 7 at Leith and 2 at Stromness, employed on target-towing and harbour duties.

Mull was soon to leave under orders for Singapore, before which she sailed to Southampton for conversion to oil-burning. Additionally, much

The 160 ft ex-Admiralty steam tawler Mull; one of the last civilian-manned sea-going vessels in the Fleet

of her accommodation (she could sleep forty-four) was converted to 550 cu.ft of refrigerated space and 160 measurement tons cargo capacity. After shakedown cruises to Hamburg she embarked on her six weeks voyage to the Far East, with a cargo of general stores. Arrived in Singapore, she was handed over to be crewed by locally engaged civilian seamen with RASC officers and senior ranks and shared a stores run to Penang with her erstwhile Cairnryan companion, *Malplaquet*. *Mull* was a smart vessel, and was once identified as the Royal Yacht by two old people on Southsea front. Some years later she returned to Cairnryan.

There were still seven coasters and ADCs on station in 1956, supported by two 28 ft open diesel launches and a 'Dickens' class launch, *Bumble*, employed on servicing naval vessels laid up in Gareloch with civilian watchmen aboard, delivering mail, supplies, reliefs, and doing multifarious other harbour duties. Fire support was provided by a RE-manned tug. *Malplaquet*, returned from her Singapore stint, had rejoined the civilian fleet; the previous year two of her crew were involved in an act of gallantry for which they received awards.

While she was berthing at the Lighterage on 25 November 1955, ABs David Kyle McCubbin and Peter Mylchreest rescued the second mate, Geoffrey Ashburn, from being crushed to death between the side of the pier and the vessel. Ashburn had fallen over the side of the ship and struck his head on a metal projection. Without hesitation and in spite of the serious risk of being crushed themselves, McCubbin and Mylchreest jumped down from the vessel on to a floating piece of timber and hauled the unconscious mate to safety. In January 1956 Maj.-Gen. R. Delacombe, GOC Lowland District, presented silver palm leaves and a Queen's Commendation for gallant conduct to each of the men. It is interesting to note that two of Capt. Jack Cains' brothers were present: Capt. Jim Cains, as Master Superintendent, and Capt. Archie Cains, as master of *Malplaquet*.

Not long afterwards, *Malplaquet* was placed under orders for Singapore. At this time, Capt. Frank Bourne was occupied at Birkenhead on the dismantling of forts. To get in some proper sea time and qualify for his mate's ticket, he volunteered for the voyage. The vessel, with a Capt. Fuller in command, sailed from Weymouth with 'a good send-off from high-ranking officers from War Office and elsewhere'.

It was by no means an uneventful trip for Bourne. 'We had a hell of a trip across the Bay of Biscay; about two days, making 3 or 4 knots.' The

Presentation of Queen's Commendations to ABs Mylchreest and McCubbin by Maj.-Gen. Delacombe. He is talking to McCubbin. The vessel is the coaster *Malplaquet*

vessel was eventually forced into Corunna, where she waited till the weather abated. Thereafter *Malplaquet* was dogged by engine trouble and only reached Aden in time to catch the monsoon weather. The vessel stayed there for a month and then returned to Port Said, where she was pressed into service to ship surplus army stores from Egypt back to Malta. On the voyage back to Port Said, however, the main engine blew up. The master sent out a Mayday signal, and hoisted a couple of sails. The signal was answered by a frigate, and *Malplaquet* was ignominiously towed into Tobruk.

This proved to be the end, at least for a time, of Frank Bourne's sea time. Arrived in Tobruk, he learned that his son had lost an eye, and it had been decided to send him home on compassionate grounds. At that time, the only way to do this was to treat him as a Distressed British Seaman (DBS). As he had only 10s. in his pocket, he was certainly well-qualified.

After a week in Tobruk he managed to get passage to Malta in a converted weather ship and was flown home. For some reason he was unable to get any money in Malta but was told to try at Gooch Street Station, familiar to wartime servicemen as the London District Assembly Centre, a rather fancy name for a Transit Camp. Fingering the 10s. in his pocket, Bourne asked how he would get there, and was told, 'Oh, you'll find a way!'. It took him two weeks finally to reach his home in Plymouth. When he reported to Plymouth Garrison at the end of his leave he was told he had no business there and should be at Cairnryan!

As indicated above, *Malplaquet* eventually completed her voyage to Singapore, and Bourne eventually got more sea time in, as we shall see.

20
CLOSING YEARS – THE VETERANS DEPART

Meanwhile, back at Cairnryan, and elsewhere around the coast, target-towing continued, both Fleet and coastal gunners sublimely unaware that the dark clouds of disbandment and redundancy were growing just beyond the horizon. At this time, however, in the early 1950s, normal service continued.

The coal-burners continued to carry out their duties in the dignified manner consonant with their age and seniority. Their tasks were many and varied, and by no means restricted to Cairnryan. *Sir Evelyn* was dispatched north to carry stores from Aberdeen to Stromness, south to the Thames during a lightermen's strike to load an ammunition vessel, then back to Cairnryan to dump phosgene gas.

In the summer of 1951 she was sent south again with *Sir Walter Campbell* to Barry to load stores for exercises with Royal Engineers TA reservists. Thus laden, the two vessels steamed to Appledore in Devon, where the soldiers were trained in off-loading stores into landing craft and discharging over the beach. A fortnight later the reverse procedure was followed. They lay at Appledore for a month and then repeated the exercise with a further group of TA soldiers. It was during this period of inactivity that the vessel was restored to her pre-war livery, as recorded in Chapter 11.

Also in attendance were two service-manned 'River' class launches. Charles Codner thought that the local pilot must have made a fortune as he was always in attendance every time the two steamers swung with the tide. 'Apparently,' he added, 'when the tide changed, especially from ebb to flood, it came with a rush. We were moored to a buoy, but had to have steam on each tide-change.'

Codner, during this period aboard *Sir Evelyn*, described her as a happy ship, the main contributory factor being the excellent 'all-in' messing arrangements and a splendid seaman cook. 'All-in' messing meant that all three daily meals were cooked centrally. This was not the general practice; more often than not, as mentioned in Chapter 8, only the main dinner meal would be a communal one. For the other meals each man (except the master) would have to shift for himself.

Later, the busy *Sir Evelyn* could be found doing a weekly run to Cherbourg, Brest, and then round to Felixstowe with cargoes of cordite from French factories.

The *Marquess* was no less busy. Like *Sir Evelyn* she did stints in support of Royal Engineers training at Marchwood. These included two cruises to the Channel Islands, during which RE personnel took over navigation and handling the ship, nervously supervised and assisted by the regular crew. On another occasion they carried RE personnel to the Arromanches beaches and on to Le Havre, where they moored at the French naval base. The highlight of this trip came when the civilian crew were cajoled into a whaler race against a French Navy crew. Presumably unable to gain access to their opponents' water tank, as on a former occasion, *Marquess* was well beaten, but royally entertained.

Another task was to tow a very large naval target from Portsmouth Harbour to Dover. During her manoeuvring she came perilously close to the Royal Yacht *Victoria and Albert* and, as Codner recalls, 'were told in beautiful RN language to "retreat!"'. This tow was almost too much for the old ship; although the sea was calm, at times she seemed to be barely moving, though she made it in the end. Back at Marchwood for another spell, she took some cadets from Southampton Nautical College to sea to give them some practicable seamanship. As a reward, the crew were invited to cricket and high tea at the college.

The *Marquess* was back on station at Cairnryan in January 1953, when the ferry *Princess Victoria* went down in the Irish Sea. Her rear doors were stove in by a following sea as she ran before a storm and 128 people lost their lives. A call had gone out for all available shipping to lend assistance to look for survivors, and as the *Marquess* was the only vessel with steam up at Cairnryan her skipper, Capt. Corvan, volunteered to go out. It was now hopeless to think of finding anyone alive as seas were still running extremely high, but the *Marquess* did bring nine bodies back. Although Corvan laughed off the experience, crew members told John Roe that it had been a hair-raising experience to go out in those conditions in an old coal-burner with a maximum speed of 8 knots!

It was later this year that the proudest moment of the *Marquess of Hartington*'s long life came, when she took part in the Coronation

Review at Spithead. Dressed overall, paintwork and brasswork gleaming, her tall slim funnel proclaiming her age, she must have presented an impressive, yet anachronistic, appearance. After all, she would then probably have been one of the oldest iron-built ships still in commission.

The secret of the longevity of the *Marquess* and *Sir Evelyn* was, of course, their iron construction. Iron rusted to a degree, and thereafter was self-preserving. John Roe says that he used to see them slipped at Grimsby for annual refit, and noticed that the plating was always in amazing condition once it had been chipped.

Grimsby was one of the few harbours which still had facilities for refitting coal-burning vessels. When refits were due they were sailed through the Caledonian Canal and down the east coast. The work took about ten weeks, and on completion, Lt. Roe and the REME workshop officer, Capt. Joe Beckett, joined the ships at Grimsby on their acceptance trials. These usually took about two days, during which the shipyard would always entertain them royally. Once, however, they refused to accept one of the ships because of unsatisfactory work. They went back a fortnight later to find the hospitality reduced to a packet of sandwiches!

The Fleet was immensely proud of the *Marquess* and her 'step sister', *Sir Evelyn Wood*. Though always associated by age and class, they were not sister ships, having been built to different designs. The *Marquess* was smaller, displacing 670 tons against the *Sir Evelyn*'s 850. Throughout their long lives, both were powered by their original twin-compound steam engines. The former was originally built for the conveyance of the then new 9.2 in coast defence gun, the barrel being stowed in the centre of the hold and the various components in two separate 'pockets' in the fore-end.

The *Sir Evelyn* had two hatch ways to her hold, with accommodation for her sails under the forecastle head. The derrick on the foremast was of considerable length to enable it to plumb the after hatchway when loading and unloading cargo. There were inner and outer topping lifts to the derrick; the falls for topping and lowering were of three-fold purchase and were also used for hoisting and lowering a foresail.

Although the civilian fleet had the greatest affection for the *Marquess* and *Sir Evelyn*, they were by no means the most comfortable of vessels. The designers of these old vessels seem to have veered between parsimony and preciosity. In both vessels the officers had comfortable cabins aft, and in the *Marquess* the saloon was in bird's eye maple, with a large crest and, beneath, Nelson's famous signal. An ornate brass lamp provided illumination; brasswork abounded everywhere, providing a never-ending source of work for idle hands. The decks, boat decks, bridges and forecastle heads were all teak.

On the other hand, the crew slept in hammocks. The least comfortable accommodation was allotted to the boy, who had to sling his hammock in the chain locker. As the anchor chain was not enclosed, the unfortunate lad would have to vacate his bedroom if the vessel were to anchor during his night watch below. In latter years, sybaritic steel cots were installed in the *Marquess*. This improvement seems to have indicated a move toward egalitarianism as, in the process, the saloon lost its bird's eye maple (and, regrettably, Nelson's exhortation) and the cabin accommodation, in Codner's words, now 'resembled a starting box for greyhounds'.

Equally spartan were the bridgeworks – not only of nineteenth-century vessels, but even of those of the 1920s. Bridges were open to the elements, the only protection being a canvas dodger, complemented by side canvases. On winter voyages, the helmsman would often swell to twice his size with sweaters, overcoats and scarves to stave off the cold. The bridges were eventually glassed in, but not until after the Second World War. The wings, however, remained open.

The open wing was very handy for one captain. He used to take great pride in coming in and rounding the end of South Deep pier and ringing down to stop engines, bringing the *Marquess* alongside without the necessity of going astern on his engines. He knew the speed and would allow for the flood tide. He kept a bicycle on the wing and when the tide was the right height he would swing the machine over onto the pier, clamber over and cycle off home.

One evening he had obviously not allowed enough for the flood tide, which was flowing quite strongly, and so for the last few yards had to ring down for 'slow ahead'. He just nudged into the berth and the vessel was made fast alongside. He put his bike over the side and made off. Lt. Roe was aboard at the time and writing up his personal log. Twenty minutes later he answered a whistle on the voice-pipe on the bridge. At the other end the plaintive voice of the chief engineer enquired, 'Can we stop engines now? We're still going slow ahead!'

In common with the *Marquess*, *Sir Evelyn* had no hot water on tap for the crew. In the former, the crew lived under the forecastle head and had wash-basins fitted in the open air. *Sir Evelyn*'s crew staggered aft to draw water in buckets from a saddle tank. There was only sufficient capacity for about four days' supply for all hands, so on voyages or bad weather delays of any length, a close watch had to be kept on consumption. Of course, the ship's ablution facilities did not run to baths, so the basic container for washing bodies and laundry was a 3 gallon bucket. Crew members of the *Marquess* were finally moved to ask if they could have hot water run off from the engine-room or galley for shaving, and this boon was granted and enjoyed for the remaining twelve months or so of the vessel's seventy-one years of military service. Hitherto hot water had usually been obtained by heating on the galley stove or, occasionally, by a friendly stoker who would use a jet of steam from the ship's condenser.

Another somewhat belated improvement was drawn to attention and made at the same time in the *Marquess*. For some time ash had been removed from the engine-room by handling buckets up a ladder. The master asked for a hoist with which to do this dirty and tedious task, whereupon a system was devised by which a cylindrical funnel was run down from the deck and a hoist system with block and tackle set up to enable buckets to be hauled up and emptied over the side. It is not known why the similar pre-war system had been abandoned, whereby ash was removed in buckets by hoists in the port and starboard ventilators to the stokehold, grabbed by a seaman and emptied overboard through a portable chute in the bulwarks. This task was carried out every four hours when fires were cleaned on change of watch and, however performed, was never a very pleasant one, particularly in bad weather.

The *Marquess* was originally built as a hybrid, a steamer also rigged as a sailing ship. She had carried a single square topsail on the foremast and square topgallants, a gaff mizzen and a flying jib and staysail, so she had three sails forward of the main mast, three square sails on the mainmast, and the mizzen. The *Sir Evelyn* had been similarly rigged, but in the 1920s the masts of both had been reduced in height, the vessels then carrying only trysails. Topsails were not used again. Capt. Jack Cains describes the use of sails:

> Both vessels had very good sea-keeping qualities in most weathers to be found around the coasts of the United Kingdom, but were very much under-powered for any bad weather which came forward of

the beam. Such weather caused considerable leeway and necessitated the setting of sails fore and aft to counteract the drift. This tendency was more pronounced in the *Sir Evelyn Wood* but the use of sails was very helpful and eased the rolling considerably. In very heavy weather it was necessary to double-bank the weather sheets. The *Marquess* would roll and go in a beam sea and achieved ten knots on occasions.

In my opinion and experience, she made better weather when caught out in a gale than did *Sir Evelyn*.

It was a very sad day when, in November 1957, these two fine old ships, the 71-year-old *Marquess* and the 61-year-old *Sir Evelyn*, slowly, reluctantly, slipped out of Cairnryan, bound for the breakers' yard. Rarely, if ever, has such a long period of unbroken service been equalled by one, let alone two, such vessels. It is indeed a matter of regret that there was no-one then to plead a case for preservation of at least one of these marvellous iron ships.

As has been shown, life was not easy or comfortable aboard these vessels, but seamen were happy to serve in them time and time again. There would scarcely have been a peacetime seaman without experience in the *Marquess* or *Sir Evelyn* – often in both. Many served as boy seamen, or stokers, then returned in higher ratings, as ABs, mates, engineers, or, the sea-going pinnacle of a Fleet career, as masters.

Many must have felt then, that with the departure of these ships, the spirit of the Fleet had departed, too. But this was not so; perhaps something intangible had gone, but a smaller fleet still continued to render the service that those old vessels had exemplified.

The retirement of the *Marquess* and *Sir Evelyn* did not end operations at Cairnryan but, in other parts of the country, where tasks had completely ceased, ties of many years between Fleet and port were sadly and quickly broken. Some long-standing connections were quietly and unobtrusively severed as vessels changed to commercial ownership for further service or for the breaker's yard while others slipped into private ownership and, their beautiful lines often ruined by self-help modifications, eked out ugly duckling existences in south coast marinas.

This was not the fate of *Fusee II*, a lovely 68½ ft GS motor launch which had been a familiar sight in Weymouth for nearly twenty-three years. The name *Fusee* had been associated with Weymouth Harbour for

The 1902 launch *Fusee* was replaced by the smart *Fusee II* (below) in 1935, to complete, in 1957, a continuous connection with Weymouth of fifty-five years

half a century; the first to bear that name, a 69½ ft steam launch, had arrived in Weymouth from Portsmouth towards the end of the first decade, never to leave until replaced by her namesake in 1935.

Fusee II left Weymouth in June 1957, to the sound of sirens and bells, dressed overall, her departure attended by Brig. W.E. MacDermott, the Deputy Director of Supplies and Transport for Southern Command and the Mayor, Mayoress and Deputy Mayor of Weymouth. The Junior NCOs Regimental Training School from the Isle of Wight provided a guard of honour. *Fusee* departed not to the breaker's yard, but to further useful employment. She went north to Liverpool for a spell as a personnel and baggage carrier, but in 1969 gained no little publicity when, as a Swansea tug, she was stranded for two days on Bude beach when her engines failed. She was successfully refloated in a salvage operation reportedly watched by hundreds.

When the last vessels left Woolwich, however, there were no flags, sirens or bells at what had been the birthplace and home of the Fleet for so many centuries. The once mighty Arsenal had long since ceased to be the Ordnance storehouse of the Empire but, throughout the war, it had still been the centre of intensive Fleet activity. When the Water Transport service was re-organized in January 1943 (see Chapter 13), 5 Company at Woolwich was divided into four companies; 629 Company became responsible for Northern Command, 630 for Eastern Command, 631 for London District, and 632 for South-Eastern Command.

The history of 631 Company gives the date of the re-organization of No. 5 Company as 16 January 1943, when the sea-going commitments of Woolwich were considerably reduced in line with the company's mainly riparian duties. The 1931 motor barge *Katharine II* remained, but the other motor barges, *Geoffrey Stanley*, and *Vawdrey*, departed to the Sheerness Company. The venerable steam target tower, *Sir Walter Nicholson*, now in her thirty-seventh year, also remained until she was sold in 1948.

By mid-1946 the civilian-manned vessels had shrunk to the motor barge *Henry Caddell*, transferred from Portsmouth, *Gog* and an ADC at Woolwich, and five launches and *Katharine II* detached at Crossness. Two 'Derby Winner' class GSLs were also detached with civilian crews at Hamburg. In addition, the company was holding a small number of vessels in temporary or permanent reserve. Two military-manned launches and the dumb barge *Arctic II* completed the sadly diminished tally.

A 90 ft motor fishing vessel of 631 Water Transport Company Woolwich unloading munitions for disposal in 1945–6. The 'Dickens' class launch *Pinch* is in attendance

(David Griffin)

The end for 631 Company came in April 1949, when the unit was disbanded; the remaining vessels became a small detachment of 632 Company, and the long association of the Fleet with Woolwich ended a few years later when 632 Company was re-organized as 18 Company (Amphibious) and departed to Fremington. *Henry Caddell* was sold to a Fawley, Southampton, shipping firm; *Katharine*, *Vawdrey* and *Geoffrey Stanley* were bought by H.R. Mitchell of Woolwich in 1959 and continued to work from Woolwich under War Department contracts until the the last chapter of a long history closed.

21
CONSTRUCTION AND REPAIR IN THE FLEET

The story of the civilian fleets through the ages would not be complete without some reference to those, equally unsung, who designed, constructed and maintained the heterogeneous fleets of the past. Sailmakers, carpenters, ropers, with needle, saw and marline spike, gave way to engineers, welders, electricians, with lathes, torches and screwdrivers, as sail gave way to steam and motor, and wood vessels were joined first by iron, then steel and finally by fibreglass constructions.

Alan Blight, the last Superintending Engineer and Constructor of Shipping, suggests that the earliest recorded fleet repair activity was in 1751 when the Ordnance Board ordered that the 'Office boat' at Woolwich be reconditioned at a cost of £5. Apparently no repairs had been done since she was built in 1746.

A few years later, in 1777, the post of Superintendent of Shipping was created, with the combined duties of operator, purveyor and repairer. It is doubtful, however, whether there was anything approaching a repair organization at this time; the majority of sea-going vessels and, quite often, lighters and barges, used by the Board of Ordnance were hired.

As described in the early chapters of this history, the Board of Ordnance had started to acquire its own vessels, but there is no direct record of the establishment of a repair organization, though from 1827 to 1845 Ordnance Estimates include repairs in the lump sums voted for 'gun hoys and floating magazines, including every expense of masters, mates, men and repairs'. Subsequent estimates provide for repair, but not separately from building, provision or purchase. In the absence of any evidence to the contrary we must suppose that repairs beyond the capabilities of the crew, would have been carried out in the shipwrights' workshops at the Royal Arsenal and the gunwharves at Portsmouth and elsewhere. In the latter part of the nineteenth century all repair became the responsibility of the Army Ordnance Department, upon whom all requisitions had to be made. Repairs beyond the scope of these Ordnance workshops were normally carried out by civilian contract. At stations abroad, naval dockyard facilities were very often used.

During the First World War and for many years after, the civilian-manned Ordnance workshop at Portsmouth employed one 'Freddy the Chippy' to make and repair Hong Kong targets, horse boats, dinghies and do minor repairs to WD vessels. In 1943 this RAOC Shipwrights' Shop was transferred to 615 Water Transport Company and became a WD Fleet responsibility. At the Royal Arsenal, Jack Cains recalls, the standard of shipwrights' work was such that they completely rebuilt the barge *Gog* after her mishap with the 12 in naval gun, as related in Chapter 10.

Cains had a lot of experience of the work of civilian contractors. Firms like Harland and Wolff, Surrey Commercial and J.S. Whites of Cowes gave excellent service, but there were others that were 'miserable, cheese-paring firms'. He remembers one firm sending out to Woolworth's (in the days when they sold nothing over sixpence (2½p)) for brass barrel bolts.

Running repairs and regular servicing on vessels were of course the responsibility of crew members, most of whom were quite capable of doing necessary maintenance work such as replacement of rigging, boat falls and lifting gear, as well as caulking and baying up of deck seams, and repairs to sails, awnings, boat covers and the re-covering of lifebuoys. Engineers were equally well skilled. Considerable ingenuity would often be displayed, not only in enabling a vessel to limp home, but in avoiding resort to workshops, subsequent awkward enquiries or that bane of all custodians of military material, a misuse and damage report.

Jack Cains gave an example. While on station at Haulbowline, Cork, in pre-war days, as a mate on the target tower *General McHardy*, he inadvertently cut the water pipe that carried water from Haulbowline to Spike Island, stripping three blades from his propeller. Luckily he had three spares aboard. His crew spent all night cutting the stumps away. This necessitated chipping away the thick coating of cement which protected the securing nuts and bolts, great care having to be taken not to damage the threads.

When the new blades were on, we covered the bosses with cement, to which was added household soda to secure a quick hardening process. The job was done on one tide and we were on range for Templebreedy 9.2s at 0930 and the military didn't know a thing about it – not the only thing they didn't know!

The *Marquess of Hartington* was involved in one emergency repair at sea
when a broken connecting rod to the main crank shaft brought her to a sudden
halt while on passage to Plymouth. Fortunately, WD vessels were always well-
found in every respect; a spare was available and replacement carried out by the
engine-room staff, taking between one-and-a-half and two hours.

The handover of the responsibility for supply of naval ordnance stores
and munitions to the Admiralty commenced in 1887. Hitherto, the
Admiralty had procured vessels for the War Department, but now this
responsibility was transferred to the War Department. In December 1890,
the Inspector of Machinery at Woolwich Arsenal became the
Superintending Engineer and Constructor of Shipping (SECS) and took
over the construction of WD vessels from the Admiralty overseer. As
recorded in Chapter 3, Mr James Hay was the first holder of the post.

The duties of the SECS at home required him to make an inspection
of all steamers and launches twice a year and of all other vessels once a
year (including those of the Submarine Mining Service) and to report
accordingly, with his financial estimates for repair and maintenance for
the following year. His reports were made to the Chief Ordnance Officer
and finished up on the desk of the Inspector-General of Ordnance at the
War Office. When new vessels were authorized, he was of course called
upon to furnish designs and specifications and see the vessel through all
its stages of construction from the placing of contracts to final payment. It
is interesting to note that, according to Regulations for Army Ordnance
Services, 1900, 'New boats should be taken on charge by the Army
Ordnance Department, and regularly issued'.

The SECS was also kept busy receiving copies of all requisitions for
work carried out on vessels, machinery, and steam boilers, as well as
details of all hydraulic and steam tests made after repair. The office
seemed to attract more and more technical duties. By 1914, this busy
official had also become responsible for provision and maintenance of all
fire appliances used by the Army, was superintending engineer to HM
Customs, and manager of the Woolwich Royal Arsenal Gasworks. He
finally jibbed at being invited to construct and maintain an inland
waterways fleet, a function which in consequence passed to the Royal
Engineers (see Appendix IV). It was not until some time in the 1920s
that the then SECS, Mr H.G. Williams-Jones, managed to shake off his
extraneous duties and revert to those for which the post had originally
been created.

On the outbreak of war in 1939 the responsibility for new construction was handed over to the new Ministry of Supply. The SECS, Rear-Admiral R.C. Boddie, RN (Retd) and most of his technical staff were transferred at the same time, leaving an Assistant SECS and two ships overseers with ADMT to deal with overhauls of WD vessels. This arrangement was short-lived.

Within a few months, the War Office (ST1) took over control of every other aspect of Fleet operation and administration from ADMT (see Chapter 13), and barely a year later welcomed Rear-Admiral Boddie and his duties into the War Office fold. To assist the SECS in his now greatly increased duties were three Deputies and twelve Assistant SECSs dealing with every technical aspect of shipping from stores supply to design and construction. Rear-Admiral Boddie had succeeded Mr Williams-Jones in 1936 and started the very successful building programmes of fast target-towing launches which rendered obsolete the graceful steam vessels that had served coastal defences so long and so well.

During his stewardship, the Fleet grew to some 1,600 vessels, of which 1,128 were designed, built, or converted, and of course maintained, under his auspices. The complexity of the task of technical control of an assortment of steam and motor coasters, motor fishing vessels, steam and diesel target towers, oil barges, cargo lighters, motor barges, fast, harbour and general service launches may well be imagined. And to this heterogeneous fleet was added, in 1945, a number of Royal Naval Landing Craft (Tank) (LCTs). One of these was a fully-equipped workshop which serviced the Ammunition Dumping Craft (ADCs) at Cairnryan.

It is also interesting to note that the SECS, whose office refused the Inland Water Transport (IWT) task in 1914, also supervised the construction and assembly of the IWT organization's Minca barges (see Appendix IV) and, through the Water Transport Companies' workshops, serviced Mulberries (the pre-fabricated harbour pontoons) for the same service.

In 1948 Fleet administration was decentralized from its War Office controlling branch (now designated ST3) and moved to Kingston as the Fleet Administrative Unit. During the immediate post-war years, Assistant SECSs were sent overseas to organize and control repairs and technical support. The last of these posts was in Hong Kong and lapsed in 1975. One notable ASECS was Mr Alfred Graham, who was made a MBE for his services to the LSTs in the Korean War.

Up until the formation of the Water Transport Companies in the early part of the Second World War, RAOC had been responsible for Fleet repair. Now, however, each company had its own workshops, which, under an RASC officer, was staffed by a civilian foreman and civilian artificers. These workshops were responsible for minor repairs and maintenance, major repairs being effected in naval dockyards through Admiralty arrangements or with civilian shipbuilders and repairers under War Office contracts. On the formation of the specialist Royal Electrical and Mechanical Engineers in 1942 the policy was reviewed, but not changed until 1947.

In that year it was established that minor repairs would continue to be a unit task, except for radio and radar equipment which would be handled by REME technicians. For major repairs differential arrangements were laid down. Hulls and motive units and engineering machinery and equipment which could not be readily removed would be repaired by shipyards or naval dockyards. All other major repairs would be handled by REME.

The RAOC, as the Army's storekeepers, had always been responsible for the issue of all stores and equipment for the WD Fleet. At the outbreak of war in 1939, however, prompted by difficulties in obtaining spares for the new generation of high-speed target towers, the first steps were taken toward transferring this responsibility to RASC. A WD Fleet store was opened at Woolwich, authorized to stock machinery spares for fast launches, and to hold sufficient vessel stores completely to fit out six motor launches.

By September 1940, the store had outgrown its Woolwich accommodation and for this and safety reasons was moved to Slough. Growth continued, keeping pace with the rapid expansion of the Fleet and nine months later the Vessels Store, RASC, as it was now called, moved to Ashchurch and became a Boat Stores Group. By April 1942, the group was holding 500 tons of stores, comprising 3,500 items.

The majority of boats and vessels stores were now transferred to RASC supply and, completing a circle, returned to Woolwich Dockyard. Renamed a Boat Stores Depot, it became the repository for all marine stores, equipment and paints, etc., for all arms of the service at home and overseas, including the then Dominion Governments. Responsibility for the provision of targets for Target Practice Seawards, including the wireless-controlled 'Queen Gull' target vessels, also became an RASC task.

By the autumn of 1943 the Depot was holding stores to the value of £1,250,000, with as much again on order, supporting 600 vessels built by 75 different builders, engined by 45 different makes and sub-divided by 125 distinct types. The volume of stores held represented a ten-fold increase in just over a year. At the war's end, the Depot held 26,500 items of stores; 10,000 tons, compared with only 5 tons in 1939! Similar Boat Stores Depots became established in all operational theatres.

On the rundown of the Woolwich water transport operations, No. 1 Boat Stores Depot, as it was now designated, moved again, this time to Barry, South Wales, shortly before the Suez operations, and later finished its days at Hilsea, Portsmouth, when, in a great rationalization exercise under which each of the three services undertook tasks common to all, marine stores were handed over to the Royal Navy.

It was not until 1951 that any major change in the repair system was made. On 1 July, the Fleet Repair Unit was formed under the Corps of Royal Electrical and Mechanical Engineers (REME) in the second phase of the re-organization of the Army's technical support system which had started in 1942, absorbing RASC technically-trained officers and NCOs.

The Fleet Repair Unit was headed by the Deputy SECS and controlled all aspects of Fleet repair, development and design. Minor repairs were still carried out by the Water Transport Company Workshops, and heavier repair and overhaul tasks by contractors, under FRU auspices. Under REME auspices the efficiency of the repair organization continued. Maj. Bill Wynn-Werninck, himself a former RASC workshops officer, comments:

> I must remark on the excellence of the work undertaken by the civilian-manned HM Gunwharf Workshop, REME, Portsmouth, under Major 'Joe' Beckett, Captain Collins and others who were hard put to it maintaining and modifying the military LCTs Mk.VIII which became based on Portsmouth. Singapore was the same; 37 Company, RASC (Water Transport) had a big workshop with Malay and Chinese fitters commanded by Major Jack Wellans, REME. They all must have saved millions in work which would have had to be done by Dockyard contract.

Very shortly afterwards completion of the re-organization, the SECS at War Office (ST3) retired, the appointment lapsing for ten years. Military officers commanded the unit during this period. In 1961, the unit was moved to Hilsea, Portsmouth and became the Fleet Repair Branch, once again entirely civilian-manned. The SECS appointment was revived and assumed by Mr Harms, the Deputy SECS.

Mr Harms retired in 1968 and was succeeded by Mr Alan Blight, who commanded the Branch for the next twenty years until his retirement in 1989. Like Frank Bourne, he too saw the last of the civilian fleet, now reduced to a handful of range safety launches, being handed over to the Director of Marine Services (Navy) on 24 September of that year.

22
SUEZ AND THE FINAL DECADES

It had been decided in November 1943 that the Fleet should be militarized, under a limit of 34 officers and 400 soldiers, the intention being that the change-over should be gradual, commencing with units involved in operational and security tasks. However, persistent shortages of military manpower prevented this policy from being put into force during the war, and the financial stringency of the immediate post-war period ensured the continuation of the *status quo* so far as the civilian fleet was concerned. The reprieve was not long-lived, however.

It was in the late 1950s that two major decisions were taken, the effects of which were to reduce the once proud civilian fleet to little more than a two-ship training organization and a flotilla of range safety craft. The first of these decisions was by far the most devastating as, virtually overnight, the civilian fleet lost its bread-and-butter commitment. On 17 February 1956, the Minister of Defence announced in the House of Commons that Coast Artillery was to be abolished. In the light of modern weapon developments he said it was clear that there was no longer any justification for maintaining coastal defences. The case was of course irrefutable and, after 31 December in the same year, Coast Artillery ceased to exist. The sad task of dismantling fortresses and batteries, some of which had been served by the Fleet under its various names for two centuries or more, became the last service to be performed for this now moribund branch of the Royal Artillery.

Needless to say, the decision sent a shock wave throughout the civilian fleet. Frank Bourne recalls that they then had a directive telling them that there would be redundancies and that with the closure of Cairnryan, Dover, Falmouth and other stations, there would eventually be only about 120 civilians in the Fleet. 'And we laughed,' he added, 'and said it was impossible. We then had over a thousand men in the Fleet and well over 200 vessels.'

The immediate effect was that the commitment to target-towing and range clearance virtually ceased and twelve high-speed target towers were taken out of commission, resulting in the redundancy of 12 masters, 12 first engineers and 30–40 crewmen. The War Office newsletter of the Institute of Professional Civil Servants (IPCS), *Pheon*, reported that the total redundancy, in terms of senior officers, would amount to 3 master superintendents, 20 masters, 35 mates and 18 first engineers. To this number must be added the 800 to 900 crew members.

The second blow came a few months later in the same year. This was the decision of the Chiefs-of-Staff Committee that the Army would in future organize and run logistic shipping for purely army operations, for which purpose it would take over, control and operate its own LCTs. These would be crewed by military manpower, thus bringing to fruition the 1943 decision.

One of the main military reasons for this decision was the fact that the build-up to the Suez operation had been hampered by a shortage of civilian commercial shipping, and the shortage of military manpower and experience to crew the available LCTs now coming to the end of their

The late Capt. Frank Bourne, last Master Superintendent of the Fleet, with a fine gallery of past RASC vessels

role as Ammunition Dumping Craft. Probably to their embarrassment, the Army chiefs had to call for volunteers from the civilian fleet to man logistic shipping to help meet Suez build-up commitments. Frank Bourne, the last Fleet Superintendent, was one of nearly seventy who volunteered to take part in this operation, and remembers it well.

Three LCTs, the Mk.IVs, L408 (J.G. Scott, master), L403 (Capt. Watt, master) and one of the first of the new Fleet, a Mk.VIII L4086 *Arromanches* (J. Bayliss, master) sailed in a small convoy for Malta escorted by a 'T' class trawler, there to await orders. Bourne's vessel, L408, was loaded, 'completely filled' with composite rations, the others with vehicles and general stores.

Thus laden the convoy then steamed off to Cyprus, taking seven to eight days, and stood off Famagusta, awaiting instructions. A day after the operation started they were ordered to Port Said and proceeded independently. On arrival after dark, L408 was met by a frigate and escorted to an anchorage for safety, the approaches having been mined. Capt. Bourne recalls:

> We lay there about half a day to a day, until the skipper made up his mind that he'd had enough and decided he wanted to go in. He managed to get a pilot, and we steamed on in. We had to go over three wrecks to get there, sailing between bridge and forecastle. Tricky, but drawing only 6 ft we were lucky – we could do it.
>
> Once we got rid of our cargo we were put to discharging lorries, etc., from the larger ships that couldn't get to the harbour. All we did was to go alongside, load up and beach on a little spit of sand right inside Port Said itself. While unloading was progressing we would have our heads down, and then it was back alongside again. This went on for about two or three weeks and then, of course, everything stopped.
>
> We were subsequently loaded with NAAFI stores, whisky, gin, cigarettes, etc. (which was very handy!), and discharged them at Famagusta. We then had a job at Limassol discharging a vessel which had a cargo of petrol in jerricans. The Harbour Master wouldn't let us alongside at night, so we were stuck out at anchor.
>
> While swimming in the clear water we found that we had somehow lost one of our two rudders. It was not possible to make the repair in Cyprus so we were sent off to Tobruk, escorted by an ex-Turkish ferry. After waiting several days at Tobruk for an escort

to Malta, a lifting vessel of the Royal Fleet Auxiliary came in. The skipper of this vessel decided that, with our speed, he would make better time to Malta by taking us in tow. However, a day out of Tobruk we hit a Force 9 gale, pretty severe for the Mediterranean. The lifting vessel was better head on in this sea, but we were better sailing beam on – if we had turned head on we would have been smashed to pieces.

So the skipper said we would have to go beam on and of course our escort, beam on also, just rolled his guts out! But he stuck it out, and we eventually found our way into Malta. Here we were repaired, got shore leave, got paid up, and eventually we were told to steam back to the UK independently, so we had a leisurely trip home, arriving in Cairnryan nearly three weeks later.

The remaining two vessels stayed in the Middle East until 1957, one returning at Easter, and the other, *Arromanches*, returning in March via Cyprus and Malta to Barry with a mixed cargo of tomatoes, gun barrels and cars.

This LCT Mk. VIII, later named *Arromanches*, was one of the first of the new fleet and took part in the Suez operation

In the meantime, to meet possible further Suez commitments (which did not materialize) eight LCTs Mk.VIII had been taken over from the Navy by more civilian volunteer seamen. These now became the first vessels of the new military Fleet and were speedily organized into a new Water Transport Unit, 76 Company, RASC (LCT) – a happy choice of number, recalling the earlier 76 Company, ASC which, over forty years earlier, had been the first to operate a military-manned craft. So quick had been the transition that, by the time the last volunteer LCT returned to the United Kingdom, the new organization was in place and operating with RASC officers and crews.

These two decisions did not instantly put an end to the civilian fleet; as recorded elsewhere, ammunition dumping at Cairnryan continued for another two to three years, and civilian-manned LCTs assisted Mk.VIIIs of 76 Company in the setting up and maintenance of the Hebrides guided weapons range. Frank Bourne's vessel took part in this operation and was the first to go alongside the new pier at Loch Carnen.

This operation became a wholly military one, with the exception that the civilian fleet's *Mull* (referred to in Chapter 19) continued in support of the LCTs, both as an escort and, later, as a winter ferry between Benbecula and St Kilda, for several years after her return from Singapore. The LCTs operated from March to October, when the sand would disappear from Village Bay, leaving only rock on which to beach. The LCTs were refitted during the sandless months, service being maintained by *Mull* for several years until finally she was paid-off, being replaced by a contract helicopter service. She had an unusual workboat, *Puffin*, a robust steel boat built to West African surfboat design modified by the Fleet Repair Branch for winter conditions in St Kilda. She had three rollers built into her hull for rock landing, and was water-jet propelled.

In the meantime the reduction of the Fleet continued. A War Office review in 1958 showed 111 vessels in commission and 58 in reserve, most awaiting disposal. Among these was the last coaster *Malplaquet*. *Katharine II*, now in 71 Company at Portsmouth, was in her last few months of Fleet service. It is interesting to note that the one surviving 69 ft 'Battle' class high-speed target tower, *Antwerp*, was still in commission, towing balloon targets for the guided weapon range at Ty Croes . . . she is believed to be the last civilian fleet vessel to be so employed.

Ironically, in 1959 shortages of military manpower resulted in the two training vessels, the 90 ft MFV *Yarmouth Navigator* and the smaller MFV

The 61½ ft motor fishing vessel *Yarmouth Seaman* as a RASC/RCT training vessel

Yarmouth Seaman, being transferred to what was left of the civilian fleet. Training voyages took them regularly to the Channel Islands and to West Country ports, these being interspersed with exercises with the Royal Navy, and range clearance patrols.

Range clearance for weapons ranges and proof and experimental establishments was a new commitment – indeed, it eventually became the only task – for the civilian fleet. Frank Bourne served for eighteen months as mate on the *Yarmouth Navigator* at Portsmouth, the training organization having moved there from the Isle of Wight, and then was appointed master of a new REME designed and built vessel, the *Trevose*. This vessel was intended to be the prototype general service launch but, proving unsuitable, was transferred to the training unit. At the same time, the 52 ft launch *Anglesey* joined the Fleet as the prototype fast launch, and was subsequently based on Tenby to spend her working life on range safety duties for the Castlemartin ranges in South Wales.

Operations started off the Royal Armoured Corps range at Lulworth, followed by the Castlemartin and Manorbier ranges in South Wales, the Royal Artillery guided missile range in the Hebrides, the Infantry ranges

The REME-designed and built *Trevose*

in the Cinque Ports training area and the proof and experimental establishments at Eskmeals in Cumbria, Pendine Sands and Shoeburyness.

The object of this task was of course to warn passing vessels of danger from overshoots. The main difficulty, apart from adverse weather conditions, was that free passage at sea could not be obstructed so that if anyone insisted on going through the danger area, as did happen, shooting had to stop. In many of the areas, however, by-laws covering inshore safety were in force and legal action could be taken where wilful obstruction of firing could be proved. In all such cases records of all messages passing between the range clearance launch and the offending vessel were passed to the shore authority for legal advice.

Once again, the civilian fleet, as it had always done, settled down to its new task, quietly and unobtrusively, still part of the RASC Fleet it had served for so long. In 1965, however, its name, its badges, its organization, changed once again, when the RASC, shedding its many non-transport duties, was metamorphosed into the Royal Corps of Transport. RASC vessels were now RCT vessels but, reassuringly, perhaps, still wore the same ensign. Life went on; from Lulworth to the far Hebrides, the range clearance task continued uninterrupted under the aegis of 18 Maritime Squadron, RCT, a unit of 20 Maritime Regiment, located at HM Gunwharf, Portsmouth.

The main characteristics of a good range clearance craft were reliable sea-keeping qualities and speed; a stable boat was essential, able to sit out on the range for anything from 8 to 10 hours a day, with a speed of, say, 15 to 16 knots. At the outset the task fell to the ageing and now much-reduced fleet of 'Derby Winner' class target towers and the 50 ft 'Dickens' class GS launches. These latter craft, although of proven reliability, had a maximum speed of only 8 knots, and so were unable to cope with the much faster coastal traffic which could, and did, invade range areas.

A number of 41 ft twin-screw fibre-glass command and control launches were therefore ordered in the late 1960s, named for seabirds. This class did not have an auspicious start as the first, *Petrel*, was returned to the builders for correction. Unfortunately, recollects Maj. Geoffrey Williamson, the cheapest tender for the building of these craft had been accepted, and they proved most unreliable, continually breaking down. None the less their 14 knot speed and reasonable sea-keeping abilities made them more suitable for the task than the ageing vessels they replaced.

The sea ranges developed into a permanent and highly important requirement of the armament industry and defence sales where no lapse could be allowed in firing programmes through failures in range clearance support. As the 41 ft craft, like the 'Dickens' class, had not provided the right answer, a number of craft in the commercial range were evaluated. The 15 m 'Talisman' class, built by James & Son, Brightlingsea, was finally selected as the replacement craft, replacing the GSLs, CCLs and *Anglesey* by the late 1970s. This new class of range safety launch, as the type was now classified, were well-equipped, comfortable vessels and a tremendous improvement on all that had gone before.

Two were named for Samuel Morley, VC and Joseph Hughes, GC, and six others for prominent ex-RASC generals, including Sir Reginald Kerr and Sir Humfrey Gale, who thus had the distinction of twice having civilian fleet vessels named for them, the earlier being the vastly dissimilar 350 ft, 2,310 ton Landing Ships (Tank) referred to in Chapter 18 as the largest ever to be operated by the RASC. In addition to this new 15 m class, a fine 24 m air-sea rescue type launch, the RCTV *Alfred Herring, VC*, was brought into service for use in the Atlantic off the Outer Hebrides. She was later to be joined by RCTV *Michael Murphy, VC*.

Alfred Herring, VC, was one of the air-sea rescue craft taken over from the RAF for range safety duties in the Hebrides

Earlier, in 1972, the Royal Aircraft Establishment at Farnborough paid the RCT Fleet the compliment of asking for assistance in operating the ex-naval inshore minesweeper they used for research work. The RAF had dropped all other maritime activities and were unable to justify maintaining an expensive shore base to run just one vessel. Furthermore, the techniques involved in the work to be undertaken required a regular crew rather than an RAF complement subject to constant change. The commitment was gladly accepted by the RCT Civilian Fleet, and the vessel, renamed the RCTV *Richard George Masters VC*, was taken over by Capt. Bourne, who had the distinction of taking her to Gibraltar and back on the last foreign-going voyage of the Fleet. The vessel was eventually replaced by an ex-trawler, the *Colonel Templer*, purchased and modified by the RAE to its special requirements. *Colonel Templer* continued under RCT control until the Army's Civilian Fleet finally received the *coup de grace*.

In 1977 Capt. Bourne was appointed Master Superintendent of the RCT Fleet, little realizing he would make a small footnote in both RCT and RN history in being the last Master Superintendent in the former and the first and only one in the latter.

This ex-Naval inshore minesweeper *R.G. Masters, VC*, was the last foreign-going vessel to be civilian-manned by the Fleet

For centuries, from the Middle Ages to the end of the nineteenth century, the Fleet, in its various guises, had served both Army and Navy impartially. As we have seen in early chapters, it had been a workable arrangement until the increasing sophistication of arms and armament had made necessary a re-appraisal. In consequence, the ASC lost a number of its vessels and their crews to the Navy. But the WD Fleet shrugged off its losses, took on target-towing and range clearance duties, and never looked back, its responsibilities and reputation growing year by year, task by task. It was ironic that, as technical advances had reduced it in the nineteenth century, so further technical developments were to decimate it in the twentieth, and at a time when its strength and reputation had never stood higher. However, it was not because of technical developments that the final blows were struck.

The Fleet had always been subject to financial scrutiny, no less than other branches of the administrative services, but had always been able to prove itself cost-effective and operationally necessary. Its former sponsors, were they Board of Ordnance, ASC or RASC, had on every occasion been able to fight off any suggestions that contractors could do its work as well, if at all. However, in the 1980s there was a new and much more severe economic climate, and there was a new concept, rationalization, as well as an old one under a new and unlovely name, contractorization.

So it was that, under the aegis of rationalization, the transfer of the remnants of the RCT civilian fleet, now 18 Maritime Squadron, RCT, Portsmouth, were handed over to the Director of Marine Services (Navy), lock stock and anchor, on 1 October 1988. It was then to be known as 'Range Safety Group DMS(N)' and to remain under the Master Superintendent, Frank Bourne. It is interesting, and surprising, to note that the declared intention was to 'contractorize' the RSG within the year *if justified*, and that, moreover, even before the transfer, DMS (N) already had the matter under consideration! In fact, this did not happen until 1991.

The civilian fleet at this time consisted of 13 Range Safety Craft, 2 Command and Control launches, the 52 ft launch *Anglesey*, 2 Harbour Launches and the training vessel *Yarmouth Navigator*, and all these vessels passed, together with the last 70 personnel, to naval control. Nor were these the only losses; at the same time, the purpose-built ammunition carrier, HMAV *St George*, 1,400 tons and the pride of the military Fleet, was transferred to the Navy's Royal Marine Auxiliary Service. The demise of 18 Squadron was marked by a melancholy review of range safety vessels at Portsmouth, the salute being taken from *St George*.

Rationalization also meant the end of the Fleet's 300-years association with HM Gunwharf. The gunwharf had been much more than a dock handling naval armament; it had developed into a complex of barracks, storehouses, armouries and workshops for every kind of military and naval purpose. Half had been given up to the Navy in 1891 following the earlier rationalization of armament supply; now, nearly a century later, the whole had become a part of the HMS *Nelson* shore establishment. The present RCT Fleet transferred its operations from Gosport to the modern Marchwood Military Port, Southampton.

There is little more to tell. Frank Bourne, who has since died, retired in February 1991 and shortly afterwards wrote:

Present situation is that the unit at Portsmouth is down to 3 officers and 4 hands. The contract for manning the vessels has gone to Messrs James Fisher of Barrow and they will take off on June 3 1991. The rest of the remaining civilian fleet is to be made redundant, which I would say is the FINAL chapter of the civilian War Department Fleet. Things will never be the same again.

APPENDIX I

1859 Regulations

(WO Circular No. 471, from the War Office, Pall Mall, 24 August 1859 (referred to in Chapter 2))

RULES and REGULATIONS to be strictly observed by Masters, Mates, and Seamen of the several Vessels belonging to or employed by the War Department

1st – On arrival at any Military Store Stations, the Master is immediately to report himself to the Senior Military Store Officer, and if any Stores are on Board, to deliver the Bills of Lading.

2nd – The Master is to attend daily at the Military Store Office at the Station where the Vessel may be lying, to receive such orders as it may be necessary to give him.

3rd – The Master is strongly enjoined frequently to examine the Hold, and to be particularly careful that all Iron Bolts, Nails, &c., are covered with Sheet Lead or pieces of Leather, and that any defects in the Vessel or Stores are immediately reported, in writing, to the Senior Military Store Officer at the Station.

4th – Previously to receiving any Gunpowder, Ammunition, &c., the Master or Mate is to take especial care to examine the Hold, and see that it is clean swept, free from grit or dust, and in a fit state to receive the Stores, which he is to report to the Senior Military Store Officer.

5th – On receiving Gunpowder, Ammunition, &c., the Master is to see that the Platform in the Vessel's Hold, the Gangways, and Comings [*sic*] of the Hatchways, are covered with Tanned Hides, that the Barrels or Boxes are carefully stowed, the Hatches properly secured and locked, and that the Key remains in his own possession.

6th – No Fires, Lights, or Smoking, are under any circumstances, to be permitted on Board at the time of Loading or Unloading, or while lying alongside (or within quarter of a mile) of any Magazine: – Fires will be provided in the Cookhouses at the several stations, when requisite for cooking the provisions. When at sea, and it is necessary to have a fire on board, the Master is to see it carefully extinguished at sunset and one hour previously to going alongside any Ship or Magazine.

7th – Having received Gunpowder, or other Ammunition, a red flag is to be hoisted at the mast-head, and kept flying until the cargo is discharged. The Master or Mate and all the Crew are to remain on Board until all the Stores are discharged, except that it may be necessary to procure Water or Provisions, of which notice is to be given to the Senior Military Store Officer.

8th – On Delivery of the above Stores the same caution is to be used as in Loading; and if any Barrels or Boxes should have been unavoidably broken, or any Powder become loose, it is to be carefully swept up and delivered at the Magazine:- and the circumstance reported by the Master to the Senior Military Stores Officer.

9th – No Lucifer Matches are at any time to be used on board any of the War Department Vessels, and any Person found to be in possession of the same will be immediately dismissed.

10th – The Master is to keep a Log Book, inserting the Daily Occurrences, and also the Receipts and Deliveries: – The Tally of all Stores passing into or out of the Vessel is to be taken by the Master or Mate, who will be held strictly accountable for the delivery of all the Stores according to the receipt tally, and any deficiency must be immediately reported by the Storekeeper to whom the Stores are consigned.

11th – In the Steamers at sea the Officer in charge is to keep his Watch on the bridge, and to see that the lamps are properly trimmed, and that a good look-out is kept by the man stationed in the bows.

12th – The Admiralty regulations respecting lights must be strictly attended to, both in the Steam and Sailing Vessels.

13th – On the arrival of the Steam Vessel in any Port, the Chief Engineer is to report to the Master or Mate that the Sea and Bilge Cocks are secure before leaving the Vessel; and the Engineer on duty, when under way, shall not under any pretence leave the Engine Room unless relieved by the Engineer off duty; and in the event of the Fires being required to be banked up, the Vessel is on no account to be left without one Engineer on board.

14th – The Stokers shall assist the crew in getting the anchor whenever required, but will not be called upon to take part in the general work of the ship on deck, except in cases of emergency at sea. On arriving at any port they shall be employed under the Engineers in cleaning the Boilers, Engines, and other work in the Engine Room.

15th – The Galley and Steam Funnels are to be kept clean swept, white-washed, and painted by the Stokers.

16th – The Galley Fire is to be extinguished at 8 p.m., and not lighted before 6 a.m. The Funnels are to be daily carefully examined and swept.

17th – All Boats, unless required for the service, are to be hoisted up at 9 p.m., and on no account to be lowered unless ordered by the Master or in his absence the Mate.

18th – When the Vessel is unloaded, safely moored, and not immediately wanted, the Master, Mate, and Crew, will be permitted, in turn, occasionally to be with their families (when the weather will allow) but Steamers are never to be left without the Master or Mate, one Engineer, one Seaman, one Stoker, and one Boy; nor Sailing Vessels without either the Master or the Mate, and one Seaman on Board, nor is any person to absent himself at any time without express permission from the Senior Military Store Officer at the Station.

19th – Each Vessel will be furnished with two Red Flags, as many Pairs of Magazine Slippers as there are men in crew, and a like number of Pairs of Trousers and Frocks, for working in the Hold, but not to be worn at any other period; these Articles will be supplied upon the Master making a requisition for them to the Senior Military Store Officer of the Station to which the Vessel belongs.

20th – When absent from his own Station, or meeting with any Accident at Sea, whereby the safety of the Vessel is endangered, or delay likely to be occasioned, the Master is to report immediately to the Senior Military Store Officer at the Station to which he belongs, and apply for assistance to the nearest Military Storekeeper, Ship, or Dockyard belonging to Her Majesty.

21st – The Master will be held strictly responsible that the service upon which his vessel is employed is performed with the utmost despatch; and, in the event of his being obliged to seek shelter, that no unnecessary delay is allowed to take place before again proceeding on his voyage. The circumstance is to be immediately reported to the Senior Military Store Officer to whom the stores are consigned.

22nd – The Master is authorised to draw half a Month's Pay, in the event of his Voyage being prolonged, by adverse Winds or unforeseen circumstances, beyond the Month in which he was originally loaded; the circumstances to be immediately reported to the Senior Military Store Officer of the Station to which the Vessel belongs.

23rd – Every man or boy employed in this service is to devote himself exclusively to it, and the Master will be held responsible for the conduct of the Mate and Crew, and in the event of any disobedience of his orders by them he is to report, in writing, to the Senior Military Store Officer at the Station to which he belongs.

24th – Any Master, Mate or Man wishing to leave the Service, must give three days' notice or forfeit pay for a similar time.

25th – When removing the Armament of any of Her Majesty's Ships, the Master is to use his utmost endeavours to prevent any article of Naval Stores being put on his Vessel with the Stores of this Department. In the event of his observing any article of Naval Stores amongst the War Department Stores, he will immediately report the circumstance to the Officer commanding the Ship from which the Armament is being removed.

26th – On all occasions before casting off, after receiving Stores from any of H.M. Ships alongside the Dockyard, the Master will apprize the Dockyard Police, in order that his vessel may be searched. Should the Ship be in the stream, he will ask the Officer commanding to send the Master-at-Arms on board his Vessel to make the examination; he will then lock the Hatch, and retain the key in his own possession, until his Vessel comes alongside Gun Wharf to unload.

27th – The Master will make out an Inventory of all the standing and running rigging, masts, blocks, anchors, cables, (stating the length of the cables), sails, and all spare stores, &c.

28th – He will transmit Demands from time to time for such Stores as may be requisite, returning the old Stores to the Military Storekeeper, to show that they have been fairly worn out.

29th – The Master will periodically examine the Forecastle, and report to the Military

Storekeeper any article of Public Stores found therein other than those belonging to the Vessel.

30th – All Stores belonging to the Vessel are to be clearly marked WD.

31st – Periodical surveys will be held by an Officer of the Military Store Department, in order to ascertain that the Stores are correct; and the Master will be held strictly responsible for all the Stores placed in his charge, as shown by the Inventory. The Military Storekeeper is to report having held the survey.

J. CRAWFORD CAFFIN
Director of Stores

To Military Store Officers in
charge of Stations,
and to the Masters of the
War Department Vessels.

APPENDIX II

Notes on the Submarine Mining Service

(Based on *The History of Submarine Mining in the British Army, 1910*, by Lt.-Col. W. Baker-Browne, RE)

The attacking of ships by floating explosive devices had been known as far back as the sixteenth century but was never taken seriously until the 1850s. The American inventor, Robert Fulton, had offered his 'torpedo', as he named it, to the British Government in 1805 but although it did sink a 200 ton brig, after some failures, they were not impressed.

Notwithstanding the apparent lack of interest in the mine or torpedo as an offensive weapon, there was an important development in 1839 when Col. Sir Charles Pasley, RE, destroyed two wrecks, the *Royal George* and *Edgar*, in what was the first application of electricity to submerged charges.

In 1854, the Russians had developed a mechanical device and one designed to explode by electricity on collision with a ship, though no evidence existed that they had ever been used. None the less interest was created anew and there was considerable further experimentation with the uses of electricity for underwater explosions. Then, during the American Civil War, the Confederate forces successfully used both mechanical and electrical devices against shipping. These, though crude, destroyed or disabled thirty-seven vessels. The naval powers sat up and took notice.

In the United Kingdom the starting point (in Col. Baker-Browne's words) 'from which sprung not only the military system of mines but also all naval mines and torpedoes in the British Service, and the systematic use of passive obstructions' was a *Memorandum of Floating Obstructions and Submarine Explosive Machines* by Gen. Sir John F. Burgoyne, the Inspector-General of Engineers, and published in 1862.

This memorandum prompted the appointment of a joint naval and military committee to investigate the questions it raised, namely the possibilities of the mine and torpedo as a defence of harbours and rivers. It took five years to complete its task and, following further discussion and committee reports, the Submarine Mining Service was set up in 1871, to be operated by the Royal Engineers. It seemed quite logical at the time that the RE should undertake this task.

The main technical difficulty at that time was to adapt the land-mine to a marine application without endangering the passage of friendly traffic. The means required was of course electricity, a comparatively recently developed form of energy. The Royal Engineers, not unnaturally, had been in the forefront of the development of this agent in the science of war; indeed, they were probably the only uniformed organization that knew anything about it and its practical application to defence.

A Gen. Harrison, in his introduction to Col. Baker-Browne's history, had no doubts:

Both electric cables, for firing and communication, as well as the mines themselves, had to be laid with care and skill; elaborate position finders had to be fixed to mark the position of ships and electric lights (searchlights) provided to enable the defence to be worked by night as well as by day. Careful organization was also required so that the necessary skilled personnel should always be ready at every defended port.

It might have been thought that defence of harbours was a naval responsibility, but Gen. Harrison goes on to say,

> In discussions with Naval Officers I often raised the question of submarine mining and its command, and my impression is that all I spoke to were of the opinion that the role of the Navy being an *active* defence, no Naval vessels should be tied to the shore.

So the best policy was to leave the sedentary defence of sea and land fortresses to the Army.

The Submarine Mining Service was set up at Chatham in 1871; progress thereafter was swift and vigorous. In the early days, the service had to make do with old mortar boats from Crimean days, for use as lighters and old 42 ft naval pinnaces, handy for laying mines, but unable to raise them. Naval tugs of all descriptions, mainly paddle-wheel, ill-adapted, and sailing vessels, were also in use. It was not until 1875 that the first specially designed boat was built for the service, the 65 ft 'Miner' class, an excellent vessel with a good steam-winch, small charthouse on deck and a bow derrick. They were later fitted with a bridge and two side davits.

The larger laying-out (of cable) vessels were first introduced in 1885, when vessels of the 'Gordon' class came into service. The *Gordon* and *Solent* were the first of this class, which varied in length from 80 to 100 ft and in displacement from 100 to 125 tons. In 1891 the 144 ton *General Skinner* and *Napier of Magdala* came into the fleet, followed by a further group of eight screw steamers. By 1898, the *Naval Service Pocket Book* was listing no less than 68 vessels, far more than the WD Fleet.

The larger vessels were fitted with mast derricks, a bow derrick, and a large steam crab with horizontal and vertical drums. The engines were compound twin-screw. There was an officer's cabin (used by the coxswain when no officer was on board!) and living accommodation for two or three deckhands, two engineers and two stokers, and a cook. The larger vessels could carry six or eight groups of electrically-controlled mines and were capable of working in fairly rough weather.

Mining vessels were deployed in key harbours around Britain and throughout the Empire and the service reached its peak strength and efficiency in the early twentieth century. However, it was not to last; like the RASC civilian fleet ninety years later, it lost out to technical and policy changes. With the arrival and acceptance of the submarine, the Navy's 'blue water' policy changed. This new type of craft had been under trial for some time and great things were expected of it.

It had, however, become apparent that the submarine would be greatly dependent upon shore support for crews and stores. Realizing this, some naval officers looked enviously at the Submarine Mining Establishments with their piers, workshops and barracks. A suggestion was then made by the Admiralty that they could allot submarines to the principal naval ports and that therefore the mining service could be withdrawn. The War Office did not give in without a fight but following considerable controversy, the Committee for Imperial Defence eventually took a decision to transfer all mine defences to the Navy, the Army, however, retaining responsibility for electric light.

At the last roll-call of the Submarine Mining Service, 1 April 1904, 5,890 officers, NCOs, men and civilians were employed throughout the Empire, of which over 2,000 were Regulars. The vessels, excluding some launches retained for harbour duties, were valued at £250,000, 21 of which were transferred to the RN, and 27 to the War Department Fleet, to meet their new target-towing and other commitments. Included in this number was the *Haslar*, 175 tons, the largest vessel built for this service. She had only been commissioned the previous year, but went on to serve the WD for forty-six years until sold out of the service in 1951.

Although the Submarine Mining Service had been short-lived, the experience gained in the handling of inshore craft would prove invaluable when, ten years later, the Inland Water Transport Organization came into being under Royal Engineers auspices.

APPENDIX III
Dress in the 1890s

(Late nineteenth-century uniform clothing regulations, as referred to in Chapter 6)

Clothing

The crews at home (with the exception of the engine-room staff, who are at present exempt) are required to wear a uniform, which they have to provide and keep up at their own expense.

CAP

Masters, Mates and Boatswains
Navy pattern, with peak and leather chin strap, with loop and slide; blue cloth, lined with crimson silk and white head leather; to have a band of black silk, oakleaf pattern, 1¼ inch lace; peak to be bound with 1¼ inch lace of a similar pattern; two small universal pattern gilt buttons at sides for chin strap.

Able Seamen, Ordinary Seamen and Boys
(1) Blue cloth, navy pattern, with black silk band lettered 'War Department' in gold; (2) Blue worsted sea kit cap.

BADGE FOR CAP

Masters, Mates and Boatswains
A large Royal crown, embroidered in gold, with crimson plush centre, supported by the letters 'WD' and surrounded by a wreath of laurel embroidered in gold.

JACKET

Masters, Mates and Boatswains
(Reefer) blue cloth, double-breasted, with body lining of black Italian cloth, and sleeve linings of striped flannel; five large universal gilt buttons upon each breast; two pockets, with flaps, on hips, and one inside pocket on left breast; lace rings of rank to commence 4 inches from bottom of sleeve.

Able Seamen, Ordinary Seamen and Boys
(Pea) blue cloth, RE, SMM (Submarine Miners), and Jersey, blue, No.1.

TROUSERS

Masters, Mates and Boatswains
Fly front, blue cloth; two side pockets of white twilled cotton.

Able Seamen, Ordinary Seamen and Boys
Blue serge, boats crews or blue tweed at the option of the men.

WAISTCOAT

Masters, Mates and Boatswains
Single-breasted, blue cloth, without collar; back and back strap of black Italian cloth, with brass buckle; lining of striped sateen; three pockets, and six small universal buttons (gilt).

BADGES OF RANK

Masters
Two rings of ½ inch universal pattern gold lace round each sleeve, with ¾ inch blue light between; the lower ring four inches from bottom of sleeve.
NB. Masters of sea-going steamers to have in addition a tracing of ⅜ inch gold braid between the rings.

Mates
One ring of ½ inch universal pattern gold lace round each sleeve; lower edge of ring 4 inches from bottom of sleeve.

Boatswains
Three small universal pattern gilt buttons in a row down lower seam of sleeve, 1 inch apart, the lowest button being 1 inch from bottom of sleeve.

The engine-room staff, i.e. engineers, engine drivers, and stokers, are provided free of cost, with two canvas suits of working clothing yearly, issued from Pimlico.

Note: All demands were forwarded through the DAAG for Transport. Masters and mates had to render a monthly certificate that all members of the crew were in possession of a clean and serviceable suit of uniform of the authorized pattern.

APPENDIX IV

Notes on the Inland Water Transport Organization RE

(Referred to in Chapter 8)

This sister service had a brief ten-year existence from 1914 to 1924, was resuscitated in 1939 and twenty-six years later was absorbed into the Royal Corps of Transport. It appears at first sight strange that, with a well-established water transport fleet already in existence, it should have been considered necessary to introduce a second, military, organization. The main reason, however, for raising this new military transport medium was to make operational use of the extensive canal system on the Continent by planning for a barge service to complement the railway system. Railways were the responsibility of the Royal Engineers, and it obviously made sense to the Quartermaster General that the two media should be under one head. He would also have been mindful of the Royal Engineers' recent experience of water operations in the Submarine Mining Service. Undoubtedly, too, it would not have been thought advisable to have a civilian-manned service in a theatre of operations, a view adopted by the WD Fleet's controllers in both world wars, when military water transport units with operational roles were raised.

The Fleet's Superintending Engineer and Constructor of Shipping (SECS) at the time was asked to construct and maintain this fleet of vessels for service on inland waterways and refused. This was not surprising as that busy official not only looked after all the War Department's vessels, but provided and maintained the Department's fire equipment, was Superintending Engineer to HM Customs and still found some time to manage the Royal Arsenal Gasworks!

Within a few weeks of the outbreak of the Great War in 1914, a small cadre was formed in the Railways Section of the War Office. This Inland Water Section, as it was designated, was headed by Commander G.E. Holland, CIE, DSO, a retired officer of the Royal Indian Marine and at that time Marine Superintendent of the London and NW Railway.

In pursuance of the principle that IWT would partly supplement and partly be a substitute for railway transport, Commander Holland was placed as a Deputy Director under the Director of Railway Transport. He had a small staff of temporary RE officers and other ranks and was charged with the purchase of barges and stores, and with the recruitment of the first Inland Water Transport units. It was not long before experience showed that in practice there was little connection between railway and water transport administration, and IWT became a separate directorate.

An Inland Water Stores and Personnel Depot was set up at Richborough, Sussex, and by 1918 had developed into a major military seaport of 2,000 acres, able to handle a weekly 30,000 tons of traffic. IWT's earlier role of carriage inland from ports of bulky traffic of no urgency, had now expanded into a regular cross-channel service, employing 242 barges. These proved invaluable for the transport of locomotives, rolling stock, heavy guns and tanks. Barges for inland waterway work were fitted out for the supply and purification of water and for the carriage of wounded.

Overseas, the IWT organization was represented in East Africa and the Middle East, and operated a lighter port at Taranto, the terminal of an overland line of communication which ran from Cherbourg, serving the Italian and Middle East theatres of operations. By far their greatest effort, however, was reserved for the Mesopotamian campaign and contributed immeasurably to its ultimate success.

This campaign had as its aim the removal of the Turks from what is now Iraq, a task the first major objective of which was the capture of Baghdad. At the outset, road communications were virtually non-existent and the only railway lay beyond Baghdad. The 500 mile meandering Tigris therefore dictated the line of march from the seaport base of Basra, and became the main line of communication, requiring an immense fleet of shallow draft river craft.

An extreme shortage of suitable craft contributed to the failure of the first phase of the campaign, which culminated in the surrender of Kut-el-Amara. Up to this time all transport arrangements afloat had been in the hands of the Royal Indian Marine but in 1916 river traffic was separated from port traffic and became the responsibility of a newly-formed Directorate of Inland Water Transport.

This organization so successfully overcame the obstacles that had helped to wreck the earlier operations, that when the second and ultimately victorious campaign opened, it was supported by nearly 750 craft of every imaginable type. As the river line extended northward beyond Baghdad, so the fleet grew to nearly 1,600 vessels.

The achievements of this new service received scant reward after the war. It fell victim to the Geddes cuts; by 1924 the Directorate of Inland Waterways and Docks had disappeared.

It was only a temporary disappearance, however, as with the outbreak of the Second World War, it rose again, phoenix-like, from its ashes. As in 1914 so in 1939, an operational role was seen for IWT on the canals of Northern France and Belgium. A Group HQ, two operating companies and an IWT workshop were set up, but not used. There was some IWT bulk petrol traffic on French canals and some coastal movement of the same commodity but further plans for the development of IWT in this theatre were overtaken by events. The Group HQ and workshops were disbanded, and the operating companies were attached to docks groups to provide lighterage service in the home ports.

Inland Water Transport Groups were, however, employed to considerable effect in the Middle East, the India Base and Ceylon, and in Burma and the Far East. Once again, too, they operated in Iraq and Persia, where they deployed 10,000 all ranks with a fleet strength of 1,300 craft, an effort quite comparable with their First World War achievements. One of the most successful of the many new types of craft developed for IWT use was a self-propelled lighter, the 'Z' craft, fabricated in India and assembled in the Middle East. This versatile craft, used for carrying personnel, vehicles and cargo, and able to undertake short sea passages unladen, became one of the standard workhorses of the IWT fleet.

So there was plenty of activity overseas; at home, however, there was not the same scope for the service until the preparations for the invasion of France, Operation Overlord, were put in hand. The Order of Battle for the force required an elaborate IWT representation which included 5 operating companies, 5 workshops and 8 floating crane sections. One of the heavy workshops companies was soon busy in the Surrey Commercial Docks adapting 400 Thames Swimhead barges ('Swimmies') to fit them for operational service. Most were fitted with engines, and the 'swim' (faired) bows were replaced by ramps to permit rapid and direct unloading to beaches. These were christened powered barges ramped (PBR) and dumb barges ramped (DBR) respectively.

At the same time, prefabricated Canadian 'Minca' barges were arriving in the United Kingdom for assembly, 400 in all, together with 96 'Sea Mules', small American tugs, and ramped cargo lighters (RCLs). These latter craft were mainly assembled by contract. An additional responsibility thrust upon the IWT organization was the erection and manning of thirty-nine 'Rhino' ferries, constructed from US naval pontoon equipment.

These latter soon proved their worth, discharging 10,882 vehicles over the Normandy beaches in the first fourteen days after the landings. All craft suffered difficulties from the bad weather during the operations and after, but by the end of July 1944, following major repair and salvage of damaged or sunken PBRs, were well able to cope with all the tonnage offered. During September the IWT effort was shifted eastwards and at last, bearing in mind the 1914 *raison d'etre* of the service, they were able to use French and Belgian canals.

It is interesting to note, however, that with the opening of the Ghent canal at Ostend in 1944, civilian barge traffic was initially requisitioned and operated by RASC for the movement of bulk petroleum and solid fuels. Only later, after the freeing of the Scheldt, was this task handed over to RE.

Prior to D-Day, the revival of IWT led to a need clearly to define the division of responsibilities for water transport between RE and RASC, as quite often these were tending to overlap. In June 1944 a directive was issued in which, broadly speaking, the RASC was made responsible for all craft required for inter-communication and distributive movement of personnel and material, while the Transportation Service was made responsible for the craft required for port working and bulk distribution of stores on the lines of communication. This was laid down as a war-time measure only and was reviewed in February 1946, when the Quartermaster General ruled that the 1944 principles should stand with possibly more careful wording. A new Army Council directive was eventually issued in September 1947 which delineated each Service's role in more specific detail.

The IWT story continued after the Second World War, the service taking a distinguished part in the Suez and Borneo operations. In the Suez campaign the regular element was ably supported by an Army Emergency Reserve Regiment called up from civilian life, operating 'Z' craft and requisitioned Canal Company vessels, including double-decker ferries. Eight of the 'Z' craft had survived a dash from Tobruk, towed by naval vessels at speeds up to 20 knots.

In Singapore, ten Port Squadron's vessels trans-shipped all services ammunition from beyond the harbour limits directly to ammunition depots, thus avoiding the dangers of road movement through Singapore City, and were prominent in supporting anti-terrorist operations in Malaya.

IWT crews were among the first to arrive at the outset of the Borneo insurrections and 'confrontation' with Indonesia. For four years, from 1962, this RE (Transportation) service operated local ramped craft and the newly developed ramped powered lighters along the coast and up to 100 miles inland on the rivers. During the whole of the period, the RE and RASC Water Transport services worked closely together. Their separate charters were disregarded to a large extent, enabling the closest possible cooperation and the development of highly effective joint systems. This was a very happy omen for the successful amalgamation which came even before the end of the operations.

Nevertheless, it was felt to be a sad day for many Royal Engineers (and Royal Army Service Corps no less) when, in 1965, the Inland Water Transport and RASC Fleets lost their separate identities in the Royal Corps of Transport. However, this rational move which united two sister services, also united two proud traditions of military service afloat.

APPENDIX V

Board of Ordnance and War Department Shipping Lists, 1844 and 1895

BOARD OF ORDNANCE VESSELS, 1844

Name of Vessel	Tonnage	Year	Station
Sir James Kempt	80	1832	
Somerset	80	1830	
The Queen	82	1839	Woolwich
Nettley	82	1841	
Lord Vivian	90	1841	
Richard	55	1808	Purfleet
Ebenezer	70	1805	
Marlborough	60	1804	Chatham
Earl of Chatham	50	1809	
Hussey	68	1836	Portsmouth
Wellington	45	1824	
Beresford	60	1828	
Gosport	68	1812	Devonport

Note: Taken from Army Ordnance Estimates 1844/45.

WAR DEPARTMENT VESSELS, 1895

Steamers

Lord Panmure	620	1859	
Marquess of Hartington	630	1886	
Sir Redvers Buller	490	1895	
Sir Evelyn Wood (building)	800	1896	Woolwich
Katharine	300	1882	
Cargo Steamer (building)	415	1896	

Name of Vessel	Tonnage	Year	Station
Osprey	225	1895	
Sir Robert Hay	225	1895	Portsmouth
Collingwood Dickson	60	1889	
Steamer (building)	–	1896	
Drake	165	1891	Devonport
Falcon	130	1874	
Advance	100	1884	Bermuda
Meteor	90	1894	Jamaica
Cambridge	100	1892	Queenstown

Steam Launches

Name of Vessel	Tonnage	Year	Station
Grand Duchess	50	1874	
Stanhope	80	1890	Portsmouth
Fuzee	50	1879	
Cecil	30	1878	Cork
Ida	25	1887	Devonport
Lizard	40	1882	Chatham
Lily	50	1878	Halifax, NS
Queen	55	1887	
Empress	50	1892	Singapore
Jubilee	57	1887	
Alexandra	57	1883	Hong Kong
Tommy Atkins	78	1883	
Sir Lintorn Simmons	27	1890	Malta
Creole	30	1890	Woolwich
Onward	35	1892	Shoeburyness
Satellite	80	1894	Harwich

Sailing Vessels

Name of Vessel	Tonnage	Year	Station
Emily	–	1867	Cork
John Adye	175	1888	Portsmouth
Lord Vivian	–	1862	
Clyde	40	1858	Bermuda
Havelock	30	1859	

Name of Vessel	Tonnage	Year	Station
Henry	160	1872	Chatham
Sir Stafford Northcote	175	1889	Devonport
Georgina	165	1889	
Othello	50	1889	
Sir George Murray	46	1880	Woolwich
Alice	48	1874	
Sebastopol	–	1857	

Note: Based on Col. Stevens, *Notes and Information*, etc., 1895.

APPENDIX VI

War Department Shipping List, 1908

VESSELS AT HOME

Name of Vessel	Tonnage	Year	Station
Freight Ships			
Marquess of Hartington	670	1886	Woolwich
Sir Evelyn Wood	850	1896	Woolwich
Target Towers			
Sir Redvers Buller	570	1895	Woolwich
Lord Wolseley	500	1896	Woolwich
Osprey	240	1895	Devonport
Lansdowne	320	1896	Portsmouth
Sir Robert Hay	270	1896	Portsmouth
Sir Henry Alderson	150	1898	Sheerness
Palliser	65	1899	Shoeburyness
Langdon	125	1902	Dover
Wyndham	125	1903	Cork
Abercorn	145	1903	Buncrana
Playfair	185	1904	Leith
Moore	185	1904	Portsmouth
Sir Frederick Walker	175	1903	Devonport
Stewart	100	1902	Weymouth
Russell	100	1902	Portsmouth
Somers	100	1902	Devonport
Haldane	125	1907	Portsmouth
Gordon	106	1907	Sheerness
Haslar	175	1903	Pembroke Dock
Special Craft			
Katharine	220	1882	Woolwich
Gog	130	1886	Woolwich
Magog	105	1900	Woolwich

Name of Vessel	Tonnage	Year	Station
Steam Launches			
Ladysmith	50	1902	Woolwich
White Rose	12	1902	Woolwich
Sir George White	35	1900	Portsmouth
Fusee	50	1902	Weymouth
Eagle	55	1895	Devonport
Ida	30	1887	Devonport
Drake	100	1891	Pembroke Dock
Mafeking	50	1902	Gravesend
Satellite	70	1894	Harwich
Cambridge	100	1892	Cork
Sail Barges			
John Adye	150	1888	Portsmouth
Sir Stafford Northcote	175	1889	Portsmouth
Sir George Murray	70	1900	Portsmouth
Seagull II	40	1901	Pembroke Dock
Henry	130	1872	Chatham
Dumb Barges			
Alice	70	1900	Woolwich
Othello	50	1892	Woolwich
Lord Vivian	120	1862	Woolwich
Sir W. Nicholson	90	1907	Portsmouth
Darenth	80	1880	Harwich
Shamrock	80	1897	Cork
Dorothy	90	1907	Cork

OVERSEAS

Vessel	Tonnage	Year	Type of Vessel
Bermuda			
Louise	145	1904	High-speed steamer
Lord Kitchener	20	1899	Steam launch
Clyde	40	1859	Sailing cutter
Havelock	30	1859	Sailing cutter

Plus: 4 barges, 2 lighters, 2 gigs, and 16 dinghies.

Jamaica

Meteor	90	1894	Steamship
Rodney	25	1902	Steam launch

Plus: 1 schooner, 1 lighter, 1 whaler, 1 gig, and 1 dinghy.

Name of Vessel	Tonnage	Year	Station
Hong Kong			
Hercules	170	1898	High-speed steamer
Jubilee	57	1898	Steam launch
Omphale	140	1905	High-speed steamer
Tommy Atkins	78	1898	Steam launch

Plus: 1 lighter, 1 whaler, 7 gigs, and 4 dinghies.

Mauritius			
Onyx	38	1902	Steam launch

Plus: 1 sailing brig, 1 whaler, and 3 gigs.

Singapore			
Moonstone	145	1904	High-speed steamer
Empress	–	1907	Powder boat
Queen	55	1887	Steam launch

Plus: 2 gigs.

Gibraltar			
May	125	1902	High-speed steamer
Quadroon	35	1898	Governor's launch

Plus: 3 cutters, 3 gigs, and 2 dinghies.

Malta			
Sir Edwin Markham	170	1898	High-speed steamer
Sir Lintorn Simmons	27	1890	Governor's launch

Plus: 7 pontoons, 1 dghaisa, 1 boat, and 1 gig.

Note: Taken from the Heath Report, 1908. (P.R.O. WO 55/5536).

APPENDIX VII

War Department Shipping List, 1914

(Abbreviations: D. = Dumb, M. = Motor, Pdr = Powder, S. = Sailing, TT = Steam Target Tower.)

Name	Type of Vessel	Built	Tonnage	Working Speed (knots)	Station
Abercorn	TT	1903	145	9.5	Lough Swilly
Alice	D. barge	1900	140	–	Woolwich
Arctic	D. barge	1900	–	–	Shoeburyness
Australia	D. barge	1906	–	–	Gibraltar
Cambridge	Launch	1892	130	8.5	Cork
Carrigaline	Launch	1892	35	8	Falmouth
Clyde	S. barge	–	–	–	Bermuda
Courier	Launch	1889	33	10	Devonport
Crystal	Launch	1902	85	8.5	Isle of Wight
Darenth	D. barge	1880	42	–	Woolwich
Dorothy	M. barge	1907	118	–	Cork
Dorothy	S. barge	1887	–	–	Jamaica
Drake	Launch	1891	100	9	Pembroke Dock
Eagle	Launch	1895	55	8	Devonport
Emerald	Launch	1899	40	8	Woolwich
Empress	Barge	1892	–	–	Singapore
Endeavour	Launch	1899	33	9	Woolwich
Forth	D. barge	1893	–	–	Shoeburyness
Fusee	Launch	1902	62	8	Weymouth
Gog	D. barge	1886	400	–	Woolwich
Gordon	TT	1907	106	9.5	Sheerness
Haldane	TT	1907	125	9.5	Portsmouth
Haslar	TT	1903	175	10.2	Pembroke Dock
Havelock	S. barge	–	–	–	Bermuda
Henry	S. barge	1872	140	–	Chatham
Hercules	Launch	1898	170	10	Hong Kong
Hurst	Launch	1904	39	12	Portsmouth
Ida	Launch	1887	30	8	Devonport
Jasper	Launch	1902	38	8.5	Malta
John Adye	S. barge	1888	185	–	Portsmouth
Joule	Launch	1890	35	9	Devonport
Jubilee	Launch	1887	60	10	Hong Kong

Name	Type of Vessel	Built	Tonnage	Working Speed (knots)	Station
Katharine	Steamer	1882	250	8.5	Woolwich
Ladysmith	Launch	1902	52	9	Cork
Langdon	TT	1902	127	9.5	Dover
Lansdowne	TT	1896	350	10	Portsmouth
Lighter (unnamed)	Lighter	1903	130	–	Portsmouth
Lord Kitchener	Launch	1899	20	9	Bermuda
Lord Vivian	D. barge	1862	–	–	Woolwich
Lord Wolseley	TT	1896	500	8.5	Woolwich
Louise	Launch	1904	145	9.5	Bermuda
Mafeking	Launch	1902	52	9	Portsmouth
Magog	D. barge	1900	260	–	Woolwich
Marquess of Hartington	Steamer	1886	670	9	Woolwich
May	Launch	1902	250	9.5	Gibraltar
Meteor	Launch	1894	78	10	Jamaica
Moonstone	Launch	1904	145	9.5	Singapore
Moore	TT	1904	185	10	Portsmouth
Omphale	Launch	1905	140	9.5	Hong Kong
Onyx	Launch	1902	38	8.5	Mauritius
Osprey	TT	1895	288	10	Devonport
Othello	D. barge	1892	60	–	Devonport
Palliser	TT	1899	65	9.5	Shoeburyness
Playfair	TT	1904	185	10	Leith
Quadroon	Launch	1898	35	9	Gibraltar
Rodney	Launch	1902	25	9	Jamaica
Russell	TT	1902	112	9.5	Isle of Wight
Satellite	Launch	1894	88	9.5	Harwich
Sapphire	Launch	1910	–	–	Singapore
Scow	D. barge	1896	–	–	Lough Swilly
Seagull II	S. hoy	1901	45	–	Pembroke Dock
Shamrock	D. barge	1897	105	–	Cork
Sir E. Markham	Launch	1898	170	10	Malta
Sir Evelyn Wood	Steamer	1896	850	9	Woolwich
Sir F. Walker	TT	1903	173	10	Devonport
Sir G. Murray	S. barge	1900	140	–	Portsmouth
Sir G. White	Launch	1900	35	9	Portsmouth
Sir H. Alderson	TT	1898	157	10	Sheerness
Sir Redvers Buller	Steamer	1895	570	9.5	Woolwich
Sir Robert Hay	TT	1896	280	7.5	Portsmouth
Sir S. Northcote	S. barge	1889	175	–	Portsmouth
Sir W. Nicholson	M. barge	1907	118	–	Portsmouth
Somers	TT	1904	150	9.5	Jamaica
Stewart	TT	1902	112	9.5	Weymouth

Name	Type of Vessel	Built	Tonnage	Working Speed (knots)	Station
Swale	Launch	1891	35	8	Sheerness
Thalia	Pdr hoy	–	–	–	Woolwich
Tommy Atkins	Launch	1898	78	10	Hong Kong
White Rose	Launch	1902	12	8	Woolwich
Wyndham	TT	1903	140	9	Cork
Oil Motor Launch	Launch	1902	3	6	Shoeburyness

Plus: 11 other unnamed lighters and 3 tow barges, tongkangs I, II and III.

Note: Details based on *Naval Service Pocket Book, 1915.*

APPENDIX VIII

War Department Shipping List, 1934–39

HOME STATIONS

Name	Tonnage	Year	Remarks
Coasters			
Marquess of Hartington	670	1886	Woolwich
Sir Evelyn Wood	850	1896	Woolwich
Sir Walter Campbell	625	1928	Woolwich
Motor Coaster			
Malplaquet	528	1939	Commissioned 1940
Steamships			
Sir John Wyndham	140	1903	Ireland – target-towing
Moore	185	1907	Portsmouth – fort duties
Hurst II	39	1913	Plymouth – target-towing
Sir Herbert Miles	–	1912	Grimsby – fort duties
Playfair	185	1904	Leith – fort duties
Sir Desmond O'Callaghan	–	1927	Sheerness – target-towing
General McHardy	100	1928	Ireland – tender
Sir Robert Whigham	152	1931	Portsmouth – target-towing
Sir Frederick Walker	175	1903	⎫
Russell	100	1902	⎪
Haslar	175	1903	⎬ Winter in reserve; target-
Gordon	38	1907	⎪ towing in summer
Stewart	100	1902	⎪
Haldane	125	1907	⎭
Steam Launches			
Ladysmith	50	1902	⎫ Coastal defence support
Mafeking	50	1902	⎭

Name	Tonnage	Year	Remarks
General Service Motor Launches			
Crystal II	32	1932	–
Marne II	–	–	–
Camel II	–	–	Sheerness
Sir Cecil Romer	–	1929	
Magpie	–	–	
Wuzzer	–	1930	Ireland
Jackdaw	–	1935	
Raven II	–	1931	
Fusee II	–	1935	Weymouth
Phoenix	–	1936	–
Titlark	–	1936	–
Motor Barges			
Geoffrey Stanley	92	1929	
Henry Caddell	104	1931	
Dorothy	118	1907	
Sir W. Nicholson	118	1907	Cargo carriers & dumb barge
Sir George Murray	70	1900	towing mainly based on
Vawdrey	98	1934	Woolwich and Portsmouth
Katharine II	195	1930	
Blenheim	115	1937	
Ramillies	–	1937	
John Adams	98	1934	Ireland
Dumb Barges			
Arctic II	–	1931	Static target-hauling
Forth II	–	1931	at Shoeburyness
Gog	400	1886	Woolwich – gun barge
Magog	260	1900	Woolwich – gun barge
Elm	–	1931	–
Chestnut	–	1931	–
Nippy	–	1931	–

57 ft High-speed target towers – 'General' class

Allenby	Kitchener	Roberts
Clive	Marlborough	Wellington
French	Raglan	Wolseley
Haig		

45 ft High-speed range clearance craft – 'Bird' class

Eagle	Kite	Swallow
Falcon	Martin	Snipe

Name		Tonnage	Year	Remarks
Grouse	*Pigeon*		*Teal*	
Gull	*Partridge*		*Vulture*	
Hawk	*Quail*		*Woodcock*	
Kestrel	*Swift*		*Widgeon*	

47 ft Special Launch

Wolfe

OVERSEAS STATIONS

Name	Tonnage	Year	Remarks
Steamships			
Sir Noel Birch	191	1926	Gibraltar
Lord Plumer	212	1927	Malta
Abercorn	145	1903	Jamaica
Moonstone	145	1904	Singapore
Omphale	140	1905	Hong Kong
Sir Hastings Anderson	–	1934	Singapore
Motor Launches			
Eliott	–	–	Gibraltar
Sir Leslie Rundle	–	–	Malta
Thrush	–	–	Malta
Sir Theodore Fraser	–	–	Singapore
Ubique	–	–	Singapore
Victor	–	–	Singapore
Hodgson	–	–	Singapore
Sir John Asser	–	–	Bermuda
Ernest Taylor	–	–	Jamaica
Steam Launches			
Victoria	–	–	Hong Kong
Tommy Atkins	12	1898	Hong Kong

Other Vessels

13 dumb barges, lighters, tongkangs, etc., including *Chang*, constructed in Singapore on similar lines to *Gog* and *Magog*, for conveying heavy guns and mountings.

Note: This list purports to show vessels which were in the Fleet at one time or another during the latter part of the 1930s. Unfortunately some of the detail is no longer available and has had to be omitted. In 1934 the Fleet's vessel strength was 66 and has been variously quoted in War Office sources as being 66, 71 and 112 at the beginning of the Second World War. The highest figure comprises 48 vessels at home and 64 overseas but it is likely that it includes local pre-mobilization acquisitions, especially as the list of overseas stations includes Port Said and Sierra Leone for the first time.

APPENDIX IX
Major Shipping Classes, 1941–6

(Note: Includes only the most important classes of vessels built or acquired from other Services during and after the Second World War, and mainly operated by the civilian fleet.)

HIGH SPEED TARGET TOWERS

48 ft 'Derby Winner' class – 1941–4
(Built by Groves & Gutteridge Ltd and J.S. White & Co., Ltd, Isle of Wight.)

Bahram	*Flying Fox*	*Manna*
Blue Peter	*Grand Parade*	*Minoru*
Captain Cuttle	*Humorist*	*Ormonde*
Coronach	*Hyperion*	*Spion Kop*
Call Boy	*Isinglass*	*Sunstar*
Cameronian	*Ladas*	*Taigo*
Felstead	*Lemberg*	*Windsor Lad*

68 ft 'Battle' class – 1944
(Built by British Power Boat Co., Ltd, Poole.)

Kemmel	*Loos*	*Scheldt*
Krithia	*Lys*	*Shaiba*
Kut	*St Julien*	*Sharon*
LaBassee	*St Quentin*	*Somme*
Langemark	*Salonika*	*Struma*
Laventie	*Sambre*	*Suvla*
Le Cateau	*Scarpe*	*Zeebrugge*

69 ft 'Battle' class – 1943–5
(Built by J.I. Thornycroft & Co., Ltd, Southampton.)

Aisne	*Armentieres*	*Bullecourt*
Albert	*Arras*	*Cambrai*
Amiens	*Bapaume*	*Ctesiphon*
Antwerp	*Bazentin*	*Courtrai*
Arleux	*Bethune*	

72 ft 'Battle' class – 1943–5 (Ex-Admiralty MTBs)
(Converted by J.I. Thornycroft & Co., Ltd, Northam.)

Mame	*Messines*	*Morval*
Megiddo	*Mons*	*Nablus*
Menin	*Montauban*	

70 ft 'Battle' class – 1943–6 (Ex-Admiralty MGBs)
(Built by Higgins of New Orleans and transferred to RN under Lend–Lease arrangements in 1940.)

Gallipoli	*Ginchey*	*Tardenois*
Gaza	*Guillemont*	*Thiepval*

Note: Three further conversions were cancelled: *Givenchy*, *Tigris* and *Tsingtao*.

GENERAL SERVICE LAUNCHES

40 ft 'Grey' class Speed Launches – 1942 (ex-RAF)
(Built by British Power Boat Co., Ltd Hythe.)

Grey Dame	*Grey Lady*	*Grey Mist*
Grey Dawn	*Grey Lass*	*Grey Nymph*
Grey Girl	*Grey Maid*	*Grey Queen*

40 ft 'Barracks' and 'Barrack Lines' class GS Launches – 1944–6
(Built by C.C. Underwood Ltd, South Benfleet, and Ranelagh Yacht Yard, Ltd, Isle of Wight.)

Alma	*Corunna*	*Salamanca*
Beaumont	*Gibraltar*	*Stanhope*
Buller	*Malta*	*Talavera*
Clayton	*Mandora*	*Victoria*
Connaught		

44½ ft 'British Rivers' class Fast Launches – 1945–6
(Built by British Power Boat Co., Ltd, Hythe.)

Adur	*Blyth*	*Coquet*
Alde	*Brora*	*Crouch*
Almond	*Bure*	*Dart*
Alness	*Burry*	*Dee*
Arun	*Butley*	*Derwent*
Avon	*Carvon*	*Dovey*
Axe	*Char*	*Eden*
Beam	*Clyde*	*Erme*
Beaulieu	*Colne*	*Esk*
Blackwater	*Conway*	*Forsa*

Fowey	Glaven	Helford
Foyle	Hamble	Humber
Frome	Hayle	Hull
Garth		

45 ft 'Shakespearian Females' class GS Launches – 1944–6
(Built by Groves & Gutteridge Ltd, and Phillips, Anderson & Co., Ltd, Isle of Wight.)

Bianca	Jessica	Paulina
Cassandra	Juliet	Perdita
Celia	Lucetta	Portia
Cleopatra	Miranda	Rosalind
Cordelia	Nerissa	Sylphia
Cressida	Octavia	Titania
Desdemona	Olivia	Ursula
Hermia	Ophelia	Viola

45 ft 'Shakespearian Males' class Passenger Launches – 1943–5 ex-RN
(Built by Phillips, Anderson, & Co. Ltd, Isle of Wight.)

Alonso	Hamlet	Orlando
Angelo	Horatio	Othello
Antony	Leontes	Pericles
Bassanio	Lysander	Peto
Brutus	Macbeth	Romeo
Claudio	Malvolio	Shylock
Falstaff	Oberon	Titus

50 ft 'Dickens' class GS Launches, Series I – 1943–6
(Built by W. Weatherhead & Sons, Cockenzie, R.A. Newman & Sons, Poole, and F. Curtis Ltd, Looe.)

Barkis	Dombey	Pecksniff
Bumble	Dorrit	Peggotty
Buzfuz	Fagin	Pickwick
Chadband	Gamp	Pinch
Chuzzlewit	Gummidge	Podsnap
Copperfield	Marley	Prodgit
Cratchit	Micawber	Quilp
Dodger	Nickleby	

50 ft 'Dickens' class GS Launches, Series II – 1945–6
(Built by Groves & Gutteridge Ltd, Isle of Wight, W. Weatherhead & Sons, Cockenzie and British Power Boat Co., Ltd, Hythe and Poole.)

Barnaby Rudge	Brownlow	Jackson
Benjamin Allen	Cherryble	Linkinwater
Bob Sawyer	Dowler	Lowten

MacStinger	Scrooge	Stiggins
Martin	Sgt. Snubbins	Tracy Tupman
Mr Toots	Sikes	Traddles
Newman Noggs	Sidney Carton	Uriah Heep
Oliver Twist	Smike	Wardle
Raddle	Snodgrass	Weller
Rose Maglie	Squeers	Winkle

MOTOR FISHING VESSELS (MFVs)

These were identified by numbers only; No. 160, a 61½ ft MFV, became the *Yarmouth Seaman*, and the 90 ft MFV No. 1502 became the *Yarmouth Navigator* (see Chapter 22). The following were the numbers taken over for civilian and military fleet use:

21	61½ ft	–	1943–5
2	45 ft	–	1943
16	75 ft	–	1945
6	90 ft	–	1945–6

In addition, twenty of various types were converted to fire boats.

LANDING CRAFT TANK (LCTs) 1945–6

These were modified and redesignated Ammunition Dumping Craft (ADC). One source quotes 103, 76 at home and 27 overseas.

160 FT ADMIRALTY STEAM TRAWLERS

Copinsay	Mull	Prospect
Foxtrot	Oxna	Sheppey
Inchcolm	Porcher	Valse

LANDING SHIPS TANK (LSTS) – 1946 (EX-ADMIRALTY)

Evan Gibb	Charles MacLeod	Reginald Kerr
Frederick Clover	Maxwell Brander	Snowden-Smith
Humfrey Gale		

PICTURE CREDITS

The author would like to thank the following for permission to reproduce illustrations:

Bekens of Cowes, pp. 105, 107; British Crown/M.o.D. copyright, by permission of the Controller, HMSO, pp. 112, 144 (below), 145, 153, 155, 187; Anne S.K. Brown Military Collection, Providence, RI, through Mr A.S. Blight, p. 5; Capt. J.F. Cains, pp. 19 (below), 67, 117, 120; Mr Eric Carlie and Wigtown Free Press (copyright), p. 161; Mrs O. Codner, p. 84; Mr E.A. Cowdry, p. 94; Mr A. Elloway (copyright), p. 60; David Griffin, p. 171; *Illustrated London News* Picture Library (copyright), p. 14; Institution of Royal Engineers, by permission of the Secretary, p. 21; RCT Maritime Heritage, pp. 66, 101, 184, 185; the Misses Reynolds, pp. 27, 40; John D. Smale Collection, pp. 13, 15, 28, 29, 68, 70, 71, 73, 80, 93, 98, 115, 125, 126, 128, 144 (above), 159, 182, 183, 188; P.A. Vicary (copyright), p. 19 (above); Mr A. Wales, p. 79; Messrs Wright & Logan, pp. 146, 151; Maj. B.V. Wynn-Werninck, frontispiece.

The John D. Smale Collection, now in the Institution of RASC/RCT Archives, was made available by kind permission of Mrs Joyce Smale. The author regrets it has not been possible, despite considerable research, to trace copyrights for many of the pictures, and apologizes for any unwitting breaches in this respect.

REFERENCES

The author gratefully acknowledges all sources and references used. The following British Crown/M.o.D. copyright publications are reproduced by permission of the Controller of HMSO:

Garrison Artillery Drill, 1897
Instructions for Practice Seawards, 1914–15
Instructions for Practice Seawards, 1931
Manual of Seamanship, Vol. I, 1937
Naval Service Pocket Books, 1899, 1907, 1915
Notes and Information on the Conveyance of Stores, etc., by Lt.-Col. Stevens, 1895
Ordnance Estimates, 1827 to 1845
Provision and Maintenance of WD GS Boats, 1897
RASC Training, Vol II. Pamphlet No. 3, 1954
Regulations for Army Ordnance Services, 1900
Regulations for WD GS Vessels and Boats, 1897
Report on the Account of Army Expenditure, 1887–88
Royal Warrant, 1900
Supplies and Transport, 1939–45, Vols I and II
Supply Transport and Barrack Regulations, 1950
Supply Transport and Barrack Services, 1900
Transportation, 1939-45
WD Fleet Regulations, 1932.

The following material was made available by permission and with the assistance of the Public Records Office.

File Gen No. 6/4730
Naval Records for Genealogists
PRO Press M 15/99B, Accession No. 363/195. (Unpublished notes on the Board of Ordnance by Brig. O.F. Hogg and J.H. Leslie.)
PRO WO 32/5536
PRO WO 32/18099
PRO WO 44/695 (25)
War Office Circulars, Nos. 266 and 471
War Office List, 1864.

BIBLIOGRAPHY

(Place of publication given only if outside London.)

Anon, *The Great War – A History*, vols IV, V, VI. Gresham Publishing Company Ltd.

ASC Journals, August 1895, December 1896, May 1897, February 1902, September 1902, May 1907, April 1912.

Baker-Browne, Lt.- Col. W., *The History of Submarine Mining in the British Army*. Chatham, Institute of the Royal Engineers, 1910.

Beadon, Col. R.H., *The History of Transport and Supply in the British Army*, vol. II. Cambridge, Cambridge Press, 1931.

Beckett, Maj. J., 'Farewell to Old Ships' in REME Magazine, 1957.

Blight, A.S., 'Fleet Repair through the Ages' in REME Journal, April 1976.

——, *List of Board of Ordnance and WD Vessels*.

Bull, P., *To Sea in a Sieve*. Heinemann (William) Ltd, 1956.

Caine, Revd C., *Martial Annals of York*, 1898. Bedford Press.

Daily Graphic, April 1895. British Newspaper Library.

City Press, 23 September 1876.

Claydon, P.A., personal correspondence incorporated in the late Mr John Smale's papers.

Gates, W.G., *History of Portsmouth*. Publisher not known, 1900.

Hansard, 14 March, 12 May, September 1893.

Hawkins, W., letter in *Ship's Monthly*, May 1991.

Hogg, Ian V., *Coastal Defences of England and Wales, 1856–1956*. Newton Abbot, David & Charles.

Hogg, Brig. O.F., and Leslie, J.H., *The History of the Royal Arsenal*. OUP, 1963.

Holmes, J.S., *Diary of the Norfolk Artillery, 1853–1909*. Norwich, Jarrold & Sons Ltd.

Institution of the RASC, *The Story of the RASC, 1939–45*. Aldershot.

Institution of the RCT, *The Story of the RASC and RCT, 1949–82*. Aldershot.

Institution of the Royal Engineers, *The History of the Corps of Royal Engineers*.

IPCS, *The Pheon*. War Office Newsletter.

Knight, C.B., *The History of the City of York*. Publisher not known, 1944, copyright C.B. Knight.

Langley, Martin, and Small, Edwina, 'The Port of Plymouth'. Unpublished.

Maurice-Jones, Col. K.W., *The History of Coast Artillery in the British Army*. Woolwich, RA Institution, 1959.

Naval Historical Branch, 'The Dunkirk Log of WDV Haig'. Unpublished.

Navy and Army Illustrated, 6 August 1897.

Nevill, C.W., personal correspondence incorporated in the late Mr John Smale's papers.

RA Institution, *The History of the Royal Artillery*, vol. I. Woolwich, RA Institution.

——, *Minutes of the Proceedings of the Royal Artillery Institution*, vol. XIII. Woolwich, RA Institution.

RASC Journals, 1934, July 1942, April 1944, September 1945, September 1957, July 1959.

RCT Archives, 'Historical Note – 632 Company (Water Transport)'. RCT Archives, unpublished.

——, '*The History of 80 Company (Water Company) RASC*'. RCT Archives, unpublished.

——, *War Office (ST1) Monograph*. RCT Archives.

RE Professional Papers, 1876. By courtesy of Maj. A.S. Hill. Chatham, Institution of RE, 1876.

Roman, Lt. S.L., RCASC, 'The Army's Navy' in *Crowsnest*, August 1959, and the RASC Review, 1959.

Royal Proclamation 1802.

Savage, C.I., *An Economic History of Transport*. Hutchinson & Co., 1959. Copyright C.I. Savage.

Skentelbery, Brig. N., *The Ordnance Board – An Historical Note*. Ordnance Board Publications, 1965.

Smale, J., 'The Government Gun' in *Coast and Country Magazine*, Parrett and Neves Ltd, 1980.

Steeple, J.W., 'The Arms and Flags of the Board of Ordnance' in *Mariner's Mirror*. The Society for Nautical Research.

Surtees, R.S., *Jorrocks Jaunts*. R.Ackerman, 1838.

Thrush, A., 'The Ordnance Office and the Navy' in *Mariner's Mirror*. The Society for Nautical Research.

The Waggoner, December 1977. Aldershot, Institution of the RCT.

Wood, D., *Powderbarge WD*. Wareman and Westcountry Barge Group of the Society for Spritsail Barge Research, 1977.

INDEX

Picture references are in bold print.